Isabelle Chrisment   Alva
Rémi Badonnel   Martin

Managing the Dynamics of Networks and Services

5th International Conference
on Autonomous Infrastructure, Management,
and Security, AIMS 2011
Nancy, France, June 13-17, 2011
Proceedings

Springer

Volume Editors

Isabelle Chrisment
Université Henri Poincaré Nancy 1
Ecole Supérieure d'Informatique et Applications de Lorraine
LORIA-INRIA Lorraine
615 Rue du Jardin Botanique, 54602 Villers-lès-Nancy, France
E-mail: isabelle.chrisment@loria.fr

Alva Couch
Tufts University, Computer Science Department
161 College Avenue, Medford, MA 02155, USA
E-mail: couch@cs.tufts.edu

Rémi Badonnel
Université Henri Poincaré Nancy 1
Ecole Supérieure d'Informatique et Applications de Lorraine
LORIA-INRIA Lorraine
615 Rue du Jardin Botanique, 54602 Villers-lès-Nancy, France
E-mail: remi.badonnel@loria.fr

Martin Waldburger
Universität Zürich, Institut für Informatik (IFI)
Binzmühlestrasse 14, 8050 Zürich, Switzerland
E-mail: waldburger@ifi.uzh.ch

ISSN 0302-9743   e-ISSN 1611-3349
ISBN 978-3-642-21483-7   e-ISBN 978-3-642-21484-4
DOI 10.1007/978-3-642-21484-4
Springer Heidelberg Dordrecht London New York

Library of Congress Control Number: 2011928561

CR Subject Classification (1998): C.2, D.2, H.4, C.2.4, D.4, D.1.3

LNCS Sublibrary: SL 5 – Computer Communication Networks and Telecommunications

Typesetting: Camera-ready by author, data conversion by Scientific Publishing Services, Chennai, India

Printed on acid-free paper

Springer is part of Springer Science+Business Media (www.springer.com)

Preface

The International Conference on Autonomous Infrastructure, Management and Security (AIMS 2011) was a single-track event integrating normal conference paper sessions, tutorials, keynotes, and a PhD student workshop into a highly interactive event. One of the goals of AIMS was to look beyond borders and to stimulate the exchange of ideas across different communities and among PhD students.

AIMS 2011—which took place during June 13–17, 2011, in Nancy, France—was hosted by INRIA Nancy Grand-Est and by ESIAL (Engineering School in Computer Science from the University of Nancy 1).

AIMS 2011 constituted the fifth edition of a conference series on management and security aspects of distributed and autonomous systems, after successful events in Oslo, Norway 2007, Bremen, Germany 2008, Enschede, The Netherlands 2009, and Zurich, Switzerland 2010. This year, AIMS 2011 focused on the theme of "Managing the Dynamics of Networks and Services."

AIMS 2011 began with 1.5 days of two courses and labs (summer school), which offered hands-on learning experience in network and service management topics and which required attendees to work in practical on-site courses combined with preceding short tutorial-like teaching sessions. The objective of the first course entitled "Using Distributed Computing Techniques and Tools to Help Network Forensics" was to show the current challenges in network analysis. The course was separated into two parts: the theoretical/engineering aspects of network forensics and a hands-on analysis lab with network data collected in honeypots and network security sensors. The second course entitled "Cloud Computing for Scalable Network Management" presented the general functioning of Hadoop, the Hadoop distributed file system, and the main paradigm behind Hadoop called Map/Reduce.

The AIMS 2011 conference continued with a keynote presentation on "IP Networks Monitoring with Netflow," delivered by Guillaume Lambert and Jean Monné from Orange Labs, France.

The four technical sessions, covering security, policy management, support technologies, and peer-to-peer and aggregation schemes, included a total of 11 full papers, which were selected after a thorough reviewing process. The majority of papers received four independent reviews and no paper had under three reviews.

The AIMS PhD workshop was a venue for doctoral students to present and discuss their research ideas as well as, most importantly, to obtain feedback from the AIMS audience about their planned PhD research work. This year, the workshop was organized into two technical sessions, where 11 PhD investigations were presented and discussed. These PhD papers included in this volume describe the current state of these investigations, including their research problem statements, investigation approaches, and outlines of results achieved so far. They were also selected through a rigorous review process, with at least three reviews per paper.

The editors would like to thank the many people who helped make AIMS 2011 such a high-quality and successful event. Firstly, the great review work performed by the members of the AIMS TPC and the PhD Workshop TPC and additional reviewers are highly acknowledged. Further thanks go to all authors who submitted their contributions to AIMS 2011. Many thanks also go to the tutorial and keynote speakers, namely, Alexandre Dulaunoy, Jérôme François, Guillaume Lambert, and Jean Monné.

Finally, the editors would like to extend their thanks to the Springer team, namely, Anna Kramer, for the smooth cooperation on finalizing these proceedings. Additionally, special thanks go to the local organizers for enabling the logistics and hosting the AIMS 2011 conference.

April 2011   Isabelle Chrisment
                                                                   Alva Couch
                                                                 Rémi Badonnel
                                                              Martin Waldburger

Organization

General Chair

Olivier Festor · · · · · · · · · · · · INRIA Nancy-Grand Est, France

Program TPC Co-chairs AIMS 2011

Isabelle Chrisment · · · · · · · · ESIAL-Université Henri Poincaré Nancy 1,
France
Alva Couch · · · · · · · · · · · · · TUFTS University, USA

PhD Student Workshop Co-chairs

Rémi Badonnel · · · · · · · · · · ESIAL-Université Henri Poincaré Nancy 1,
France
Martin Waldburger · · · · · · · University of Zürich, Switzerland

Summer School Co-chair

Radu State · · · · · · · · · · · · · ESIAL-Université Henri Poincaré Nancy 1,
France

Publications Chair

Burkhard Stiller · · · · · · · · · University of Zürich, Switzerland

Steering Committee

Mark Burgess · · · · · · · · · · · HIO, Norway
Jürgen Schönwälder · · · · · · Jacobs University Bremen, Germany
Aiko Pras · · · · · · · · · · · · · · University of Twente, The Netherlands
Burkhard Stiller · · · · · · · · · University of Zürich, Switzerland
Olivier Festor · · · · · · · · · · · INRIA Nancy-Grand Est, France
David Hausheer · · · · · · · · · University of Berkeley, USA
Rolf Stadler · · · · · · · · · · · · KTH Royal Institute of Technology, Sweden

Technical Program Committee AIMS 2011

Claudio Bartolini	HP Labs, USA
Torsten Braun	University of Bern, Switzerland
Guillaume Doyen	Université Technologique de Troyes, France
Gabi Dreo Rodosek	University of Federal Armed Forces Munich, Germany
Dominique Dudkowski	NEC Europe Ltd., Germany
Metin Feridun	IBM Research, Switzerland
Samir Ghamri-Doudane	Alcatel-Lucent Bell Labs, France
Imen Gridabenyahia	Orange Labs, France
David Hausheer	University of Berkeley, USA
Jérôme François	University of Luxembourg, Luxembourg
Georgios Karagiannis	University of Twente, The Netherlands
Antonio Liotta	Eindhoven University of Technology, The Netherlands
Emil Lupu	Imperial College, UK
Hanan Lutfiyya	University of Western Ontario, Canada
Philippe Owezarski	LAAS-CNRS, France
Aiko Pras	University of Twente, The Netherlands
Bruno Quoitin	University of Mons, Belgium
Danny Raz	Technion, Israel
Ramin Sadre	University of Twente, The Netherlands
Jürgen Schönwälder	Jacobs University Bremen, Germany
Joan Serrat	Universitat Politecnica de Catalunya, Spain
Michele Sibilla	Paul Sabatier University, France
Burkhard Stiller	University of Zürich, Switzerland
Robert Szabo	Budapest University of Technology and Economics, Hungary
Filip De Turck	Ghent University — IBBT, Belgium
Kurt Tutschku	University of Vienna, Austria
Lisandro Zambenedetti Granville	University Federal do Rio Grande do Sul, Brazil

PhD Student Workshop Committee

Marinos Charalambides	University College London, UK
Marc Chiarini	Harvard's School of Engineering and Applied Sciences, USA
Yacine Ghamri-Doudane	ENSIIE Evry, France
Thomas Schaaf	LMU Munich, Germany
Anna Sperotto	University of Twente, The Netherlands
Sven van der Meer	Waterford Institute of Technology, Ireland

Table of Contents

Security Management

PhD Workshop: Autonomic Network and Service Management

Policy Management

Support Technologies

P2P and Aggregation Schemes

PhD Workshop: Monitoring and Security

Cleaning Your House First: Shifting the Paradigm on How to Secure Networks

Jérôme François[1], Giovane C. M. Moura[2], and Aiko Pras[2]

[1] University of Luxembourg - Interdisciplinary Centre for Security, Reliability and Trust
jerome.francois@uni.lu
[2] Centre for Telematics and Information Technology (CTIT)
Faculty of Electrical Engineering, Mathematics and Computer Science (EEMCS)
Design and Analysis of Communications Systems (DACS)
Enschede, The Netherlands
{g.c.m.moura,a.pras}@utwente.nl

Abstract. The standard paradigm when securing networks is to filter *ingress traffic* to the domain to be protected. Even though many tools and techniques have been developed and employed over the recent years for this purpose, we are still far from having secure networks. In this work, we propose a paradigm shift on the way we secure networks, by investigating whether it would not be efficient to filter *egress traffic* as well. The main benefit of this approach is the possibility to mitigate malicious activities before they reach the Internet. To evaluate our proposal, we have developed a prototype and conducted experiments using NetFlow data from the University of Twente.

1 Introduction

When it comes to protecting their networks, Internet Service Providers (ISPs) and businesses employ a large set of specialized tools aiming at mitigate attacks targeting their networks. Examples of such tools include network firewalls, Network Intrusion Detection Systems (NIDS), antivirus, web proxies, and mail filters. Stills, we are far from having secure networks. To better illustrate this, take as example one of the largest security threats on the Internet nowadays: botnets [1]. By definition, a *botnet* is a network of compromised hosts (also known as *bots/zombies*) controlled by a botmaster, via a Command and Control (C&C) channel. They are used for different purposes, such as phishing, malware propagation, distributed denial of service (DDoS), and spamming. It is estimated 85% of the more than 100 billion daily spam messages are sent by bots [2].

Behind the current security problems, there might be a subtle defense approach decision: ISPs and businesses usually focus on protecting their own network from the outside world, filtering mostly *ingress traffic*. However, much less attention is usually given to *egress traffic*, meaning that malicious traffic find little or no barrier to leave the originating domain. One example is spam – most companies filter heavily incoming mail, but usually they do not much when their own users spam other domains [3]. Due to that, by the time a security event is detected, it has already taken its own share from routers, network links and computers that it had to go through to reach its final target, imposing direct and indirect costs.

I. Chrisment et al. (Eds.): AIMS 2011, LNCS 6734, pp. 1–12, 2011.

This left us wondering if it would not be the case of *changing the paradigm* on how we secure our networks, filtering egress traffic as well. Thus, this leads us to the following research question: *what can be achieved by filtering egress traffic from a particular domain?* – that is, why not "clean your house before looking for dirty at other's houses?"

Some research works suggest that is worth doing. Van Eeten *et al.*, for example, have shown that 10 ISPs account for 30% of unique IP addresses sending spam worldwide [4]. According to that, by filtering outgoing mail from only 10 ISPs, we could reduce almost one third of all spam. In another work, de Vries *et al.* [3] have shown that egress mail traffic can be easily filtered with higher detection rates.

In order to filter *egress traffic*, many sources of data can be employed, such as mail server logs, network traces, DNS blacklists. In this work we propose the use of flow records [5]. The main advantage is scalability, since flow records provide summarized information about the network traffic, thus coping much better with cfurrent high speed multi-gigabit lines. Besides that, by using flows records, the communication patterns in a network can be evaluated instead of having to process the content of each packet [6]. Finally, flows records are application independent, so they can potentially be used to detect and block any type of malicious activity in the network.

To analyze flow records, in this work we employ cluster analysis, since it is a unsupervised learning technique that does not require *a priori* knowledge about malicious communication patterns (in contrast to signature-based NIDS). The assumption is that we can detect different types of malicious traffic using flow records and cluster analysis. To prove technical feasibility of our proposal, we have developed a prototype and conducted an evaluation on network flows obtained from the University of Twente.

The rest of this paper is organized as follows: Section 2 provides background information and introduces the architecture proposed for detecting intra-domain malicious hosts. Next, Section 3 details the clustering algorithms employed. After that, Section 4 covers the experiments and the results obtained. Next, Section 5 presents the related work. Finally, Section 6 concludes the paper and proposes future work.

2   Intra-domain Malicious Hosts Detection Architecture

Figure 1 shows the proposed architecture for detecting intra-domain malicious hosts. NetFlow-enabled routers export flow records to a collector. This information is stored on a database and fed into the Anomaly Detection Engines (step 1 – in between parentheses – in the same figure) which are responsible for analyzing the input data. A broad range of attacks can be analyzed such as DDoS or port scan but we focus on spamming since botnets are well used for spamming [7].

Hence, we aim to find bots by looking at group of hosts having similar communication patterns with some of them involved in spamming activity. In this way, detecting spammers helps to figure out entirely botnet related traffic (C&C as well as other malicious activities). To do that, we first obtain a list email senders (step 2 in Figure 1) and exclude legitimate mail servers from our domain (step 3). Next, hosts sending many more emails than others are considered as potential spammers (step 4).

After obtaining a list of spamming hosts, we compute the following aggregated metrics (obtained from Botminer [8]) for all flows: the average number of individual flows

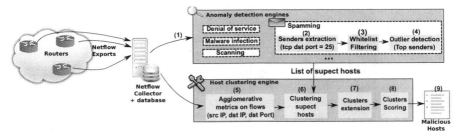

Fig. 1. Intra-domain malicious hosts detection architecture

per hour (*fph*), the average number of packets per flow (*ppf*) and the average number of bytes per packet (*bpp*).

In the end, for each flow we have the following tuple: <source IP address, destination IP address, destination UDP/TCP port, fph, ppf, bpp>. These metrics (step 5) allow to easily compare flow records from different hosts in order to find shared communication patterns (step 6). For example, if messages sent by a bot master reach two different hosts in our network, it is expected that they have similar properties, such as similar number of packets and bytes. In the same way, bots from a peer-to-peer botnet should exhibit similar communications to route the messages and to maintain the coherency of routing tables when nodes join or leave the network.

Once these agglomerative metrics are computed, the next step is to compare such metrics for flows related to hosts exhibiting abnormal activities in order to cluster them (step 6). It is important to note that it is applied on flows and not on hosts. It means that it also helps to distinguish the malicious traffic pattern from the benign ones for a single host.

The major advantage is the reduction the number of flows to be analyzed. Then, we extend the clusters to other flows (step 7) by comparing them with flows related to suspect hosts, reducing the overall complexity of the algorithm. Finally, a score is computed (step 8) for each cluster based on the similarity of flows within it and the number of hosts it contains which are tagged as suspect. Hosts as source of Netflow included in highly scored clusters are declared as malicious (step 9).

3   Detection Algorithms

3.1   Anomaly Detection Engine – Top Email Senders

On step 2 in Figure 1, we have to find a list of spamming hosts. After listing all hosts that have connections to mail servers *outside* our domain (machines have outgoing TCP connections on port 25), we remove legitimate IP addresses of legitimate mail servers from UT (step 3). Finally, we compute two metrics for each remaining host:

- n_i: the number of mail flows records per the host i,
- b_i: the total volume of email data sent per host i (in bytes).

The idea behind combining these metrics is that we can detect both hosts contacting many different mail servers and hosts sending too much mail data (specially related with spam campaigns that include attachments, such as PDF files). A more complex approach to detect spam using flow records was proposed by Sperotto *et al.* [9]. However, in our case we employ a faster and simpler approach because the output is the list of potential spammers for which no decision have to be taken and so can include benign hosts which will be discarded afterwards.

Therefore, a host is considered as a spamming one if the number of emails and bytes sent is higher than the observed average plus a margin expressed as a multiple of the standard deviation. Considering all hosts, the average number of emails sent by an individual host is avg_n and the corresponding standard deviation is std_n. In the same way, avg_b and std_b refer to the number of bytes. i is a spamming host if:

$$(n_i > avg_n + \sigma std_n) \; or \; (b_i > avg_b + \gamma std_b) \tag{1}$$

In this paper, γ and σ are set to 3 based on preliminary experiments. The corresponding hosts form the set S which is constructed in a linear time (iteration over all email senders).

3.2 Email Senders Clustering

Before starting the clustering algorithm, we obtain the following tuple for each single flow: <source IP address, destination IP address, destination UDP/TCP port, number of bytes, number of packets>. After that, we divide this set into two subsets: F_s, a subset that contains all the flows related to the spamming hosts and F_a, that contains all the remaining flows from the other machines. Then, we compute for each flow $f \in \{F_s \cup F_a\}$ the metrics introduced in section 2 (fph_f, ppf_f, and bpp_f).

In order to reduce the computational complexity, the first clustering process focuses on the suspect IP addresses (potential spammers) and creates clusters containing aggregated flow information from F_s. Hence, the goal is to find similar communication patterns involving multiple suspect hosts. Without any prior knowledge, unsupervised clustering is required. Besides, there is no assumption about the shape of clusters (following a certain distribution) and that is why nearest neighbor clustering [10] is fitted in our case. Medoids based methods are excluded because they entail computational overhead.

Nearest neighbor clustering assumes that two data points belong to the same cluster if the distance, $dist(d_1, d_2)$, between them is lower than the threshold θ. Regarding our context, each data point represents a tuple f as a vector $[fph_f, ppf_f, bpp_f]$. After normalizing the values, we applied the Euclidean distance on the vectors since this is commonly used in various contexts with multidimensional data.

The algorithm iterates over all f_i of F_s and compute $dist(f_i, f_j)$ for all $f_j \in F_s$ and $f_j \neq f_i$. The pairs of points which the resulting distance is lower than θ are aggregated into one cluster. If the aggregated points were prior assigned to another clusters, all points belonging to them are also aggregated (merging). The result is a set of clusters C.

Like many unsupervised algorithm, computing the distance between each pair of data points is needed which implies a quadratic complexity. Thus, this clustering process is only applied to a limited subset of points which were previously selected and form the set F_s.

3.3 Extending Clusters

The assignation list represents for each flow, the cluster where it is affected. Assuming K clusters, $C = \{c_1, \ldots, c_K\}$, the assignation list is $A = \{a_1, \ldots, a_{|F_s|}\}$ such that $a_i = c_j$ if the flow $f_i \in F_s$ is assigned to the cluster c_j. Each remaining non suspect point is assigned to the closest cluster except if this distance is too high that lead to consider the host as a benign one. They are represented by points outside of clusters in Figure 2a which shows a toy example in two dimensions. There are a first set of initial clusters constructed in the previous step and then the clusters are extended.

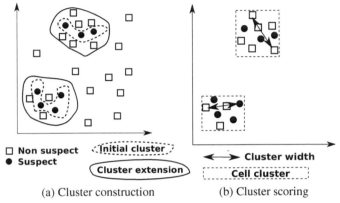

□ **Non suspect** ⟨Initial cluster⟩	◀──▶ **Cluster width**
● **Suspect**	
⟨**Cluster extension**⟩	**Cell cluster**

(a) Cluster construction · · · · · · · · · (b) Cluster scoring

Fig. 2. Clustering algorithms on a toy example

The distance between a new point to assign and a cluster is the minimal distance between this point and any point of the cluster. The assignation list denoted $A' = \{a'_1, \ldots, a'_{|F_a|}\}$ is defined as follows:

$$a'_i = \begin{cases} a_k \ if \ f_k = \underset{f_j \in F_s}{\arg\min} \, dist(f_i, f_j) \ and \ dist(f_i, f_k) < \theta' \\ unassigned \ else \end{cases} \tag{2}$$

From a computational point of view, the distance between each non suspect data point and suspect data points have to be computed. It is equivalent to $|F_s| \times |F_a|$ iterations. Considering the quadratic complexity of the constructions of clusters in the previous step, the total number of iterations is $|F_s| \times (|F_s| + |F_a|)$ whereas naive clustering of all flows would have led to $(|F_s| + |F_a|)^2$ iterations.

3.4 Scoring

Once clusters are created, the goal is to identify those containing hosts with higher probability of being malicious. Since our approach relies on the malicious activities and the similar communication patterns, a score is assigned to each cluster based on these criteria. In brief, the first component of score named $score\_anomaly_i$ represents the proportion of hosts related to malicious activities in the cluster c_i:

$$score\_anomaly_i = \frac{|\{f_j \in F_s, a_j = c_i\}|}{|\{f_j \in F_s, a_j = c_i\}| + |\{f_k \in F_s, a_k = c_i\}|} \tag{3}$$

The other component of the global score considers also the similarity among the flow information containing in the cluster. The lower the distances between the points of a cluster, the higher the score is. This can be regarded as the width of the cluster (maximal distance between two internal points as shown in figure 2b). The computation of the width can be long since clusters should contain hundreds or thousands of points and computing all pair-wise distance is quadratic. Therefore, we propose a simple method inspired from grid clustering techniques [11] where each cluster is represented as a squared cell like in the toy example in figure 2b. Only one iteration per point is needed to compute the coordinate of the cell since the goal is to find the maximal and minimal value for each dimension (two in the toy example and three in our context). Assuming the cluster c_i, the similarity score is defined:

$$score\_sim_i = dist(FMin_i, FMax_i) \tag{4}$$

where $FMin_i$ and $FMax_i$ are fictive points containing minimal and maximal values for fph_f, ppf_f and bpp_f subject to f assigned to c_i. For example, the first feature of $FMin$ is:

$$\min_{\{f_j \in F_s, a_j = c_i\} \cup \{f_j \in F_a, a'_j = c_i\}} fph_{f_j}$$

Since, the iterations have only to cover each point one time, the complexity is $O(n)$ where n is the number of points in a cluster. Traditional methods have to compute pair-wise distances for extracting then the minimal, maximal or the average one. Unlike our method, the complexity is $O(n^2)$.

Finally, the global score of the cluster c_i is the usual mean of both scores:

$$S_i = \frac{score\_anomaly_i + score\_sim_i}{2} \tag{5}$$

If the score is higher than the threshold ψ, all source IP addresses related to the cluster are considered as malicious. It includes spamming hosts as well as other ones thanks to the cluster extension process.

4   Experimental Evaluation

In this section we describe the evaluation conducted to prove technical feasibility of our proposal. As describe in Figure 1, the first step is to obtain NetFlow data from external data sources. For this experiment, we have obtained two NetFlow datasets from the University of Twente (a /16 network):

- **Dataset A**: 1 hour of flow records (April 10th, 2010, from 5:00 PM to 6:00 PM CEST) – a total of more than 12 million records;
- **Dataset B**: 2 hours of flow records (April 10th, 2010, from 3:00 PM to 5:00 PM CEST) – more than 24 million records.

Dataset A was used in the anomaly detection engine in Figure 1, while the dataset B was used in the host clustering engine. Next we present the detection results and the validation.

4.1 Malicious Host Detection

After obtaining the aforementioned datasets, we analyze the first one (A) to find hosts that have contacted more mail servers outside of our domain (steps 2 and 3 in Figure 1). Then, we removed legitimated mail servers from this list, and two hosts have been automatically selected to be fed into the host clustering engine. The first host was tagged as suspect since it has contacted 45 distinct mail servers outside our domain (some of them more than one time) within one hour, in a total of 250 flow records. Thus, we can assume that at least 250 accounts were target. The other host tagged as suspect has contacted 12 distinct mail servers in a total of 12 flow records.

Next, we have computed the metrics defined in Section 2 for the dataset B (step 5). In the end, we had 5,424,333 entries in the metrics table with the following format: IP source/destination, destination port, fph, ppf, and bpp. It is important to emphasize that we have computed these metrics for not only mail flow records, but all flow records. By doing that, our algorithm is suitable detecting common communication patterns and not only spam. So even, it helps to distinguish potential C&C flows from other ones even if there are few hosts.

In step 6 and 7, two level clustering is applied on the metrics obtained in the previous step, regard the parameter θ. We assume that $\theta = \theta'$ (the similarity within a cluster has to be same when comparing spamming hosts or any other hosts). Therefore, when θ increases, more points are grouped within each cluster and so the total number of clusters decreases. This is shown in Figures 3a and 3b where each cluster is represented by two points (the score and the size equivalent to the number of distinct source IP addresses among all flows of the cluster). The x-axis represents only an arbitrary cluster index but also indicates the total number of clusters which is the maximal index. More complex method, based on cluster characteristics, might be used to fine-tune the parameters similar to [12].

In Figure 3a, there are two main groups of clusters. Firstly, many clusters have a very low scores. They represents normal group of IP addresses which the underling applications exhibit different patterns. Secondly, there are many clusters with high score (> 0.5). In fact, the corresponding sizes are very low (one or two IP addresses). Therefore, the high score is only due to the bias introduced by the anomaly score (*score_anomaly*) equal 1. Indeed, such clusters may easily contain 100% of flows related to potential spammers since they contain only one or two IP addresses. That is why these clusters are discarded for further analysis. However, there is a third group of outlier scores below 0.1 between these extrema.

In order to figure out them easily, θ is increased in Figure 3b to merge clusters with few IP addresses. This case is an extreme one showing very few clusters and highlighting only one score greatly higher than others (the second index on x-axis). Therefore, this case was chosen in the end of the clustering process. The selected cluster contains 100 different flow tuples from 52 distinct IP addresses under University of Twente domain, which represent the list of malicious hosts obtained in the step 7.

4.2 Complexity

The core construction of initial clusters is quadratic (section 3.2) due to the calculation of all pairwise distances. To avoid this drawback, some samples (potential spammers)

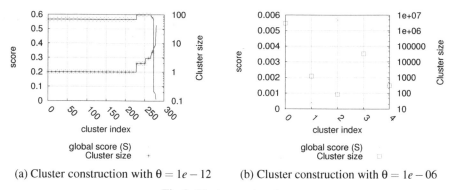

(a) Cluster construction with $\theta = 1e - 12$ (b) Cluster construction with $\theta = 1e - 06$

Fig. 3. Cluster construction

are selected in a linear time (33k iterations) regarding the number of SMTP flows (section 3.1). Then, the two selected hosts coverages $143k$ records. It leads to $143k^2$ calculations for the initial clustering. Then, $143k \times 24M$ operations are necessary for the cluster extension which represent around 0.6% if no prior selection and clustering were performed ($24M^2$ iterations to compute all pair-wise distance). Finally, the scoring process has to deal with about 3,000,000 points in the worst case (the biggest cluster). The complexity of our scoring method is linear whereas traditional approaches are quadratic (section 3.4). So, the number of iterations is also divided by 3M.

Even our approach has similarities with other ones [8], we have really focus on reducing the running time by optimizing the algorithms. This is particularly important when monitoring large networks.

4.3   Validation and Egress Traffic Filtering

When evaluating the performance of techniques for intrusion detection, researches usually rely on labeled datasets, which contains meta-information about the attacks observed. Usually such kind of datasets are available in pcap format, *i.e.*, complete network traces. Since our technique is based on flow records instead, we could not benefit from these datasets. Even though Sperotto *et al.* [13] have provided the first labeled dataset for flow-based intrusion detection, this could not be used in our research, since in this work we evaluate egress traffic instead. More than that, their dataset is based on a single host – which is not suitable for our clustering technique. Due to that, we have to check manually the flow records associated to the 52 malicious hosts obtained as a result of our detection technique to try to find whether malicious behavior was observed or not. Some interesting findings were obtained:

– One desktop PC was found having 7151 SMTP flows to 245 different mail servers located in many different countries for a 24 hours period. Since flows contain only a summary of a connection, we cannot tell how many messages are sent per flow. Assuming, in this case, that only one message was sent per flow, we have a total of almost 5 mail messages send per second, which is very unusual for a desktop. Figure 4 shows the number of SMTP flows to each mail server. Moreover, the same

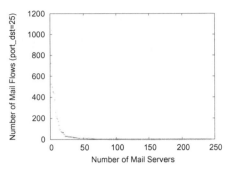

Fig. 4. Number of flows from one suspect host to different mail servers

machine have contacted two different IRC servers, in a total of 1193 flows. Such behavior is typical for a machine belonging to a spamming IRC botnet.

– One Windows desktop found running a non-authorized service on UDP and TCP port 56168. After checking with the Security Administrator at UT, it was found that this machine was the desktop of a professor that was unaware of it. He was promptly notified. In this two hour period, this machine has been contacted by 72579 different IP addresses on the aforementioned port, transmitting more than 66MB of data. Also, a hidden web server was found on this machine, which was contacted by 353 different hosts. We have extended the analysis for this machine and found out that 330,925 different IP addresses reached it on April 10th 2010 – a very suspect behavior for a desktop. We suspect this machine may be working as a botmaster (remotely controlled) or as a coordination point for botnets like those used by Storm [14].

– Another computer on the wireless network – which, by definition, should not run any services – was found running a suspect service on port 23352, for TCP and UDP (mostly UDP). In this 2 hours period, the machine was contacted by 96.609 different hosts from various countries. Since this machine is mobile, we could not reach it by the time of the analysis. For this period, 19GB of data was transfered to these different hosts.

– One machine from the student network was also running a suspect service on UDP and TCP port 32861, which was contacted by 77,434 different hosts in two hours. 67 MB of data were transfered in this case.

– Another host was found running a suspect service on TCP and UDP port 39563, contacted by 79824 distinct IP addresses from various locations. 66 MB of data were transfered in this two hours.

Even though the validation process was manually and not extensively executed, this results shows that our approach was able to detect the involved hosts based on very small list of potential suspect addresses – 2 spamming hosts detected before applying clustering. By blocking such malicious hosts in our domain ("cleaning our houses first"), we can avoid their malicious activities to reach the Internet. Some estimates can be calculated from blocking malicious hosts: assuming that every flow of the spamming bot we found represents a single spam, by blocking only this host, we could avoid 7151 spam messages to reach the Internet. If the botnet this host is part has a size of 100k bots, by dismantling it (looking at the IRC traffic) we could potentially avoid 715 millions spam messages to reach the Internet in a single day. That represents 878.2 GB of data by extrapolating the monitored metrics. The same reasoning can be extended to other machines that our previous analysis has figured out and as well to other source of network attacks, such as DDoS. The more egress filtering is employed by ISPs and businesses, the more malicious traffic can be blocked from the Internet.

5   Related Work

Van Eeten *et al.* [4] have evaluated a dataset of 63 billion spam messages obtained between 2005 and 2008. By analyzing the IP addresses of the sources, they observed that 10 ISPs account for 30% of unique IP addresses sending spam worldwide, 50 ISPs for half of all sources. Even though this study was performed on a not up-to-date data set, it suggests the benefits that can be achieved by filtering egress traffic of few ISPs.

In another work, de Vries *et al.* [3] have shown that egress mail traffic can be easily filtered using lightweight techniques. However, in this work the authors rely on the message's content when filtering the traffic. A survey on flow-based intrusion detection, on the hand, was presented by Sperotto *et. al* [6]. Differently from this work, the authors focus on detecting malicious host on the Internet, while in this work we target intra-domain malicious hosts.

Deploying a honeypot to be infected by a bot software is usually a direct and convenient way to study a botnet but it may not be efficient [15]. Tracking infected hosts can also be done by monitoring DNS requests of the machines [16] especially for an IRC botnet. A lot of techniques detect a botnet relying on the malicious activities such as scanning or denial of service attacks [17]. In our approach, we leverage the same knowledge but then we improve the botnet detection by detecting common communication patterns of the C&C channel. P2P botnets are usually detected by active techniques such as in [18]. Graph algorithms may be also employed to infer interesting properties of bots relationships [19].

In this work, we have conducted a study case on spamming hosts. We based our work on two works by Gu *et. al* [8] [20]. In our work, we correlate malicious activities with C&C detected communication patterns. The main difference between BotMiner [8] and our approach is that we apply clustering only to a small subset of Netflows resulting in clusters which are extended afterwards to all Netflows. It leads to a huge improvement of the complexity and so the running time.

6   Conclusions and Future Work

In this paper we propose a new paradigm to be employed by ISPs and businesses for protecting their own networks. Instead of solely filter ingress traffic, in this work we investigate the benefits that can be achieved by filtering *egress* traffic as well (cleaning our own house first). The motivation is that if such policy is widely adopted, the overall amount of malicious traffic on the Internet could be significantly reduced. That would ultimately lead to saving considerable amounts of money and computer/network resources.

Therefore, in this paper we investigated the following research question: *what can be achieved by filtering egress traffic from a particular domain?* To answer this question, we have refined clustering techniques to analyze flow records from the University of Twente. As our results have shown, we were able to detect many suspect hosts. By detecting and blocking one of these hosts, for example, we could have been able to avoid that 7151 spam messages could reach the Internet in first place. The same reasoning applies to the other suspect hosts. More than that, our results have shown that such filtering could help to detect and dismantle botnet operations *outside* the monitored domain. The benefits of egress filtering would only increase as more ISPs and businesses adopt it as a common practice.

As future work, we intend to combine surpervised detection methods (since they are more efficient to detect known attacks) with clustering analysis. The idea is to combine both methods for improving the detection accuracy in various scenarios. Finally, we plan to obtain an economic model in order to estimate how much can be saved by filtering egress traffic.

Acknowledgments. The authors would like to thank Radu State, Anna Sperotto, Marc Berenschot, Ramin Sadre, and Olivier Festor for their valuable comments, suggestions, and contributions for this work.

References

1. Arbor networks. Worldwide infrastructure security report (2009 report). Technical report (2010)
2. John, J.P., Moshchuk, A., Gribble, S.D., Krishnamurthy, A.: Studying spamming botnets using Botlab. In: NSDI 2009: Proceedings of the 6th USENIX Symposium on Networked Systems Design and Implementation, pp. 291–306. USENIX Association, Berkeley (2009)
3. de Vries, W.W., Moreira Moura, G.C., Pras, A.: Fighting spam on the sender side: A lightweight approach. In: Aagesen, F.A., Knapskog, S.J. (eds.) EUNICE 2010. LNCS, vol. 6164, pp. 188–197. Springer, Heidelberg (2010)
4. van Eeten, M., Bauerb, J.M., Asgharia, H., Tabatabaiea, S., Randc, D.: The Role of Internet Service Providers in Botnet Mitigation: An Empirical Analysis Based on Spam Data. In: WEIS 2010: Ninth Workshop on the Economics of Information Security (2010)
5. Cisco Systems. Cisco IOS NetFlow (August 2010)
6. Sperotto, A., Schaffrath, G., Sadre, R., Morariu, C., Pras, A., Stiller, B.: An Overview of IP Flow-Based Intrusion Detection. IEEE Communications Surveys Tutorials 12(3), 343–356 (2010)
7. Xie, Y., Yu, F., Achan, K., Panigrahy, R., Hulten, G., Osipkov, I.: Spamming botnets: signatures and characteristics. SIGCOMM Comput. Commun. Rev. 38(4), 171–182 (2008)
8. Gu, G., Perdisci, R., Zhang, J., Lee, W.: Botminer: clustering analysis of network traffic for protocol- and structure-independent botnet detection. In: USENIX Security Symposium (SS), San Jose, CA, pp. 139–154 (July 2008)
9. Sperotto, A., Vliek, G., Sadre, R., Pras, A.: Detecting spam at the network level. In: Oliver, M., Sallent, S. (eds.) EUNICE 2009. LNCS, vol. 5733, pp. 208–216. Springer, Heidelberg (2009)
10. Day, W.H., Edelsbrunner, H.: Efficient algorithms for agglomerative hierarchical clustering methods. Journal of Classification 1(1), 7–24 (1984)

11. Schikuta, E.: Grid-clustering: a fast hierarchical clustering method for very large data sets. In: Proceedings 15th Int. Conf. on Pattern Recognition, pp. 101–105 (1996)
12. François, J., Abdelnur, H., State, R., Festor, O.: Automated Behavioral Fingerprinting. In: Kirda, E., Jha, S., Balzarotti, D. (eds.) RAID 2009. LNCS, vol. 5758, pp. 182–201. Springer, Heidelberg (2009)
13. Sperotto, A., Sadre, R., van Vliet, F., Pras, A.: A Labeled Data Set for Flow-Based Intrusion Detection. In: Nunzi, G., Scoglio, C., Li, X. (eds.) IPOM 2009. LNCS, vol. 5843, pp. 39–50. Springer, Heidelberg (2009)
14. Porras, P., Sadi, H., Yegneswaran, V.: A Multi-perspective Analysis of the Storm (Peacomm) Worm
15. Wang, P., Wu, L., Cunningham, R., Zou, C.C.: Honeypot detection in advanced botnet attacks. Int. J. Inf. Comput. Secur. 4(1), 30–51 (2010)
16. Rajab, M.A., Zarfoss, J., Monrose, F., Terzis, A.: A multifaceted approach to understanding the botnet phenomenon. In: ACM SIGCOMM conference on Internet measurement (IMC), pp. 41–52 (2006)
17. Karasaridis, A., Rexroad, B., Hoeflin, D.: Wide-scale botnet detection and characterization. In: First Workshop on Hot Topics in Understanding Botnets (HotBots). USENIX (2007)
18. Holz, T., Steiner, M., Dahl, F., Biersack, E., Freiling, F.: Measurements and mitigation of peer-to-peer-based botnets: a case study on storm worm. In: LEET 2008: Proceedings of the 1st Usenix Workshop on Large-Scale Exploits and Emergent Threats, pp. 1–9. USENIX Association, Berkeley (2008)
19. François, J., Wang, S., State, R., Engel, T.: BotTrack: Tracking Botnets using NetFlow and PageRank. In: Domingo-Pascual, J., Manzoni, P., Palazzo, S., Pont, A., Scoglio, C. (eds.) NETWORKING 2011, Part I. LNCS, vol. 6640, pp. 1–14. Springer, Heidelberg (2011)
20. Gu, G., Porras, P., Yegneswaran, V., Fong, M., Lee, W.: Bothunter: detecting malware infection through ids-driven dialog correlation. In: USENIX Security Symposium (SS) (August 2007)

Efficient Distributed Signature Analysis

Michael Vogel, Sebastian Schmerl, Hartmut König

Brandenburg University of Technology, Cottbus
Computer Science Department
{mv,sbs,koenig}@informatik.tu-cottbus.de

Abstract. Intrusion Detection Systems (IDS) have proven as valuable measure to cope reactively with attacks in the Internet. The growing complexity of IT-systems, however, increases rapidly the audit data volumes and the size of the signature bases. This forces IDS to drop audit data in high load situations thus offering attackers chances to act undetected. To tackle this issue we propose an efficient and adaptive analysis approach for multi-step signatures that is based on a dynamic distribution of analyses. We propose different optimization strategies for an efficient analysis distribution. The strengths and weaknesses of each strategy are evaluated based on a prototype implementation.

1 Introduction

Intrusion detection systems (IDS) have been proven as an important instrument for the protection of computer systems and networks. Nowadays, most IDS use a centralized approach and apply misuse detection (signature analysis). They mainly use single-step signatures to identify harmful behavior in a stream of audit data or network packets, respectively. This will change in next years, since multi-step signatures, in contrast to single step signatures, allow it to model attacks much more precisely, in particular the specific characteristics of the attack traces, existing dependencies, and the chronological order of the attack steps. This will reduce significantly the false alarm rate. Multi-step signatures can store state information to track the attack through its different stages. This supports in particular the attack detection in application layer protocols as well as in Web 2.0 applications which are of increasing importance. Many semantic aspects of today's attacks cannot be modeled by single-step signatures at all or only insufficiently. Therefore, we focus our work on multi-step signatures.

A challenge that all intrusion detection systems are facing is the increasing performance of networks and end systems. This leads to a rapid growth of audit data volumes to be analyzed. On the other hand, the growing complexity of IT systems creates novel vulnerabilities and offers new possibilities for running attacks so that the number of signatures to be analyzed increases as well. Already now intrusion detection systems are forced to reject audit data in high load situations or to delay the analysis of security violations significantly. Thus, counter-measures become impossible or lose their impact. As consequence, systems become unprotected, when they are intensively used.

I. Chrisment et al. (Eds.): AIMS 2011, LNCS 6734, pp. 13–25, 2011.
© IFIP International Federation for Information Processing 2011

To cope with this situation several approaches have been proposed, e.g. the detection of intrusions based on an analysis of more compact, less detailed audit data [2, 3] and network flows [1] as well as various optimizing analysis methods for signature and network based single-step intrusion detection systems. For example, [6] describes an approach for the IDS SNORT that transforms signatures into a decision tree to reduce the number of redundant comparisons during analysis. Optimized string matching algorithms are proposed in [5]. These approaches aim at optimizing the non-distributed, single threaded signature analyses. A distributed approach like GNORT [8] utilizes the massive parallel computing capabilities of graphic processors (GPUs), but it only doubles the analysis throughput compared to the sequential Snort. So far, network-based IDS only apply primitive means to parallelize analyses by load balancing [10, 11]. There are also almost no approaches to parallelize host-based IDS analyses [9].

On the other hand, free computing resources are available in any network. CPU technology will provide only slightly more computation power per core in the future. In this paper we present a distributed signature analysis approach to use free resources in networks to overcome this issue. In Section 2 we introduce a generic model for multi-step signatures to discuss distribution strategies. Next, in Section 3 we introduce several distribution strategies and outline their benefits and constraints for multi-step IDS. In Section 4 we evaluate the strategies based on measurements of a prototype implementation and discuss their applicability. Some final remarks conclude the paper.

2 Modeling Multi-step Signatures

We first introduce a generic model for multi-step signatures which covers all existing multi-step-signature languages and related intrusion detection systems. The model confines to typical characteristics of multi-step signatures and their analysis. The core concept of a multi-step signature language is its ability to store information about attacks, system states, and related changes. Accordingly, a multi-step signature can be defined as a directed, labeled graph $MS = \{V, E, EvT, SI, f, state, sens, cond, mark, trans\}$ with:

- V – set of state nodes, representing the stages of an attack,
- $E \subseteq V \times V$ – set of edges representing valid state transitions,
- EvT – finite set of types of security relevant events (audit events), e.g. different types of system calls or network events,
- SI – set of state information representing the state and the stage of a certain attack,
- $state: V \rightarrow \wp(SI)$ – a function which labels state nodes with a set $si \subseteq SI$ of state information,
- $f \in V$ – a final node indicating a detected attack as soon as labeled by $state(f)$,
- $sens: E \rightarrow EvT$ – a function which labels each graph edge with an event type, whereby the occurrence of an event of the specified type can trigger a state transition represented by the edge,
- $cond: E \rightarrow B$ – a function labeling each edge $(a, b) \in E$ with a Boolean condition $B: SI \times Ev \rightarrow \{0, 1\}$ which specifies arbitrary expressions (arithmetic, string matching, …) between features of state information $si \in state(a)$ of node a and the occurring event $ev \in Ev$, whereby a state transition requires a fulfilled condition,

- *mark: V × SI → V* – a labeling function which adds state information *si* to node *v*, whereby *mark(v, si) = v'*, with *state(v') = state(v) ∪ si*,
- *trans: E × Ev → V* – transition function that evaluates for each occurring event *ev* of type *evType ∈ EvT* whether edge *e = (a, b) ∈ E* is sensitive to this event type (*sens(e) = evType*) and whether its condition *cond(e)* is fulfilled. In this case, the transition *(a, b)* is executed by reading state information *si* of node *a* by *state(a)*, modifying *si* (its features) to *si'*, and moving *si'* to node *b* by applying *mark(b, si')*.

The detection of a multi-step attack can be outlined as follows. For each occurring audit event *ev* and for each edge *e = (a, b) ∈ E* of the signature, the function *trans(e, ev)* is executed. This function evaluates by *sens(e)* whether edge *e* is sensitive to the type of event *ev* which may triggers a state transition. In this case, the edge condition *cond(e)* is evaluated by correlating features of event *ev* with state information *si ∈* state(a) of node *a* which represents the stage of the attack and contains aggregated information of former state transitions. If the edge condition *cond(e)* is fulfilled the state transition *(a, b)* is executed in two steps: (1) State information *si ∈ state(a)* is read and updated or modified with information from the current event *ev*. (2) Next, the successor node *b* is labeled with the modified state information *si'* by *mark(b, si')*. This evaluation process is executed for each edge of the signature and all signatures. It must be repeated for each occurring audit event. An attack is detected if the final node *f* of a signature is reached and labeled with state information.

Now we extend the model for the needs of a distributed analysis by defining functions for statistical data collection to derive optimal distribution decisions.

- *C* – a cluster representing a virtual analysis unit with limited computation capacities to assign signature fragments (state nodes) to,
- *cl: V → C* – a function which assigns each state node to a cluster, whereby initially each node is assigned to a unique cluster,
- *compC: E → N* – a function labeling each edge *e ∈ E* with the value of the computation effort (e.g. #cpu cycles), which was consumed in the previous time frame to evaluate the edge condition of *e*.
- commC: *E → N* – a function labeling each edge *(a, b) ∈ E* with the value of the communication effort (e.g. #bytes) which was consumed in the previous time frame to transmit state information from *a* to *b*.
- *evC: E → N* – a function labeling each edge *(a, b) ∈ E* with the value of the communication effort which was consumed in the previous time frame to transmit audit events of type *sens(a, b)* from a sensor to node *a*.

3   Distributed Audit Data Analysis Strategies

In signature based intrusion detection systems the analysis of audit data requires considerable computation efforts. Signature bases that cover all currently known vulnerabilities of the protected systems may easily consist of thousands of signatures. In high load situations, when large amounts of audit data are recorded, the resource consumption of the analysis system grows rapidly and exceeds frequently the available resources. For very short time periods (seconds), buffering can be an appropriate measure, but as soon as the buffer capacities are exhausted the analysis system has to drop audit data and becomes useless and blind for attacks.

In order to reliably prevent such overload situations the analysis efforts of a signature based IDS should be kept continuously on a reasonable low level. This can be achieved by distributing and balancing the required analysis efforts among free resources in the protected domain. So it is more appropriate to utilize five analysis units with a load of 20 % each, instead of only two systems with 50 % load each. This allows it to keep sufficient, free resources needed for analysis efforts in high load situations. As known, analysis distribution causes additional communication overhead which burdens the network and may lead to transmission delays. To ensure that the transmission of audit data in high load situations does not delay the analysis, sufficient bandwidth has to be provided. These demands, however, are conflictive and cannot be achieved at the same time.

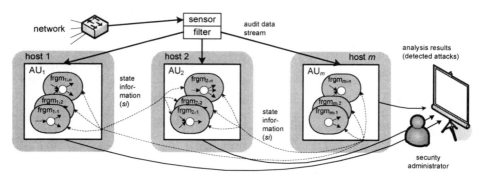

Fig. 1. Elements of a distributed signature analysis

Fig. 1 shows the elements of a distributed audit data analysis. A *sensor* logs audit events which are forwarded to *analysis units*, in our example AU_1 to AU_3. Each analysis unit AU_i evaluates a subset of the signatures. The audit events are classified into different event types EvT. To reduce the network utilization a configurable *filter* discards non-relevant audit events of types which are not needed by the respective analysis unit. For example, only events of type EvT in $\cup_{a,b \in V_1} sens(a, b)$ are forwarded to AU_1, where V_1 is the set of state nodes assigned to AU_1. The analysis units transmit state information $si \in SI$ between each other if needed. Analysis results are reported to a central component. Based on this concept we present below five distribution strategies.

A) Distributing Complete Signatures

The first approach simply distributes complete signatures to different analysis units AU_i. Hereby, a simple optimization can be performed balancing the number of assigned signatures to each analysis unit. Additionally, a finer-grained optimization can be achieved if statistics on resource consumption are gathered continuously for each signature. So CPU hardware counters can be used [7] to determine the number of clock cycles utilized to evaluate audit events and edge conditions for each signature. For this, the signatures' edges e are labeled with these values by function $compC(e)$ to estimate the resource consumption of each signature. An example for a respective signature distribution is depicted in Fig. 2. Edges are labeled with required computation effort and examined event types as defined by *compC(e)* and *sens(e)*, respectively.

This simple strategy causes, however, two major problems. (1) If an overload situation is mainly caused by a certain signature the performance problem will be solely moved to another analysis unit (another CPU or host) and the strategy to distribute whole signatures fails. (2) A typical signature *MS* usually correlates different types of audit events. Particularly, *MS* analyzes all audit events of types in $\cup_{a,b \in V} sens(a, b)$, where *V* is the set of state nodes of *MS*. If whole signatures are distributed nearly all audit events captured by a sensor have to be sent to the related analysis units. This multiplies the communication effort by *n* (number of used analysis units). This is unacceptable for most IT-infrastructures. Fig. 2 depicts these problems exemplarily.

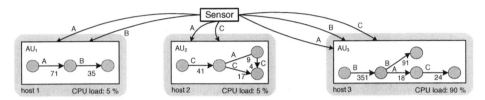

Fig. 2. Example of a simple, non-fragmented signature distribution

First, the three signatures MS_1 to MS_3 are assigned to AU_1 to AU_3. An optimal distribution would strive for a balanced load on all three systems of 33 % each. But, the analysis of signature MS_3 utilizes 90 % of the available resources of the respective analysis unit, while the analyses of MS_1 and MS_2 require only 5 % each. Secondly, additional communication is caused through event duplication. So the sensor has to triplicate type *A* events because they are analyzed by all three signatures. Analogously, type *B* and *C* events have to be duplicated for two analysis units. Therefore, further distribution options are required to balance the computation load finer-grained and to reduce the communication overhead.

B) Fragmenting Signatures
A more fine-grained signature distribution can be achieved by distributing signature fragments. This allows it to minimize audit event duplication. One or many state nodes (fragments) of a signature can be assigned to various analysis units, as depicted in Fig. 1. Now the distribution strategy can pool nodes having outgoing state transition edges which are sensitive to the same audit event types (label *sens(a, b)*) onto the same analysis units. So, audit events only have to be duplicated for few analysis units. Fragmentation also supports a better balance of the analysis efforts among the units. Signatures that require the majority of available computation resources of an analysis unit, as discussed above, can be split up now. An optimization strategy though which only aims at pooling signature fragments that analyze the same audit event types on the same analysis unit is not desirable. If two state nodes $a, b \in V$ are connected by an edge (a, b) and a and b have been assigned to different analysis units AU_1 and AU_2 ($cl(a) \neq cl(b)$), then state information $si \in SI$ must be transferred from AU_1 to AU_2, whenever transition condition *cond(a, b)* is fulfilled. The transfer of state information

has to be minimized as well. To sum up, signature fragmentation allows a better balance of the computation load among analysis units and reduces audit event duplication. Fragmentation though may cause additional communication to transfer state information between analysis units.

C) Additional Reduction of the Communication Costs

Our next optimization does not primarily aim for an optimal balance of the computation efforts among the analysis units. Instead it takes the required communication effort to transmit audit events from the sensor to the analysis units into account as well as the transfer of state information between the distributed units.

To achieve this, the sensor has to gather a statistics that logs how often audit events of different types occur. The average data amount of an audit event is almost the same ($evSize = 100 \ldots 1000$ bytes). The communication costs to transmit events of different types from the sensor to each analysis unit are labeled to the event types by function $evC(evType) = \#events * evSize$. Additionally, each analysis unit continuously maintains a statistics that logs the number and size of transferred state information separately for each edge of the multi-step signature. The statistical values are labeled at each edge (a, b) of the signature by function $commC(a, b)$. They allow determining the communication effort for audit event duplication and state information transfers for arbitrary signature distributions as an optimization criteria. For a given signature distribution, the event duplication effort can be determined according to equation (1).

$$\sum_{i=1}^{\#AU} \sum_{evT \in S_i} evC(evT), \text{ where } S_i = \bigcup_{a \in V_i, b \in V} sens(a, b) \quad (1) \qquad \sum_{(a,b) \in E, cl(a) \neq cl(b)} commC(a, b) \quad (2)$$

Here, S_i is the set of event types examined by the subset V_i of signature fragments ($V_i \subset V$) that is assigned to AU_i. Similarly, the statistics permits to calculate the communication costs for state information transfers among different AUs by eq. (2). We apply the cluster component of our signature model (cf. Sect. 2). Each state node a is mapped onto a cluster by function $cl(a)$, virtually representing an analysis unit. Only state information transfers between nodes a and b assigned to different AUs (clusters) cause real communication costs. Transfers between nodes on the same AU use shared memory.

Based on the statistical data, we can determine a communication efficient distribution of signature fragments by using a Greedy clustering algorithm. For this, we initially assign each state node of the signatures to an exclusive cluster. This initial state represents a virtual signature distribution for a maximum number of analysis units. In this case, all communication costs labeled to clusters and the signature edges are relevant because the audit events have to be duplicated for various analysis units and all state information has to be transferred between nodes assigned to different analysis units. Therefore, the initial stage represents the worst case communication scenario. The communication overhead, as defined in equations (1) and (2), can now be minimized by an iterative merging of clusters. We merge stepwise two clusters C_i and C_j that possess the maximum cumulated communication costs ($\Sigma_{(a, b) \in E} commC(a, b)$, with $cl(a) = C_i$, $cl(b) = C_j$) on edges leading from nodes of C_i to nodes of C_j or vice versa. This merging process is repeated until the desired number of analysis units (e.g. 3) is reached. Since the clustering algorithm only optimizes the communication costs, it is necessary to limit the number of assigned state nodes and thus the computation effort required to evaluate the transition conditions for each cluster. As a result, our clustering algorithm creates signature distributions with a minimal communication overhead and an acceptable balance of analysis effort.

D) Detection of Repeated Dependencies between Audit Events

A fine-grained signature distribution, as described above, induces new challenges. When fragmentation is applied and the nodes of a signature are assigned to different analysis units, state information may arrive delayed at the successor nodes due to network latencies. An attack, however, can be only detected in the audit event stream if all preceding attack steps, described by the state information, have been recognized before. This is not possible, when the state information arrives too late. There is a simple solution for this problem. Since audit events from the same sensor can be ordered chronologically, state information can be related to the audit events. This can be achieved by enumerating all emitted audit events consecutively with a unique ID in the sensor. Each state information si is labeled with the ID of the related audit event. Thus, the analysis units can easily identify delayed state information by comparing their IDs. Fig. 3 illustrates the problem.

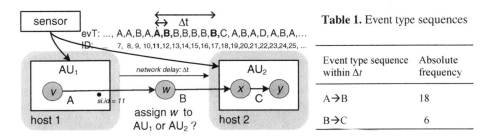

Table 1. Event type sequences

Event type sequence within Δt	Absolute frequency
A→B	18
B→C	6

Fig. 3. Unfavorable sequence of audit events

It shows a fragmented signature consisting of four nodes. The nodes v, x and y are assigned to the analysis units AU_1 and AU_2, respectively. Which is the optimal assignment of node w? The assumed sequence of audit events emitted by the sensor is indicated above the AUs. Since type B events often occur after type A, while type C events rarely occur after B, node w should be assigned together with v to AU_1 to prevent delayed state information arrivals at node w. If delayed state information arrives the related audit event has to be re-evaluated. This requires that the audit events are buffered in the analysis units for a short time. When new state information arrives all audit events that are older than the received one can be removed from the buffer. Therefore, the required buffer memory is assumed to be constant and is not discussed further here.

The repeated evaluation of audit events though may lead to a significant additional computation effort. We demonstrate this with the example above and assume now that node w has been assigned to AU_2. If a type A event triggers a transition the respective state information has to be placed on node w. We assume that the information is delayed by Δt due to network latencies. The absolute frequency of type B and C events occurring after type A and B events within Δt is listed in Table 1. When events of type B occur after A within a time window of Δt, they have to be buffered in AU_2 for repeated evaluation. An event sequence in the audit data stream containing events of type i and j within Δt is called *critical* if it may cause repeated evaluations. This is the case, if an applied signature contains edges which are sensitive to i and j, respectively, and a type j event is expected after analyzing a type i event. Now, the sensor and the analysis units can dynamically update the statistics how often such critical sequences occur in the audit event stream. Each analysis unit also continuously logs number and types of repeatedly evaluated audit events. Based on this statistics, the responsible transition edges of a signature can be assigned to the same unit to avoid repeated analyses.

E) Iterative Adaptation of Signature Distributions

The characteristics of the audit data stream can change frequently. Therefore, the statistics on critical event sequences has to be updated continuously and the signature distribution has to be adapted accordingly. All optimization strategies described above determine an entirely new signature distribution. This requires high reorganization efforts because usually many state nodes have to be moved to other analysis units. Therefore, these strategies should only be applied to get an optimal initial signature distribution. They may be repeated perhaps 2–6 times per day. For the normal analysis process, an iterative adaptation strategy should be preferred which adapts the signature distribution with minimal reorganization continuously. If the resource consumption of the distributed analysis systems runs out of balance signature fragments from high loaded analysis units should be reassigned to less occupied ones. The fragments to be moved can be selected accordingly to one of the following procedures. (a) A fragment from the most occupied analysis unit is reassigned to the least occupied unit. (b) Like (a), but the most suitable fragment is selected whose reassignment rebalances the computation load best. This can be achieved by evaluating the computational loads of the analysis units using the analysis statistics based on equation (2). (c) That fragment is chosen from the highest loaded unit which mostly requires repeated event analysis due to delayed state information. Again, the analysis statistics have to be evaluated to select the responsible signature fragment. We consider again nodes v and w of the above example. Let node v be the source of the delayed information and $(v, w) \in E$, then node w is reassigned to the same analysis unit as node v. No additional effort for repeated event analysis will be induced by state information transfers between v and w during further analysis.

After finishing a reorganization step the efficiency gain has to be evaluated. If the adapted analysis distribution is not better than the previous one the reorganization step can be easily taken back due to the low reorganization effort required for single fragments. Thereafter an alternative fragment can be chosen for reassignment.

4 Evaluation

The distribution strategies described in the last section have been implemented and evaluated using the distributed intrusion detection system DSAM (distributed signature analysis module) that utilizes EDL multi-step signatures [4]. DSAM sensors are configurable and forward audit events only to analysis units where they are required.

The DSAM analysis units are configurable as well. A set of signature fragments (state nodes) is assigned to each of them. The analysis units transfer automatically state information via the network if needed. For the performance measurements, we applied three typical signatures and examined all possible partitions (assignments) of the contained signature fragments to three analysis units. We evaluated each of the 965 possible partitions. These partitions include very efficient distributions as well as completely inefficient ones which cause an unfavorable computation or network load or both. Because of limited space we only give a brief overview about two of the applied signature examples (see Fig. 4).

The first example (Fig. 4 (a)) describes a link shell attack which exploits a vulnerability of a specific shell function and the SUID (set user ID) mechanism of the Solaris OS. If a link refers to a shell script and the scripts file name starts with a hyphen "-" an attacker can get an interactive shell with the access rights of the script owner (e.g. root) by executing the link. The second signature – the SUID script attack (Fig. 4 (b)) – describes how to gain administrative privileges in Solaris by exploiting a vulnerability of the extended file access rights.

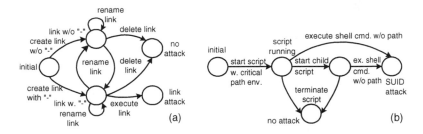

Fig. 4. (a) Shell link and   (b) SUID script attack

To evaluate the analysis efficiency of DSAM in a high load situation we used a generic set of audit data. This set was created by capturing system calls of a host, while the described attacks were executed. All logged system calls that did not belong to the attacks were discarded manually. Thus, the audit data set only contains relevant attack traces of the applied signatures. Concerning the required analysis effort, this represents a stress test and a worst scenario. Additionally, the captured attack traces have been duplicated to create a sufficiently large audit data file of 6,000 events (system calls). The experiments were conducted on four machines (Intel Xeon "Prestonia", 2.66 GHz, 512 KB L2 cache, 2 GB RAM) connected by 1 GE links. One machine executed the sensor; the others run an analysis unit. First we applied the generic audit data set and evaluated the strategy A of Section 3 by assigning the three example signatures to different AUs without fragmenting them. Then we applied the strategy B to fragment and to assign fine-grained signature parts to the analysis units. We evaluated all 965 possible distributions of the signature fragments on the three AUs and measured the runtime separately for each unit. Table 2 contains the values for some selected distributions.

The sensor runtime is related to the slowest AU, as the sensor terminates after transmitting the last audit event to the slowest AU. The third column (ID 0) represents

Table 2. Runtimes of selected distributions

distribution ID		0	96	302	626
sensor	real [s]	47.95	29.63	110.64	19.72
AU₁	real [s]	47.63	37.72	110.66	19.75
	user [s]	46.89	28.67	108.47	17.95
AU₂	real [s]		29.33	116.34	25.44
	user [s]		9.83	33.89	18.08
AU₃	real [s]		32.39	113.72	23.45
	user [s]		7.84	17.97	17.97

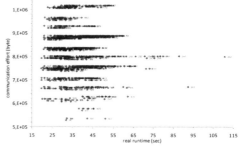

Fig. 5. Runtime and communication costs for different signature distributions

the non-distributed case, where only one AU is used that receives all signatures. This is the benchmark for any optimizations of the described strategies. The fourth column (ID 96) represents the simple, non-fragmented distribution for three AUs. The runtime shows a relevant improvement for the distributed case. The other columns represent the least and most efficient distribution. The diagram in Fig. 5 shows for each of the 965 signature distributions the sensor runtime and the required communication effort (bytes) for transmitting state information and audit events. Each point in the diagram represents a signature distribution and is enumerated with a unique ID. The diagram shows many analysis distributions (at the bottom) that require a low computation effort. Furthermore, the step-wise increase of the communication effort for audit event duplication can be seen. The figure indicates that there are many distributions with reasonable computation and communication effort (lower left corner) that should be selected for efficient analyses.

In order to select a suitable analysis distribution for a given network and CPU utilization a metrics based approach can be used. The metrics shall determine a suitability degree for each signature distribution and resource utilization. We defined a metrics that maps features of the audit event characteristics monitored by the sensor as well as the statistics maintained by the analysis units for a specific signature distribution onto a metrics value M. Simplified, M is defined by equation (3).

$$M = \alpha \sum_{i=1}^{\#AU} \sum_{evT \in S_i} evC(evT) + \beta \sum_{\substack{(a,b) \in E, \\ cl(a) \neq cl(b)}} commC(a,b) + \gamma \sum_{e \in E} compC(e) + \delta \sum_{c \in C} bal(c) \qquad (3)$$

The metrics combines and weights four features of a signature distribution by weight factors $(\alpha, \beta, \ldots)$: (a) the communication cost for audit event duplication from equation (1), (b) the state information transfers between analysis units from equation (2), (c) the computation effort for transition condition evaluation (IDS core functionality), and (d) a load balance function $bal(c)$ which determines for each analysis unit (cluster c) the deviation of the actual load from the average load of all units. Nevertheless, our experimental evaluation shows that the applied worst case scenario (the events contain a large number of attack traces) is misleading, as we were not able to find a reasonable metrics. The problem results from the additional computation effort for repeated event analysis for delayed state information. This effort changes significantly if the distances between critical event sequences change only slightly. Therefore, the computation overhead for repeated event evaluations dominates the overall runtime of unfavorable signature distributions and cannot be predicted by metrics M. Fig. 6 depicts the logged runtime (sec) together with the metrics prognosis (normalized to range [0,1]) for all 965 distributions. We tried different weight factors as well as additional distribution features to find a reasonable metrics, but we could not identify a common relation between metrics prediction and real runtime (see Fig. 6).

Hence, this kind of metrics cannot be used to predict optimal analysis distributions for the worst case, since they do not take all important computation dependencies between the signature fragments into account. Moreover, a further enhancement by additional statistical information is not desirable because CPU and network consumption change continuously and even minor changes would lead to entirely different distributions. Such a metrics can only discover an initial distribution with a satisfying analysis performance that must be adapted periodically. So, we applied next the iterative optimization strategy E for the worst case. When the dynamically updated sensor statistics and the analysis units suddenly indicate significant changes in the audit data characteristics the current distribution has to be iteratively adapted. In typical IT infrastructures this happens inevitable by changing user and system activities (e.g. daily schedules).

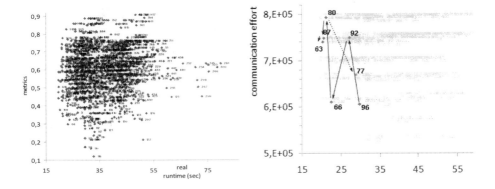

Fig. 6. Metrics prognosis and real runtime   **Fig. 7.** Iterative optimization of distributions

Our iterative optimization strategy minimizes first the effort for repeated event evaluations by reassigning the responsible signature fragments. For this, fragments are iteratively selected and moved according to selection procedure (c) of strategy E until no computation effort is spent for repeated event evaluations. Then, as a second objective, the load balance of the analysis units is improved iteratively by selecting signature fragments according to procedure (b). For this, a suitable fragment is chosen from the most loaded analysis unit and reassigned to the least loaded unit. If the subsequent performance evaluation turns out that the new distribution performs worse than the previous one the previous distribution is restored. This causes only minor reorganization effort, as only a single signature fragment is reassigned. Fig. 7 depicts the iterative adaptation of the signature distributions by an annotated fragment of Fig. 5.

Starting from the simple non-fragmented distribution (ID 96), where each of the three signatures is assigned to a different analysis unit, the distribution was adapted by consecutively reassigning single signature fragments generating the distributions with the IDs 92, 66, 80, 77, 80, 87, and 63. Distribution 77 was found to perform worse compared to the previous one after some analysis time. Therefore, it was reverted to ID 80 and another suitable fragment was reassigned (ID 87). The iterative adaptation of the signature distribution stops with distribution 63, when no suitable fragment for a further reassignment step can be found. This happens, when a pretty good balanced (and efficient) signature distribution is reached, such that also the "lightest" fragment from the most loaded analysis unit that requires least computation resources will impair the overall load balance, even if it will be reassigned.

To sum up, in worst case situations we always can apply the iterative optimization strategy starting with a sufficiently efficient non-fragmented signature distribution. Minor changes in the distribution can be easily taken back if they turn out to be misleading. The communication overhead can be estimated in advance. Thus, we can prevent high network utilizations. This strategy may only find semi-optimal distributions, but even these perform better than the distributed analysis of complete signatures.

5 Summary

The increasing performance of IT systems leads to a rapid growth of audit data volumes. This represents a major challenge for signature based intrusion detection systems, which already have to cope with growing signature databases. In this paper we presented various optimization strategies which aim at balancing the analysis load of complex signature based IDS over distributed analysis units. We focused on the analysis of multi-step signatures because complex attacks, i.e. on application level protocols (Web 2.0), will be much more important in the future, while simply structured attacks can be successfully prevented by today's proactive measures (e.g. address space layout randomization, stack protection). A prototype implementation was used to evaluate the achievable performance improvements by the various proposed optimization strategies. Our results indicate that relevant improvements in the efficiency of audit event analyses can be only obtained by a fine-grained assignment of fragmented signatures. But, the results also indicate that poorly chosen distributions require much more computation effort than the non-distributed baseline. Our results also show that a dynamic approach which iteratively adapts the signature distribution to the current analysis situation during runtime should be favored over a statically determined optimal signature distribution. As future work, we plan to integrate our prototype into a multi-agent platform to build up a distributed intrusion detection system responsible for securing an IT infrastructure (e.g. a company network). The system will analyze audit events from many widely distributed sensors and adapt dynamically to changes of the audit stream characteristics, analysis load, available free computation resources, and network bandwidth.

References

1. Cisco Systems Inc.: NetFlow Services and Applications. White Paper (2002),
   `http://www.cisco.com/warp/public/cc/pd/iosw/ioft/neflct/`
   `tech/napps_wp.htm`
2. McHugh, J.: Set, Bags and Rock and Roll – Analyzing Large Datasets of Network Data.
   In: Samarati, P., Ryan, P.Y.A., Gollmann, D., Molva, R. (eds.) ESORICS 2004. LNCS,
   vol. 3193, pp. 407–422. Springer, Heidelberg (2004)
3. Sommer, R., Feldmann, A.: NetFlow: Information Loss or Win? In: 2nd ACM SIGCOMM
   and USENIX Internet Measurement Workshop (IMW 2002), Marseille, France (2002)
4. Meier, M.: A Model for the Semantics of Attack Signatures in Misuse Detection Systems.
   In: Zhang, K., Zheng, Y. (eds.) ISC 2004. LNCS, vol. 3225, pp. 158–169. Springer, Heidelberg (2004)
5. Anagnostakis, K.G., Markatos, E.P., Antonatos, S., Polychronakis, M.: E2xB: A Domain
   Specific String Matching Algorithm for Intrusion Detection. In: 18th IFIP International Information Security Conference (SEC 2003), pp. 217–228. Kluwer Academic Publishing,
   Dordrecht (2003)
6. Yang, L., Karim, R., Ganapathy, V., Smith, R.: Improving NFA-based Signature Matching
   Using Ordered Binary Decision Diagrams. In: Jha, S., Sommer, R., Kreibich, C. (eds.)
   RAID 2010. LNCS, vol. 6307, pp. 58–78. Springer, Heidelberg (2010)
7. Shemitz, J.: Using RDTSC for Pentium Benchmarking. Visual Developer Magazine, Cori-
   olis Group, Scottsdale, AZ, USA (June/July 1996),
   `http://www.midnightbeach.com/jon/pubs/rdtsc.htm`
8. Vasiliadis, G., Antonatos, S., Polychronakis, M., Markatos, E.P., Ioannidis, S.: Gnort:
   High Performance Network Intrusion Detection Using Graphics Processors. In: Lippmann,
   R., Kirda, E., Trachtenberg, A. (eds.) RAID 2008. LNCS, vol. 5230, pp. 116–134. Springer, Heidelberg (2008)
9. Krügel, C., Tóth, T., Kerer, C.: Decentralized Event Correlation for Intrusion Detection.
   In: Kim, K.-c. (ed.) ICISC 2001. LNCS, vol. 2288, pp. 114–131. Springer, Heidelberg
   (2002)
10. Colajanni, M., Marchetti, M.: A Parallel Architecture for Stateful Intrusion Detection in
    High Trac Networks. In: IEEE/IST Workshop on Monitoring, Attack Detection and Miti-
    gation. IEEE Press, Los Alamitos (2006)
11. Schaelicke, L., Wheeler, K., Freeland, C.: SPANIDS: A Scalable Network Intrusion Detec-
    tion Loadbalancer. In: 2nd Conference on Computing Frontiers (CCF 2005), pp. 315–322.
    ACM, New York (2005)

Econometric Feedback for Runtime Risk Management in VoIP Architectures

Oussema Dabbebi, Rémi Badonnel, and Olivier Festor

INRIA, Nancy University

Abstract. VoIP infrastructures are exposed to a large variety of security attacks, but the deployment of security safeguards may deteriorate their performance. Risk management provides new perspectives for addressing this issue. Risk models permit to reduce these attacks while maintaining the quality of such a critical service. These models often suffer from their complexity due to the high number of parameters to be configured. We therefore propose in this paper a self-configuration strategy for supporting runtime risk management in VoIP architectures. This strategy aims at automatically adapting these parameters based on an econometric feedback mechanism. We mathematically describe this self-configuration strategy, show how it can be integrated into our runtime risk model. We then evaluate its deployment based on a proof-of-concept prototype, and quantify its performance through an extensive set of simulation results.

1 Introduction

Voice over IP (VoIP) has become a new paradigm in the area of telephony. It contributes to the convergence of services and permits IP providers to offer telephony service with a higher flexibility than traditional PSTN (Packet Switch Telephony Networks). The interoperability amongst VoIP equipments is supported by the standardization of dedicated protocols, including signaling protocols such as SIP (Session Initiation Protocol) for establishing phone sessions, and media transport protocols such as RTP (Real-time Transport Protocol) for transporting communications. The large scale deployment of VoIP infrastructures has introduced new security issues, including security threats inherited from the IP layer, such as denial of service and IP spoofing, but also security threats specific to VoIP protocols such as SIP flooding and SPIT (Spam over Internet Telephony) [1,2]. A large variety of security mechanisms (firewalls and intrusion prevention systems) are available for preventing these threats. However, the application of these security mechanisms on such critical infrastructures may seriously impact on the performance and usability of telephony service.

Risk management provides new opportunities for addressing this trade-off between security and performance [3]. It aims at quantifying the potentiality of threats and selecting suitable security safeguards in order to minimize the impact the VoIP infrastructure. In that context, we have already argued in favor of the application of risk management at runtime, by extending and applying the Rheostat model to VoIP architectures [4]. The parameterization of a risk

I. Chrisment et al. (Eds.): AIMS 2011, LNCS 6734, pp. 26–37, 2011.
© IFIP International Federation for Information Processing 2011

model is a key challenge.We therefore propose in this paper a self-configuration strategy for supporting runtime risk management in VoIP infrastructures. This approach permits to simplify the configuration of such risk models, by refining at runtime the model parameters based on an econometric feedback mechanism. We define this strategy in a theoretical manner and then describe how it can be integrated into our runtime risk model for VoIP architectures. We consider the model parameter which characterizes the cost of a safeguard as the case study of this work. This parameter is crucial because risk management aims at minimizing this cost while maintaining a low risk level. Our approach is generic and can easily be applied to the other risk model parameters. The main contributions of this paper are: (a) the design of a self-configuration strategy for VoIP risk models, (b) its specification based on an econometric feedback mechanism, (c) its integration into our runtime risk model, (d) its implementation into our Asterisk-based prototype (e) its evaluation based a set of simulation results.

The paper is consequently organized as follows. Section 2 describes the key concepts of runtime risk management in VoIP networks. Section 3 describes our self-configuration strategy and the considered parameters. Section 4 details the econometric feedback mechanism supporting our strategy. Section 5 presents the integration of this mechanism into our proof-of-concept prototype. Section 6 evaluates the performance of our solution through a set of experimental results. Related work are described in Section 7, and Section 8 concludes the paper and points out future research efforts.

2   Runtime Risk Management

Risk management is typically defined as the management process which consists in assessing risks and treating them i.e. taking the steps required for minimizing them to an acceptable level in the infrastructure. When we analyze existing work in the area of VoIP networks, we can observe that the first phase is covered by approaches for assessing threats (such as honeypot architectures and intrusion detection systems based on signatures, or based on anomalies [5]), and also by approaches for assessing vulnerabilities (such as auditing/benchmarking tools [6]). The second phase is covered by different types of treatments, in order to eliminate risks (risk avoidance) by applying best practices, to reduce and mitigate them (risk optimization) by deploying protection and prevention systems [7], to ensure against them (risk transfert) by subscribing an insurance contract or to accept them (risk retention) [3].

Runtime risk management aims at applying a continuous control of the infrastructure exposure to threats through the activation or deactivation of safeguards (as an instantiation of [3]). Rheostat instantiates such a dynamic schema [8]. We have previously shown how it can be applied to VoIP infrastructures [4]. Let a be a security attack part of A (the set of attacks), Rheostat quantifies the risk level $\mathcal{R}$ based on three parameters $\mathcal{P}(a)$, $\mathcal{E}(a)$ and $\mathcal{C}(a)$, as defined in Equation 1. $\mathcal{P}(a)$ stands for the potentiality of the threat associated to the attack a. $\mathcal{E}(a)$ defines the exposure of the infrastructure, which depends on the vulnerabilities of the system with respect to this attack. Finally, $\mathcal{C}(a)$ stands for the consequences of a successful attack on the infrastructure resources. This last parameter quantifies the degradation of the assets.

$$\mathcal{R} = \sum_{a \in A} \mathcal{P}(a) \times \mathcal{E}(a) \times \mathcal{C}(a) \tag{1}$$

Rheostat exploits two algorithms for controlling the exposure of the infrastructure. These algorithms aim at maintaining the risk level to an acceptable level (less than a threshold $\mathcal{R}_{threshold}$ while reducing the costs of safeguards (see Equation 2, with the ith safeguard being noted sf_i).

$$minimize(\sum_i cost(sf_i)) \ and \ \mathcal{R} < \mathcal{R}_{threshold} \tag{2}$$

The risk restriction algorithm activates security safeguards in order to reduce the risk level when the potentiality of a threat is high, while the risk relaxation algorithm deactivates theses safeguards when the potentiality is low in order to reduce the costs induced by safeguards.

Configuring the parameters of a risk model is an important and difficult activity, because the number of parameters may be high (parameters $\mathcal{P}(a)$, $\mathcal{E}(a)$ and $\mathcal{C}(a)$ are themselves dependent on other parameters) and also because parameters may vary with respect to the context. Several parameters are particularly hard to configure in our scenario. A first one is the impact of a security safeguard. It quantifies the capability of a security safeguard to protect the VoIP infrastructure with respect to a security threat. While this quantification is sometimes obvious (application of a specific patch), in most cases this parameter is difficult to quantify, in particular in case of unwanted communications (such as SPIT). We only focus here on the impact on the attack, not the impact on the threat itself. It is also interesting to quantify this second parameter, even if this impact is often low in case of attacks generated by bots. The second one is the cost of a security safeguard, which specifies how the safeguard deteriorates the performance of the service telephony. It is often defined in terms of service availability or usability. It is also possible to quantify it based on the number of innocent suspects that have to pass the security safeguard. At the extreme case, the cost of a safeguard can be considered as infinite when it consists in stopping the telephony service. This safeguard should only be executed when no alternative has been found for treating the considered risk. The last one is consequence of a successful attack, which is typically quantified in terms of confidentiality, integrity and availability. The objective is to determine if an attack will generate important damages or not on the VoIP infrastructure. While availability can be calculated in a dynamic manner in specific scenarios, privacy and integrity are more challenging and often require to be estimated by experts.

3   Self-Configuration Strategy

We propose in this paper to define a self-configuration strategy for improving runtime risk management in VoIP infrastructures (see Figure 1). Risk models

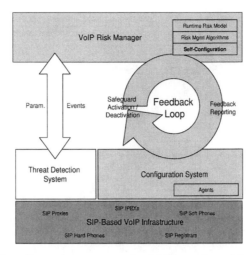

Fig. 1. Self-configuration strategy for VoIP runtime risk management

suffer from their complexity due to the high number of parameters. This automation is a key requirement in order to simplify this task and in order to adapt and refine risk model parameters with respect to their context. We consider an economic feedback mechanism to support our self-configuration schema. The objective is to take into account the experience in order to adapt the parameterization and to build a higher added-value modeling. As depicted in Figure 1, our VoIP architecture is composed of three components: (1) a detection system responsible for quantifying the potentiality of security threats, (2) a risk manager responsible for selecting safeguards based on the runtime risk model and based on the management algorithms, and (3) a configuration system which executes the safeguards on the VoIP infrastructure. The self-configuration strategy permits to establish a feedback loop based on the reporting performed by agents deployed on VoIP equipments. Thanks to this reporting integrated into the risk model, each application of security safeguards permits to perform additional observations and to leverage our risk management strategy. We have voluntarily focused our study on the cost of safeguards, in particular on safeguards based on audio captcha tests [9]. It has been shown that several hundred million captchas are filled out every day, and that these captchas could represent a cost of one billion dollars in terms of productivity loss [10]. Even if this value is probably over-estimated, it illustrates the importance of well-configured risk models. After the application of a safeguard, the agent estimates its cost and reports it to the configuration server. The server collects and aggregates these statistics that are forwarded to the risk manager. The risk manager then exploits these data to refine the cost of the considered safeguard.

We consider a VoIP infrastructure based on the SIP protocol. SIP is an open standardized protocol for managing sessions in VoIP telephony [11]. It handles the authentication and location of multiple participants, and supports the negotiation of media types using SDP (Session Description Protocol) messages. Let

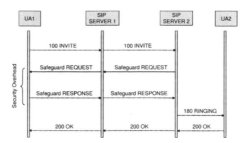

Fig. 2. SIP session initiation with security safeguard

consider the case of an agent UA1 establishing a VoIP communication with another agent UA2, as described in figure 2. The agent UA1 first sends an INVITE message to initiate a session with the second agent. If the potentiality of an attack is high, the SIP proxy of the second domain may require the application of a security safeguard in order to protect the VoIP equipments against attacks that could be generated by the first agent The agent UA1 is then invited to respond to this safeguard. For instance, in our case, the SIP proxy can apply an audio captcha test, such as requesting the typing of a specific code If the second agent UA2 provides a correct answer , the session initiation can continue normally with a RINGING message and an OK message. The application of the safeguard has introduced an additional overhead during the session initiation. In our scenario, we quantify the cost of the captcha safeguard in terms of delay.

4   Econometric Feedback Mechanism

Our self-configuration strategy is supported by an econometric feedback mechanism. The objective is to exploit the results of previous safeguard applications in order to refine the risk management model and determine the cost of next applications in a more efficient manner. A large variety of methods and techniques are available for performing such a forecasting with different performances, in particular in the area of econometry. We considered the commonly used ARMA analysis technique. While it presents some limitations, this technique is fully adequate with our runtime constraints, and our observations can easily be mapped to time series [12].

4.1   Refinement Modeling

An ARMA model is typically defined as the combination of two models: the first one is an autoregressive model of order p and the second one is a moving average model of order q. It can therefore be mathematically defined as given by Equation 4.

$$y_t = \sum_{i=0}^{p} \phi_i y_{t-i} - \sum_{j=0}^{q} \theta_j \epsilon_{t-j} + \epsilon_t \qquad (3)$$

In this equation, the variable y_t stands for the forecasted value, while the $\{y_{t-i}\}$ variables represent the previous forecasted values. ϵ_t provides the error of the prediction method following the law $BB(0, \sigma_t)$. The $\{\phi_i\}$ and $\{\theta_i\}$ variables are the coefficients (positive or negative) to be determined. These coefficients can be estimated with the maximum likelihood method.

We apply the ARMA analysis technique in order to refine the cost of the security safeguards. We note $fcCost$ as the forecasted cost and $efCost$ as the effective cost of the security safeguard. In that case, the forecasted cost $fcCost_t$ at an instant time t is given by Equation 4 with ϵ_{t-j} standing for the difference between the effective safeguard cost $fcCost_{t-j}$ and the forecasted safeguard cost $efCost_{t-j}$ at time t and ϵ_{t-j} standing for the cost error.

$$fcCost_t = \sum_{i=0}^{p} \phi_i fcCost_{t-i} - \sum_{j=0}^{q} \theta_j \epsilon_{t-j} + \epsilon_t \qquad (4)$$

As a consequence, the management algorithms (risk restriction algorithm and risk relaxation algorithm) permit to minimize the refined values corresponding the cost of security safeguards, while maintaining the risk level to an acceptable value, as described by Equation 2.

4.2   Analysis and Validation

This analysis technique is typically specified into five phases, and includes a validation test [13]. We briefly describe below its application in our scenario of runtime risk management. The first phase consists in identifying and filtering periodicity; this task can be performed by analyzing simple and partial correlograms or by applying a dedicated test such as the augmented Dickey-Fuller test or the Philips-Perron test. The second phase permits to determine the orders p and q of the ARMA model ; this task is typically done again based on the analysis of simple and partial correlograms. The autocorrelation function measures the correlation between $efCost_t$ and $efCost_{t-k}$, and the influence of the other variables $(efCost_{t-i})_{0<i<k}$ having been withdrawn. The autocorrelation coefficient of order k is given by Equation 5.

$$\rho_k = \frac{cov(efCost_t, efCost_{t-k})}{\sigma_{efCost_t} \sigma_{efCost_{t-k}}} \qquad (5)$$

The third phase estimates the coefficients $\{\phi_i\}$ and $\{\theta_i\}$ of the ARMA model. The coefficients weight respectively the variables $fcCost_{t-i}$ and ϵ_{t-j} (see Equation 4). Their estimation is obtained by exploiting the maximum likelihood method. The fourth phase represents the validation of the ARMA method. This first consists in analyzing the coefficients and the residuals and then to apply the autocorrelation test of Box and Pierce using a static quantity Q which is given by this equation: $Q = n \sum_{k=0}^{K} \rho_k^2$. In this equation, n stands for the number of observations and ρ_k represents the autocorrelation coefficient of order k of the

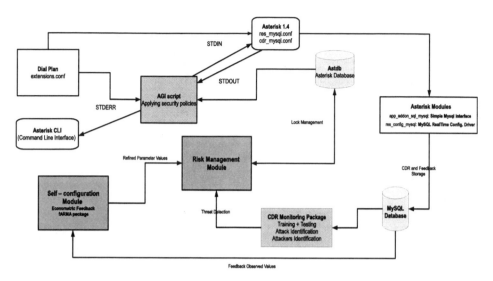

Fig. 3. Integration of the self-configuration strategy into our Asterisk-based prototype

estimated residuals. This validation permits to determine the error term with respect to the sample size. The last phase consists in quantifying the predicted cost of the safeguard based on the established modelling, using Equation 4.

5   Prototype Integration

We have integrated our self-configuration strategy into an Asterisk-based VoIP environment. We have exploited built-in Asterisk drivers, and implemented the self-configuration module based on AGI (Asterisk Gateway Interface) scripts using the AGI python toolkit. This prototype detects suspicious actors based on an anomaly detection algorithm detailed in [4]. This algorithm (monitoring package) identifies the presence of SPIT or other abnormalities based on Call Detail Records (CDRs). The identity of the suspicious actors is represented by the user account for a registered user and by the IP address for external calls. The monitoring package forwards the results to the risk management module. This one stores and manages the list of suspicious actors and assigns safeguards for each actor based on our runtime risk model. The AGI script takes the Asterisk channel parameters as arguments and determines if any safeguard has to be applied before calling the extension. Our prototype currently supports several safeguards, such as responding with a busy message for the first call tentative, asking to dial a specific DTMF tone in order to establish the call, and redirecting the call to another destination. After each application of a safeguard, the prototype stores the effective cost of the activated safeguards into the database. The self-configuration module analyses the series of cost values, and quantifies a refined value for the safeguard by applying our econometric feedback mechanism. It directly calls the ARMA (p,q) functions of the fArma package [14] and forwards the refined value to the risk management module. We have experimented this feedback mechanism with the audio captcha safeguard (5 x 30 samples) and have determined an error term which serves as a basis for simulation experiments.

6   Experimental Results

We have considered the scenario of SPIT attacks, as SPIT is a very common threat in VoIP infrastructures. Our purpose is to evaluate the impact of our econometric feedback mechanism on the runtime risk management schema. The call arrival is represented by a Poisson law and a mean of 100 calls per unit of time. The call duration is represented by an exponential law and a mean of 10 seconds. The attacks are represented by 4 different types with increasing SPIT intensity (from 10 to 1000 SPIT calls per unit of time). We define from 5 to 20 different safeguards where each safeguard is characterized by three variables: the cost (representing the additional delay introduced by the safeguard, with an error term between 1% and 10%), the probability that a malicious call bypasses the safeguard (following a uniform distribution in the $[0.8; 1]$ interval), and the probability that an honest call bypasses the safeguard (following a uniform distribution in intervals between $[0.8; 1]$ (best cases) and $[0; 0.2]$ (worst cases). We have conducted 10,000 Monte Carlo simulations per scenario, which permits to reduce sufficiently the simulator error term. We use the same seed number for the pseudo-random number generation of all scenarios. Next, we expose a subset of our experimental results. We are in particular interested in evaluating the benefits and limits of the econometric feedback mechanism our runtime risk management performance. In a first series of experiments, we have investigated the impact of the feedback mechanism on the risk amplitude. Figure 4 represents the risk distribution for three different cases: a cost with an error term of 0% (scenario A), a cost with an error term of less than or equal to 5% (scenarios B_{1a} and B_{2a}), and a cost with an error term between 5% and 10% (scenarios B_{1b} and B_{2b}). We can clearly observe on the first subfigure 4(a) corresponding to an error term with a positive direction that the risk amplitude is higher with the scenario A than the two other scenarios B_{2a} and B_{2b}. The distinction between scenario A and the other scenarios starts with a risk amplitude greater than 0.14. The two curves corresponding to the scenarios B_{2a} and B_{2b} are converging to the same distribution. We observe the same phenomenon with the second subfigure 4(b). We have plotted the three same scenarios A, B_{1a} and B_{1b}, but in that case with a negative direction. The risk amplitude is once again higher with scenario A than with the two other scenarios B_{1a} and B_{1b}, and the distribution of these two last scenarios are also converging. However, the difference between scenario A and the scenarios B_{1a} and B_{1b} is less important than in the first subfigure. These results are in coherence with our runtime risk management strategy. The objective of the risk management algorithms is to minimize the cost of activated security safeguards while maintaining the risk amplitude less than a threshold value, which permits to explain the experimental results observed in the two subfigures 4(a) and 4(b). In the first subfigure 4(a), the difference between scenario

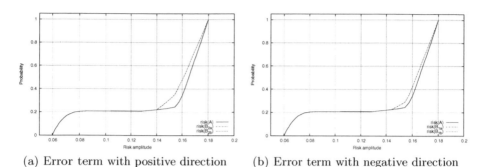

(a) Error term with positive direction   (b) Error term with negative direction

Fig. 4. Impact of feedback on risk amplitude

A and scenarios B_2 (B_{2a} and B_{2b}) is due to the activation of a security safeguard with an impact higher than effectively required. The error rate with a positive direction contributes to the selection of such a safeguard at an earlier stage, as its cost looks less expensive than the effective cost. In that case, the error term leads the runtime risk model to generate a restriction on the infrastructure exposure more important than required. This minimizes the risk amplitude in a more significant manner, but the cost due to activated safeguards is not optimized. This means the risk management module will activate security safeguards that are not necessarily required for protecting the VoIP infrastructure, and will introduce an additional delay in the service functioning. The difference between the B_{2a} and B_{2b} error terms has not been sufficient to modify the selection of security safeguards in these two scenarios. We can observe a similar behavior with the second subfigure 4(b), while we expected the opposite phenomenon: a risk amplitude less important with scenario A than with scenarios B_1. In this case, the cost of the security safeguard is decreased (negative direction) of up to 10%. The considered safeguard seems less expensive than its effective cost, this leads once again the risk management algorithms to select a more impacting safeguard than effectively required with respect to the potentiality of the threat. A lower risk amplitude with the two scenarios B_{1a} and B_{1b} does not mean the performance results are better, but that the risk management solution has underestimated the cost of the safeguard, which may generate a significant impact on the service performance. Another interesting question is to determine to what

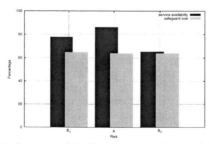

Fig. 5. Impact of feedback on service availability

extent the econometric feedback mechanism impacts on the service performance. We have therefore evaluated in a second series of experiments, both the service availability and the total cost of security safeguards. We have plotted on figure 5 a diagram representing these two metrics in a normalized manner (availability values and cost values estimated between 0% and 100%), for the three previously mentioned scenarios A, B_1 and B_2. We observe on this diagram that scenario A offers a lower effective cost due to security safeguards in comparison to scenarios B_1 and B_2. It also shows the best service performance with a value of up to 86%, while scenarios B_1 and B_2 provide respectively a value of up to 77% and up to 65%. Indeed, the VoIP infrastructure is overprotected in these two last scenarios because risk model parameters are not properly configured, which argues in favour of our refinement mechanism. It is also important to evaluate how the number of available security safeguards may impact on the service performance when the economic feedback mechanism is activated. We have quantified the service performance while varying the number of safeguards from 5 to 20. The risk management system behavior depends on the distribution of cost values on the set of security safeguards. The more the costs of two consecutive safeguards is important, the more the runtime risk management is sensitive to the error term. If we consider a distribution of costs sufficiently homogeneous amongst security safeguards, then a high number of security safeguards reduces the cost difference between two safeguards. As a consequence, the runtime risk model less tolerate on average the error term in that case. In the same manner, a low number of security safeguards increases the interval between the costs of two safeguards, and then reduces on average the sensitivity with respect to the error term value.

7   Related Work

A few work really address risk management and its runtime instantiation in the area of VoIP infrastructures. Related work mentioned in section 2 only cover the risk management process in a partial manner, and do not integrate any risk model. This can be explained by the complexity to establish and configure risk models. Risk management is however a key requirement for protecting efficiently such a critical service. We have proposed in [4] a strategy capable to identify and treat risks at runtime in a VoIP environment. This solution is based on the extension of the Rheostat risk modeling and permits to prevent SPIT attacks based on a set of safeguards. We have observed in that context that the parameterization and maintenance of a risk model is expensive. We have therefore design our self-configuration strategy in order to address this issue. The management of unwanted communications, in particular SPIT, has been extensively studied because of its importance for the future of VoIP. Quittek et. al. [15] apply hidden Turing tests on the caller side and compare their results to typical human communication patterns. For passing these tests, significant resource consumptions at the SPIT generating side would be required which contradicts the spammer's objective of placing as many SPIT calls as possible. VoIP SEAL [16] implements a two-stage decision process: the first stage contains modules which analyze a call only by looking at information which is available before actually answering the call. The second stage consists of modules which actually interacts with the caller or the callee to refine the detection. Since the second stage modules introduce some inconvenience, a scoring system is deployed at the first stage to determine if they will be used or not. Rather than Turing tests, other modules include white/black list, simultaneous calls, call rate, and URI's IP/domain correlation. Finally, the end-user feedback is taken into account if the SIP-client is instrumented for that. This work is the most similar to our work but does not explicitly propose a risk model. The end-user feedback could be easily integrated into our self-configuration schema. A survey of protection techniques against SPIT is given in [17]. The authors argue in favor of combining complementary techniques, which is fully in coherence with our dynamic solution and its automation. More elaborated econometric techniques [18] could be considered to instantiate our self-configuration approach, in particular techniques such as FFNN (Feed Forward Neural Network) and SVR (Support Vector Regression) [19].

8   Conclusions and Future Work

VoIP networks are exposed to multiple security threats, as they are less confined than traditional PSTN networks. Protection mechanisms are available, but their activation in such a critical environment may induce a signification deterioration of the service performance. Applying risk management in VoIP infrastructures is therefore a key requirement for protecting VoIP communications while maintaining the service usability. In that context, we have previously shown how the Rheostat runtime risk model can be extended to support risk management in VoIP infrastructures. We have also shown how the parameterization of such risk models can be difficult to maintain. In order to address this issue, we propose in this paper a self-configuration strategy for supporting risk management in VoIP networks. The objective is to dynamically adapt and refine the risk model parameters based on a econometric feedback mechanism. We have first remained the challenges of runtime risk management for such critical environments. We have then describe our self-management schema and shown how it can be deployed into a SIP-based architecture. We have mathematically detailed the econometric feedback mechanism. We have evaluated to what extent our solution can integrated into our implementation prototype. We have evaluate the performance of our approach through a set of simulation experiments. In particular, we have quantified the impact of feedback on risk amplitude and service performance. The error term due to poorly configured models can limit the benefits of risk management and induce an additional overhead. Our automation permits to reduce the complexity of risk model parameterization and to perform a better treatment of risks in VoIP networks. As future work, we are interested in experimenting and evaluating alternative econometric techniques for adjusting our runtime risk models and improving the selection of security safeguards.

We are also planning to investigate the deployment of our risk management approach into decentralized environments such as VoIP infrastructures exploiting the P2PSIP protocol.

References

1. Voice over IP Security Alliance, VoIP Security and Privacy Threat Taxonomy (October 2005), http://www.voipsa.org/Activities/taxonomy.php
2. Thermos, P., Takanen, A.: Securing VoIP Networks: Threats, Vulnerabilities, and Countermeasures. Addison-Wesley Professional, Reading (2007)
3. ISO/IEC 27005, Information Security Risk Management, http://www.iso.org
4. Dabbebi, O., Badonnel, R., Festor, O.: Automated Runtime Risk Management for Voice over IP Networks and Services. In: Proc. of the 12th IEEE/IFIP Network Operations and Management Symposium, NOMS 2010 (April 2010)
5. Dantu, R., Kolan, P., Cangussu, J.W.: Network Risk Management using Attacker Profiling. Security and Communication Networks 2(1) (2009)
6. Bunini, M., Sicari, S.: Assessing the Risk of Intercepting VoIP Calls. Elsevier Journal on Computer Networks (May 2008)
7. d'Heureuse, N., Seedorf, J., Niccolini, S., Ewald, T.: Protecting SIP-based Networks and Services from Unwanted Communications. In: Proc. of IEEE/Global Telecommunications Conference (GLOBECOM 2008) (December 2008)
8. Gehani, A., Kedem, G.: RheoStat: Real Time Risk Management. In: Jonsson, E., Valdes, A., Almgren, M. (eds.) RAID 2004. LNCS, vol. 3224, pp. 296–314. Springer, Heidelberg (2004)
9. Soupionis, Y., Tountas, G., Gritzalis, D.: Audio Captcha for SIP-Based VoIP. Springer Journal 41, 25–38
10. Computer Literacy Tests: Are You Human?, Grossman. Times Magazine (2008)
11. Russell, T.: Session Initiation Protocol (SIP): Controlling Convergent Networks. McGraw-Hill, New York (2008)
12. Hamilton, J.: Time Series Analysis. Princeton Univ. Press, Princeton (1994)
13. Caldwell, J.G.: The Box-Jenkins Forecasting Technique. Ph.D. dissertation, University of North Carolina (1971)
14. R language, R project, http://cran.r-project.org/
15. Quittek, J., Niccolini, S., Tartarelli, S., Schlegel, R.: Prevention of Spam over IP Telephony (SPIT). NEC Technical Journal 1(2) (2006)
16. Schlegel, R., Niccolini, S., Tartarelli, S.: Spam over Internet Telephony (SPIT) Prevention Framework. In: Proc. of the IEEE GLOBECOM, San Francisco (2006)
17. Quinten, V.M., van de Meent, R., Pras, A.: Analysis of Techniques for Protection Against Spam over Internet Telephony. In: Pras, A., van Sinderen, M. (eds.) EUNICE 2007. LNCS, vol. 4606, pp. 70–77. Springer, Heidelberg (2007)
18. Vitalta, R., Apte, C.V., Hellerstein, J.L., Ma, S., Weiss, S.M.: Predictive Algorithms in the Management of Computer Systems. IBM System Journal 41(3) (2003)
19. Hossain, A., Nassar, M., Rahman, A.: Comparison of Finite mixture of ARMA-GARCH, Back Propagation Neural Networks and Support-Vector Machines in Forecasting Returns. Departement of Finance & Banking, Rajshahi University

Finding and Analyzing Evil Cities on the Internet

Matthijs G.T. van Polen, Giovane C. M. Moura, and Aiko Pras

Centre for Telematics and Information Technology (CTIT)
Faculty of Electrical Engineering, Mathematics
and Computer Science (EEMCS)
Design and Analysis of Communications Systems (DACS)
Enschede, The Netherlands
matthijs@vanpolen.biz, {g.c.m.moura,a.pras}@utwente.nl

Abstract. IP Geolocation is used to determine the geographical location of Internet users based on their IP addresses. When it comes to security, most of the traditional geolocation analysis is performed at country level. Since countries usually have many cities/towns of different sizes, it is expected that they behave differently when performing malicious activities. Therefore, in this paper we refine geolocation analysis to the city level. The idea is to find the most dangerous cities on the Internet and observe how they behave. This information can then be used by security analysts to improve their methods and tools. To perform this analysis, we have obtained and evaluated data from a real-world honeypot network of 125 hosts and from production e-mail servers.

Keywords: Geographical Analysis, Bad Neighborhoods, Internet Geolocation, IP Geolocation, Spam, Network Attacks, Honeypots.

1 Introduction

IP Geolocation aims to determine the Internet users' geographical location based on their IP address [1]. It has been used by industries and businesses for many purposes, including targeted advertisement (e.g., a global portal can deliver customized ads according to the user's location), fraud detection (e.g., online stores can check the physical location of a client against its billing address), media licensing (e.g, broadcasters, such as those on Hulu [2], only stream content to IPs belonging to certain countries) and even spam filtering [3].

In relation to security, most of the current Internet Geolocation analysis is done only at the country level. For example, the latest 'State of the Internet' report by Akamai shows only the top 10 countries from where attacks originated [4] [1]. Another example of country-level analysis is the daily generated map provided by Quarantainenet BV [5].

In this paper, we address the Internet Geolocation for security on a city level instead. The assumption is that countries are too big and heterogeneous so their cities/towns are expected to exhibit different behavior in relation to security. The motivation for doing so is that it would allow provide security developers with hints on how to better

---

[1] In this work, by originated we mean where the attack came from. We do not consider if there were other hosts controlling the attacking one.

I. Chrisment et al. (Eds.): AIMS 2011, LNCS 6734, pp. 38–48, 2011.

tweak/improve their tools. Therefore, the main research question addressed in this paper is: *"Which cities in the world are responsible for most of the security incidents?"* Following the main research question, in this paper we address other sub questions:

- *Are there cities that are relatively more 'evil' than others?* Some cities might be more evil than others (that is, they generate more attacks than others), in some cases just because this city has more inhabitants, which leads to more computers and a higher probability of starting attacks. This sub research question addresses the evilness of cities taking into account its number of attackers per inhabitants. The idea is to observe if and how the evilness of a city changes according to its population.
- *Are the cities where the most attacks originated located in the countries where the most attacks originated?* If this would be the case, then filtering on a city level would not be very necessary, since filtering on a country level would yield the same results. However, if the answer to this question is 'no', then filtering on a city level might lead to more accurate results. If there are countries that cause a small number of attacks, but there is a city in that country that does cause a relatively large number of attacks, it might be a good idea to mistrust only the city and not the whole country.
- *Is there much change over time in the list of the most evil cities?* The list of countries where the most attacks come from doesn't change much, as can be observed for the map generated by Quarantainenet [5]. There is a mild variation during the day (probably due to day/night), but seen over the course of a week this list stays mostly the same. Would this behavior hold when cities are evaluated?
- *Do the evil cities change according to the type of attack?* In this question we verify whether the list of evil cities remains the same for different types of security attacks. If the list remains the same, it suggests, for example, that a list of cities where the most SSH attacks originate can be fed into a spam filter when scoring IPs based on their geolocation. If not, then a list of evil cities should be obtained per application.

The remainder of this paper is organized as follows: Section 2 discusses the related work. Section 3 presents our approach on how to find evil cities and describes our data sets. Section 4 addresses the main research question, providing analysis on the most malicious cities. Section 5 aims at the first sub research questions, in which the evilness of cities is evaluated taking into account its population. Section 6 presents results on the second sub question, evaluating whether the most evil cities belong to the most evil countries. Next, Section 7 covers the third sub question, in which the list of evil cities changes over time. After that, we evaluate how the evil cities change according to the type of attack in Section 8. Finally, Section 9 presents our conclusions and remarks for future work.

2   Related Work

Most of the current research works focusses on geographical location at the country level. For example, Jiang *et al.* [6] propose a spam filtering technique that uses country-level geographical information, which lead to a reduction of 13.9% in their experiments.Even though they were able to reduce the number of spam messages, the authors do not describe what could happen if city-level information would be used instead of country level for filtering spam.

Sobel *et al.* [3], on the other hand, hold a U.S. patent for use of geolocation data for spam detection. It is stated in the patent that "the geolocation data may be any type of geographical information such as city, country, state or presence within a pre-selected radius of a geographical point". As a patent, the method is only described while its effectiveness is not addressed. Other non-scientific reports on the number of attacks per country also exist. For example, the Internet hosting company Akamai provides a quartely report named 'The State of the Internet' [4], which is obtained from the analysis of users that access Akamai servers (many sites, such as Hulu, BBC iPlayer and the White House use the Akamai content distribution network). In their latest report, they have observed attacks from 209 countries/regions, with the U.S. being the first one, in terms of traffic (12%). However, only 10 countries are mentioned in the report, and they do not provide analysis at city-level. Quarantainenet also provides a daily map of the countries that have attacked their honeypot infrastructure [5].

Other work is also related to ours. In a previous piece of work, Van Wanrooij and Pras [7] employ the concept of 'Internet bad neighborhood' – that is, there are certain IP blocks on the Internet more evil than others – to filter mail messages. Using data from blacklists, the authors were able to filter detect 95% of the spam messages. However, in their work, no geographical information is used. The research questions in our work address the existence of malicious cities on the Internet, instead of network blocks. In another work , Koike *et al.* [8] perform data visualization on the origin of attacks at IP block level or country level. Finally, Muir *et al.* [1] present a survey on the current Internet geolocation methods.

In the next section we describe the dataset and the approach used in our study to find evil cities on the Internet.

3 Dataset and Approach

3.1 Quarantainenet Honeypot Data

In order to answer our research questions, the first step was to obtain reliable data from real world attacks. In our case, we have obtained full non-anonymized data from Quarantainenet B.V [9], a Dutch company that develops network management and security tools and provides admission control and malware detection for their customers, including more than half of Dutch universities. Quarantainenet has a honeypot infrastructure which is distributed mostly over the Netherlands. In total, 125 machines are used for this purpose. Each has multiple IP addresses assigned to it to increase the chance of it being targeted by attackers.

Quarantainenet collects information from each honeypot and combines it into one single database. By definition, every new attack is logged. However, if the same IP address attacks a same honeypot multiple times within 48 hours, only the first incident is recorded. This is employed in order to keep the database more concise. For example, a host performing SSH dictionary attacks could be logged many times if this would not be employed. However, for our research, this does not represent a problem, since we are interested in the IP addresses of attackers, instead of the number of attacks.

Each honeypot is able to log many different type of attacks. Among them are *SSH*-attacks, *Conficker* [10], known exploits of Microsoft Windows and others. Attacks that are as of yet unknown, are forwarded to Qnetlabs, the sister company of Quarantaine-net, for further analysis. The honeypots used are passive, which means they wait for incoming connections that are then analyzed to see whether they are malicious.

The data provided by Quarantainenet is not publicly available, as it, of course, contains IP addresses of the attackers. Under Dutch law IP addresses can be *'persoons-gegevens'*, personal data. It is illegal to make them public. Therefore all IP addresses were processed automatically. Then they were discarded, leaving only an internal ID and a location.

For this research, we have evaluated a one week period from Quarantainet database – from October 29th to November 4th, 2010. During this period 25474 attacks were logged, from 23814 different IP addresses. Of these attacks, 20174 came from a form of the *Conficker* worm, a worm that targets the Windows operating system. The next largest number of attacks, namely 2052, were attacks trying to take advantage of the vulnerability in certain Windows-versions dubbed MS08-067 by Microsoft[2].

In the Sections 7 and 8 we have used different periods, which are detailed in the same sections. Next we describe the method we have employed to obtain Internet Geolocation information.

3.2   Method for Obtaining IP Geolocation

After having obtained the IP addresses for the monitoring period, we have mapped them to their geographical location using GeoPlugin [11]. GeoPlugin is a free online API which uses Maxmind database [12] to resolve Internet Geolocation. They provide the following data for a particular address: city, region, area code, dma code , country name, country code, longitude, latitude, currency code, currency symbol and exchange rate. For our experiments, we needed only city and country code.

The main problem with using GeoPlugin that it relies on the accuracy of Maxmind database [12], of which numbers on accuracy are available [13]. Even though the database is not 100% precise, (Maxmind claims that their "GeoIP databases are 99.8% accurate on a country level, 90% accurate on a state level and 83% accurate for the US within a 25 mile radius"), we believe the results obtained would still hold, even though with some margin for errors.

For the sub-research question in which the number of inhabitants is taken into account, this was manually done using numbers obtained from Wikipedia. We intend as future work to develop a more automated and precise way to perform this using an online database, so that all cities can be checked, and not just the top 20. It would also be fitting to use the number of internet subscribers in a certain city, but at the time of writing this paper a database with information on the number of internet subscribers per city could not be found.

In the next sections we present the analysis for the research questions addressed in this paper.

---

[2] Please see http://www.microsoft.com/technet/security/bulletin/ms08-067.mspx for details from Microsoft TechNet.

4 Which Cities Are Responsible for Most of the Security Incidents?

To answer this question, we have evaluated the dataset described in Section 3. Table 1 shows the top 20 cities from which most of attackers were present, in absolute numbers.

Table 1. Top 20 attacking cities

#	City	Ctry	# of attacks	#	City	Ctry	# of attacks
1	Seoul	(KP)	735	11	Guangzhou	(CN)	219
2	Taipei	(TW)	618	12	Shanghai	(CN)	210
3	Beijing	(CN)	563	13	Ho Chi Minh City	(VN)	179
4	Jakarta	(ID)	362	14	Kuala Lumpur	(MY)	177
5	Buenos Aires	(AR)	351	15	Bogota	(CO)	162
6	Bangkok	(TH)	308	16	Saint Petersburg	(RU)	160
7	Moscow	(RU)	268	17	Rio De Janeiro	(BR)	152
8	Hanoi	(VN)	267	18	Caracas	(VE)	143
9	Santiago	(CL)	246	19	Bucharest	(RO)	139
10	Sao Paulo	(BR)	229	20	Chelyabinsk	(RU)	129

Analyzing this table, we can observe that, despite most of Quarantainenet's honeypot infrastructure being located in Europe, we have observed only one European city (Bucharest) among the top 20 evil cities. In addition, 9 of the top attacking cities are located in Asia and other 6 in South America, while no evil city from North America was found among the top 20. Three evil cities are located in Russia and other three in China. Figure 1 shows the attackers concentration in the world map, from the top 20 cities. As can be seen, most of attackers are located in Asia.

Taking the numbers into account, we observe that for that evaluated period most of attacks were originated in Seoul. The reasons for that might be due to Seoul has a huge

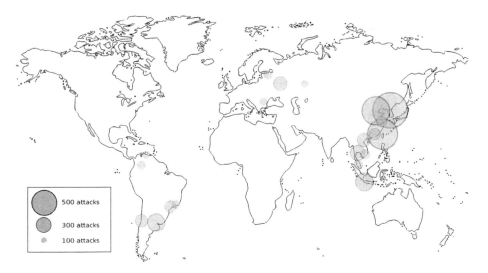

Fig. 1. Attacks on Dutch networks from 2010-10-29 until 2010-11-04

number of inhabitants – Seoul metropolitan area has more than 24 million people (that is more than the population of the Netherlands, for example) combined with a high Internet penetration level [4]. Another reason could be the precision of the MaxMind database – they claim that 75% of all IP addresses that are located in South Korea are correctly placed within 25 miles of their true location [13]. However, even with such precision, Seoul would still be responsible for many attacks in absolute numbers.

On the next section we present the results for the most evil cities taking into account its number of inhabitants.

5   Are There Cities That Are Relatively More 'Evil' Than Others?

In the previous section we have presented the most evil cities ranked according to the number of attackers observed. In this section we present how evil they are, taking into account the number of inhabitants of each city. Table 2 shows the results.

In this table, each city is ranked according to the number of attackers per million inhabitants. In the third column, the number behind each city name shows the position the city was in Table 1, which only takes into account the absolute number of attackers. One can notice that results change when the population is taken into account. Chelyabinsk, in Russia, is the city with more attackers per inhabitants, while it was number 20 in absolute numbers. Seoul, which was the first, is ranked as 5th in this table. Chelyabinsk has ten times more attacks per inhabitant than Shanghai does, which was not clear looking only at the previous section.

However, we do see that the top four cities don't differ that much; at least not enough to call Chelyabinsk a more evil city than Buenos Aires, for example. Lower down the

Table 2. Top 20 evil cities taking into account the population

#	Ctry	City	# of attackers	# inhabitants	Att/10^6inhab.
1	(RU)	Chelyabinsk (20)	129	1078300	119.63
2	(AR)	Buenos Aires (5)	351	3050728	115.05
3	(MY)	Kuala Lumpur (14)	177	1809699	97.81
4	(TW)	Taipei (2)	618	6776264	91.20
5	(KP)	Seoul (1)	735	10208302	72.00
6	(RO)	Bucharest (6)	139	2151880	64.59
7	(CL)	Santiago (9)	246	5278044	46.61
8	(VN)	Hanoi (8)	267	6500000	41.08
9	(ID)	Jakarta (4)	362	9580000	37.79
10	(RU)	Saint Petersburg (16)	160	4661219	34.33
11	(TH)	Bangkok (6)	308	9100000	33.85
12	(CN)	Guangzhou (11)	219	7841695	27.93
13	(VE)	Caracas (18)	143	5196514	27.52
14	(RU)	Moscow (7)	268	10126424	26.47
15	(CN)	Beijing (3)	563	22000000	25.59
16	(VN)	Ho Chi Minh City (13)	179	7162864	24.99
17	(BR)	Rio De Janeiro (17)	152	6186710	24.57
18	(CO)	Bogota (15)	162	7392241	24.91
19	(BR)	Sao Paulo (10)	229	11037593	20.75
20	(CN)	Shanghai (12)	210	19210000	10.93

list the results change. For example, Shanghai, while being on the twelfth position for absolute number of attacks, is on the twentieth position on the relative table. This might be a relatively small drop, however this is because only the absolute top twenty of cities was evaluated.

Finally, looking at these results, one can conclude that there are also significant differences when evaluating cities' evilness according to the number of inhabitants.

6   Are the Cities Where the Most Attacks Originated Located in the Countries Where the Most Attacks Originated?

Table 3 shows the 20 countries that have started more attacks to the Quarantainenet honeypots. As one can notice, China is the leading country, followed by Brazil, U.S. and Russia. This table can be compared with the the list provided by Akamai in their report [4]. In this report, they present the top 10 countries originating attacks, using a different metric: volume traffic, instead of number of incidents. In their report, 6 of the top 10 countries match our results (China, Brazil, U.S., Russia, Taiwan and Italy), despite different ordering, being the U.S. the first country in their results.

Table 3. Top 20 attacking countries

#	Country	# of attackers	#	Country	# of attackers
1	China	2532	11	France	772
2	Brazil	1943	12	Germany	746
3	United States	1815	13	Ukraine	658
4	Russia	1733	14	Vietnam	622
5	Italy	1690	15	Malaysia	590
6	Spain	955	16	Japan	577
7	Republic of Korea	936	17	Thailand	454
8	Argentina	907	18	United Kingdom	448
9	Indonesia	870	19	Romania	431
10	Taiwan	832	20	Poland	413

To answer the research question addressed in this section, we should compare Table 3 to Table 1. In Table 1, the most evil city is Seoul. However, The Republic of Korea (South Korea) ranks at the 7th position when we aggregate the number of attackers per country. On the other hand, China tops the list as the most evil country, while it has 3 cities among the top 20 (Beijin, Guangzhou and Shanghai). While only one European city is among the top 20 cities, 8 countries are among the top 20 most evil countries. Finally, there are countries among the top 20 that have no city among the top 20 (e.g., Italy and Spain).

This results shows that there is little correlation between the most evil cities and the most evil countries. There are countries (e.g, Italy, U.S.) that have no cities among the most evil, but when attacks are aggregated at the country level their evilness is revealed. Therefore, filtering traffic taking into account the originating country is a risky approach, and a much more precise solution is to use cities instead.

7   Is There Much Change over Time in the List of Top Offenders?

In order to answer this research question, we have obtained a list of the top 20 cities for each day of the evaluated week. Table 4 shows the obtained results. Due to space constraints, we do not show the number of attackers.

Table 4. Top 20 evil cities over one week

#	Day 1	Day 2	Day 3	Day 4	Day 5	Day 6	Day 7
1	Seoul	Seoul	Seoul	Taipei	Seoul	Seoul	Seoul
2	Taipei	Taipei	Taipei	Beijing	Beijing	Taipei	Taipei
3	Beijing	Beijing	Beijing	Seoul	Taipei	Beijing	Beijing
4	Jakarta	B. Aires	Jakarta	B. Aires	Bangkok	Jakarta	Jakarta
5	Bangkok	Bangkok	S. Paulo	Bangkok	B. Aires	B. Aires	B. Aires
6	Moscow	Hanoi	B. Aires	Jakarta	Jakarta	Moscow	Hanoi
7	B. Aires	Jakarta	Santiago	S. Paulo	Hanoi	Bangkok	Santiago
8	Santiago	Guangzhou	Bangkok	Hanoi	Moscow	HoChiMinh	Guangzhou
9	Hanoi	Santiago	R.deJaneiro	Santiago	Shanghai	Shanghai	Moscow
10	Shanghai	Bogota	Hanoi	Cairo	Guangzhou	Hanoi	Bangkok
11	S.Petersburg	S. Paulo	Moscow	Guangzhou	K.Lumpur	Santiago	S.Paulo
12	K.Lumpur	Moscow	Caracas	Moscow	Chelyabinsk	S. Paulo	Shanghai
13	S. Paulo	S.Petersburg	Chelyabinsk	Shanghai	HoChiMinh	K.Lumpur	Bogota
14	Guangzhou	Caracas	Bucharest	Chelyabinsk	S. Paulo	Guangzhou	S.Petersburg
15	R.deJaneiro	Shanghai	HoChiMinh	Rome	Madrid	Bucharest	Rome
16	Bucharest	K.Lumpur	S.Petersburg	Madrid	S.Petersburg	Caracas	K.Lumpur
17	Rome	R.deJaneiro	Bogota	Bogota	Bogota	R.deJaneiro	R.deJaneiro
18	Caracas	HoChiMinh	Madrid	S.Petersburg	Bucharest	Bogota	Bucharest
19	HoChiMinh	Chelyabinsk	Brasilia	Caracas	Tokyo	Cairo	HoChiMinh
20	Shenzhen	Mexico	Guangzhou	K.Lumpur	Santiago	Madrid	Caracas

As can be seen, Seoul is the most malicious city for 6 of the 7 days. In addition, the top 3 cities are always Seoul, Taipei or Beijing for each day. The one time Taipei was number one, the difference between the two was only two attackers. However, the mid-section was also quite stable. There were changes between cities already on the list, but only rarely did a city make the list for a day that wasn't already on the top twenty list of the entire week.

So, all in all, the top twenty list of cities is quite stable. This means that it can be used as the foundation of a set of rules for day-to-day use. There were no cases of a city making the overall top twenty list because there was a one-day spike of traffic. This suggests that is not necessary to update the list of malicious cities on a daily basis.

8   Do the Evil Cities Change According to the Type of Attack?

To investigate if the evil cities differ or not according to type of attack, we have analyzed data from two different datasets: (*i*) Quarantainenet database and (*ii*) log files from e-mail servers of the Electrical Engineering, Mathematics and Computer Science Department at University of Twente (EWI/UT). The difference between the datasets is that the first one lists IP addresses of hosts performing different types of brute force/break-in attempts (as described in Section 3), while the second one lists spamming hosts.

In order to have a more fair comparison, we have evaluated the IP addresses of malicious hosts for the same day: April 22nd, 2010. In this very day, Quarantainenet dataset had 6,797 IPs as malicious. The mail log files from EWI/UT, on the other hand, contained 240,733 spam messages from 70,546 different IP addresses. The IP addresses of both datasets were resolved to city level and then analyzed.

Table 5 presents the Top 20 evil cities for both datasets. At a first glance, one could notice that 9 out of 20 cities are found in both cases (highlighted in boldface). In fact, out of top 100 evil cities, 50 are found for both datasets, and 105 cities are present in both cases when comparing the top 200 evil cities. Even though the position in tables might change for each city, around 50% of the cities remains the same. This could be used, for example, to application level filters (such as mail filters, http proxies), in which cities would get lower scores levels for a certain type of application just by being evil for other applications. However, further research is need to investigated the feasibility of this proposal.

Table 5. Top 20 evil cities for differents type of attacks

#	QNET-Attacks Cities	# of attackers	#	Spamming Cities	# of spammers
1	**Seoul**	190	1	**Seoul**	1759
2	Beijing	176	2	Mumbai	1488
3	**Taipei**	147	3	**Hanoi**	1364
4	Buenos Aires	107	4	New Delhi	797
5	**Jakarta**	106	5	**Ho Chi Mihn**	790
6	Santiago	87	6	Delhi	752
7	Guangzhou	75	7	Riyadh	731
8	**Sao Paulo**	75	8	**Bogota**	717
9	**Bogota**	75	9	Jiddah	682
10	Moscow	73	10	**Sao Paulo**	677
11	Saint Petersburg	70	11	**Bangkok**	677
12	**Bangkok**	56	12	Bangalore	676
13	**Hanoi**	50	13	**Taipei**	604
14	**Bucharest**	50	14	**Bucharest**	593
15	Shanghai	49	15	Madras	576
16	Rio de Janeiro	49	16	Hyderabad	525
17	**Ho Chi Mihn**	40	17	Santiago	516
18	Rome	37	18	Kiev	467
19	Caracas	35	19	**Jakarta**	429
20	Shenzhen	32	20	Cairo	428

In the table, we can also observe that, for both cases, Seoul is the city where most of attackers and spammers come from. This is an interesting fact that shows us a different side of Seoul (as in Section 4): South Korea is usually regarded as the country with the highest level of broadband adoption, including its capital Seoul[3]. However, as shown

---

[3] Seoul was ranked the 9th city in the world with the highest average measured connection speed by Akamai Networks [4] – an average of 14.4 Mpbs (all top 11 cities were in South Korea for the reporting period).

by our results, more broadband penetration does not mean higher security levels. Seoul network administrators should be aware of this fact in order to improve security levels in their networks.

Finally, we can conclude that around 50% of malicious cities remains the same for different types of attacks, even when analyzing data from different domains.

9 Conclusions and Future Work

In this paper we have employed Internet Geolocation in order to find what are the most evil cities on the Internet. To achieve this, we have obtained IP addresses from malicious hosts from 125 honeypots maintained by Quarantainenet [5], over a period of one week. Then, we have used Geoplugin [11] which, in turn, employs the Maxmind database to obtain the geographical information associated to a particular IP address.

The main research question addressed in this paper is: *"Which cities in the world are responsible for most of the security incidents?"*. As detailed in Section 4, Seoul is the most dangerous city on the Internet, having 735 malicious hosts attacking Quarantainenet infrastructure. In addition, the results have shown that just one European city is among the top 20 most evil cities on the Internet, while 9 of the top 20 evil cities are located in Asia.

The main research question was followed by four sub-questions. The first one was if *"Are there cities that are relatively more 'evil' than others?"*. In this sub-question we take into account the number of inhabitants per city to determine how evil they are. We can conclude that there are indeed cities that are relatively more evil than other cities. For example, Seoul caused the highest absolute number of attacks. When the number of inhabitants is taken into account, Seoul ends up on the fifth position. The number of attacks per inhabitant is lower than for example in Taipei.

The next addressed subquestion was *"Are the cities where the most attacks originated located in the countries where the most attacks originated?"*. In our results, we have observed that most of the attackers are in China, Brazil and then in the U.S.. While only one European city is among the top 20 evil cities, 8 countries are among the top 20 most evil contries. The answer to this question is that there is little correlation between the most evil cities and most evil countries. This means that using a list of evil cities to finetune firewalls or filters would yield better results than using a list of countries.

The next sub-question investigated was *"Is there much change over time in the list of top offenders?"*. The top twenty of evil cities is pretty invariable. While lower on the list changes do occur over time (e.g. looking at different weeks or different days within a week), Seoul is (almost) always on top, followed by Taipei, Bejing, etc. This makes using the data easier, as there is no need to gather new data on a daily basis.

Finally, the last sub-question was if *"Do the evil cities change according to the type of attack?"*. To answer this question, we have compared the Quarantainenet database against the spam log files from two mail servers from the University of Twente for a period of one day. The answer to this question is that around 50% of the cities remain the same, independently from the type of attack. This suggests that geographical information from one type of attack might be used as input to other types of attacks.

As future work, we intend to improve our approach by using a online database for the number of inhabitants per city. In addition, we intend to conduct a evaluation over a longer period of data (a year) to observe how evil cities change according to time, if there is any sort of pattern. We also intend to perform the same analysis on different datasets. Finally, the next step is to to find out if spam filters and/or firewalls can indeed be made more precise by utilizing information about evil cities. One way might be to automate the process of calculating the most dangerous cities over, for example, the last week. The data gathered from this could be incorporated into automated generating of spam rules.

Acknowledgments. The authors would like to thank Quarantainenet B.V. for granting us access to their honeypot data, in special Casper Joost Eyckelhof. Also, many thanks to Marc Berenschot for his suggestions and contribution to this work.

References

1. Muir, J.A., Van Oorschot, P.C.: Internet geolocation: Evasion and counterevasion. ACM Comput. Surv. 42, 4:1–4:23 (2009)
2. Hulu: Hulu - What your favorites. Anytime. For free, http://www.hulu.com (accessed on February 2011)
3. Sobel, W.E., McCorkendale, B.: Use of Geo-Location Data for Spam Detection. U.S. Patent #7,366,919 issued April 29 filed (2008)
4. Akamai: The State of the Internet, 3rd Quarter, 2010. Technical report, Akamai, http://www.akamai.com/stateoftheinternet/ (accessed on February 2011)
5. Quarantainenet, B.V.: Virus attacks, http://quarantainenet.com/?language=en;page=infections (accessed on February 2011)
6. Jiang, Y., Zhang, N., Fang, B.: An email geographic Path-Based technique for spam filtering. In: 2007 International Conference on Computational Intelligence and Security, pp. 750–753 (2007)
7. van Wanrooij, W., Pras, A.: Filtering spam from bad neighborhoods. International Journal of Network Management 20(6), 433–444 (2010)
8. Koike, H., Ohno, K., Koizumi, K.: Visualizing cyber attacks using IP matrix. In: IEEE Workshops on Visualization for Computer Security, vol. 0, page 11. IEEE Computer Society, Los Alamitos (2005)
9. Quarantainenet, B.V.: Quarantainenet, http://quarantainenet.com/ (accessed on February 2011)
10. Microsoft. Computer Worms - Conficker — Microsoft Security, http://www.microsoft.com/security/pc-security/conficker.aspx (accessed on February 2011)
11. Geoplugin: Geoplugin, http://www.geoplugin.com (accessed on February 2011)
12. Maxmind: Maxmind, http://www.maxmind.com/ (accessed on February 2011)
13. Maxmind: Geolite city accuracy, http://www.maxmind.com/app/geolite_city_accuracy (accessed on February 2011)

Autonomous Service Composition in Symbiotic Networks

Tim De Pauw[1,2], Filip De Turck[1], and Veerle Ongenae[2]

[1] Department of Information Technology (INTEC)
Ghent University – IBBT, Gaston Crommenlaan 8 bus 201, 9050 Ghent, Belgium
[2] Faculty of Applied Engineering Sciences (INWE)
University College Ghent, Schoonmeersstraat 52, 9000 Ghent, Belgium
`tim.depauw@intec.ugent.be`

Abstract. To cope with the ever-growing number of wired and wireless networks, we introduce the notion of so-called *symbiotic networks*. These networks seamlessly operate across layers and over network boundaries, resulting in improved scalability, dependability, and energy efficiency. This particular Ph.D. research focuses on software services operating in such symbiotic networks. When two or more networks merge, the services provided on them may be combined into a service composition that is much more than the sum of its parts. Driven by two distinct use cases, we aim to enable fully autonomous service composition and resource provisioning. For the first use case, an in-building over-the-top service platform, we describe a software architecture and a set of generic resource provisioning algorithms. The second use case, which focuses on wireless body area networks, will allow us to expand our research domain into highly dynamic symbiotic network environments, where services appear and disappear more frequently.

1 Introduction

In the future home and office, a large number of networks will be active simultaneously. There will be the public cellular networks used for voice and data services, competing with WiMAX. In addition to wired and wireless LANs, networks used in building automation, such as wireless sensor networks [1], will be commonplace. All in all, the growing number of mobile applications leads to an increasing density of colocated networks and devices.

We aim to bring these networks closer together through the introduction of the concept of *symbiotic networks*: independent, colocated, homogeneous and heterogeneous, wired and wireless networks, which operate across all layers and over network boundaries. This will be realized through advanced sharing of information, infrastructure and networking services. In this particular Ph.D. research, we aim to enable novel cross-network services through dynamic service composition in such symbiotic networks. This should ultimately contribute to networks with improved scalability, dependability and energy efficiency.

I. Chrisment et al. (Eds.): AIMS 2011, LNCS 6734, pp. 49–52, 2011.

2   Research Questions

Establishing and maintaining symbiotic networks implies the exploitation and sharing of services that execute in different networks and with varying requirements. Our research focuses on forming symbioses between such services. We aim to answer the following research questions:

1. *How should resource and service parameters be modeled?*
   When a symbiotic network is formed, many parameters can be decisive toward collaboration at the application level. The identification and representation of these parameters is our first goal.
2. *How can the parameters' values be monitored?*
   Once key parameters have been identified, we need to determine how to measure them, how often they should be collected, andsoforth. Aggregation and caching may help reduce overhead, at the expense of some precision.
3. *How can an effective service composition be reached?*
   Based on parameters extracted from the environment, the actual symbiosis needs to be realized. The composition of services and the allocation of resources are subject to numerous constraints, calling for efficient algorithms.
4. *How should changes in the environment be handled?*
   The service composition should be dynamic. Changes in the environment must therefore be analyzed to see if the existing composition should be updated to reflect them. Ideally, this would be handled transparently.
5. *Which supporting components should enable the symbiosis?*
   To actually allow software components to operate in a symbiotic fashion, an enabling software platform must be available. The design of this platform forms another one of our goals.
6. *What makes a realistic test scenario?*
   For the validation of our findings, they need to be applied to representative scenarios. On one hand, random yet realistic scenarios can be generated. On the other hand, a real-life test case could also be interesting.

3   Approach

Our research focuses on two use cases for symbiotic networks. The first one emphasizes the case of static service composition, where new networks and services rarely appear. It serves as a stepping stone for the second case, where the symbiotic network and its service composition are highly dynamic in nature.

We envisage a context-aware **in-building** service platform to streamline day-to-day life in homes and offices. Context awareness means that the platform is driven by environment information such as the location of a user, his personal preferences, and his calendar, but also temperature measurements, cafeteria menus, andsoforth. The platform will help users find friends or coworkers, send them personalized recommendations, etc., and interact with their mobile devices, but also display information on wall-mounted screens, for instance.

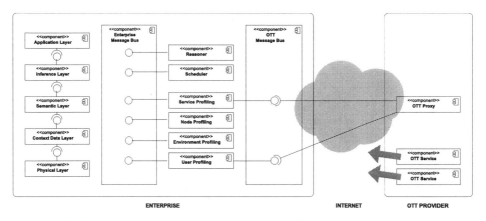

Fig. 1. Component diagram showing the in-building context-aware platform

The services supporting this platform's operation are quite diverse. Therefore, it is wise to delegate them to external service providers. By deploying the *over-the-top* paradigm, we allow these providers to inject their services into the platform and access its hard- and software components, while the platform itself remains in charge of monitoring and resource arbitration. Thus, implicitly, at least two symbiotic networks are formed. In [2], we described a software architecture to enable such a context-aware over-the-top service platform, thereby presenting initial steps toward answering research question 5. It is displayed in Fig. 1. On the left are five layers commonly found in context-aware applications. [3] Via the *Enterprise Message Bus*, they communicate with a number of enterprise services; among them are profiling services, which maintain context information about key parts of the operating environment. The *OTT Message Bus* allows for interaction with external service providers; via the *OTT Proxy*, a provider may inject his service components into the platform.

Resource provisioning is a core responsibility of symbiotic networks. In response to research question 1, we devised a generic resource model, which copes with the heterogeneity of the infrastructure. Building upon this model, we applied *bin packing* heuristics to the problem of scheduling tasks in heterogeneous environments, thereby providing a preliminary answer to research question 3. Both the model and the scheduling algorithms are detailed in [4].

In the case of in-building service provisioning, the service composition is expected to be rather static. Moving on to research question 4, regarding *dynamic* symbiotic networks, we will be paying attention to **wireless body area networks**. In such networks, sensors are placed on the human body to monitor physiological parameters like heartbeat, body temperature, motion, etc. A symbiotic body area network originates, for instance, when a driver's network merges with his vehicle's to prevent him from falling asleep. Furthermore, that symbiotic network could in turn merge with nearby cyclists', thereby again reducing the chance of accidents. Especially in this second scenario, additional networks appear and disappear quite frequently, calling for immediate response.

4   Validation

We aim to validate the in-building service platform through deployment on our test bed *WiLab*, composed of several hundred wireless mesh network nodes equipped with sensor boards. [5] This will allow us to conduct realistic experiments in a real-life office environment, with actual users.

In an attempt to answer research question 6, we will equip the service platform with an over-the-top service that analyzes context information to identify opportunities for public notices and advertisements, and subsequently broadcasts video streams to mobile devices and fixed displays. Initial benchmarks on WiLab have yielded favorable results, but further experimentation is needed. [2]

We are still in the early stages of researching *dynamic* service composition. The body area network scenario will therefore be addressed further when we have sufficiently researched the case of mostly static in-building services.

5   Conclusion

We introduced the concept of symbiotic networks, which operate across network boundaries to provide a more dependable infrastructure. Guided by the use cases of in-building over-the-top services and body area networks, we aspire to enable fully autonomous service composition in such network environments. Research is currently being carried out toward the first of these use cases. The second will provide insight into highly dynamic symbiotic network scenarios.

Acknowledgment

Tim De Pauw would like to thank the University College Ghent Research Fund for financial support through his Ph.D. grant. Part of this work has been funded by the IWT SBO SymbioNets project.

References

1. Romer, K., Mattern, F.: The Design Space of Wireless Sensor Networks. IEEE Transactions on Wireless Communications 11(6), 54–61 (2004)
2. De Pauw, T., Volckaert, B., De Turck, F., Ongenae, V.: On the Design of a Flexible Software Platform for In-Building OTT Service Provisioning. In: IFIP/IEEE Workshop on Distributed Autonomous Network Management Systems (2011) (accepted)
3. Ailisto, H., Alahuhta, P., Haataja, V., Kyllönen, V., Lindholm, M.: Structuring Context Aware Applications: Five-Layer Model and Example Case. In: Workshop on Concepts and Models for Ubiquitous Computing (2002)
4. De Pauw, T., Verstichel, S., Volckaert, B., De Turck, F., Ongenae, V.: Resource-Aware Scheduling of Distributed Ontological Reasoning Tasks in Wireless Sensor Networks. In: IEEE International Conference on Sensor Networks, Ubiquitous and Trustworthy Computing (2010)
5. Tytgat, L., Jooris, B., De Mil, P., Latré, B., Moerman, I., Demeester, P.: WiLab: A Real-Life Wireless Sensor Testbed with Environment Emulation. In: European Conference on Wireless Sensor Networks, adjunct poster proceedings (2009)

An SLA Support System for Cloud Computing

Guilherme Sperb Machado and Burkhard Stiller

Department of Informatics IFI, University of Zurich
Binzmühlestrasse 14, CH—8050 Zürich, Switzerland
{machado, stiller}@ifi.uzh.ch

Abstract. Nowadays, even with the existence of many Cloud Providers (CP) in the market, it is still impossible to see CPs who guarantee, or at least offer, an SLA specification to Cloud Users (CU) interests: not just offering percentage of availability, but also guaranteeing specific performance parameters for a certain Cloud application. Due to (1) the huge size of CPs' IT infrastructures and (2) the high complexity with multiple inter-dependencies of resources (physical or virtual), the estimation of specific SLA parameters to compose Service Level Objectives (SLOs) with trustful Key Performance Indicators (KPIs) tends to be inaccurate. This paper proposes the initial design and preliminary approach for an SLA Support System for CC (SLACC) in order to estimate in a formalized methodology — based on available CC infrastructure parameters — what CPs will be able to offer/accept as SLOs or KPIs and, as a consequence, which increasing levels of SLA specificity for their customers can be reached.

1 Introduction

Within CC environments a contract or a Service Level Agreement (SLA) needs to exist between two parties: Cloud Providers (CP) and Cloud Users (CU), *e.g.*, organizations or individuals. These two parties need to agree on a set of parameters expressed through the SLA. However, even with the existence of many CPs in the market (*e.g.*, Amazon, Sales-Force, Rackspace, or Google), it is still impossible today to see CPs, who guarantee or at least offer an SLA specification tailored to CU's interests; however, tailoring interests have a great importance for tomorrows CC, since very general requirements (such as the "availability needs of a given service" [1], [8], [3]) do not match commercial needs for guaranteed CC services. Thus, CPs need accurate definitions of objective values that can be derived automatically and offered to their customers. An example of a specific SLA parameter is the Return to Operation (RTO) time, in case of virtual machine failures. If the RTO is estimated beforehand (and continuously), CPs can compose a Service Level Objective (SLO) offering guarantees of Key Performance Indicators (KPI) with a high precision (*e.g.*, RTO under 3 minutes, measured by the bootstrap time of virtual machines). Nevertheless, due to (1) the huge size of CPs' IT infrastructures and (2) the high complexity with multiple inter-dependencies of resources (physical or virtual), the estimation of specific SLA parameters to compose SLOs with trustful KPIs tends to be inaccurate. This inaccuracy can result in penalties for a CP, if an unrealistic set of values was proposed and consequently agreed upon in an SLA. Therefore, the lack of an automated system that maps and aggregates low-level measures into SLOs is the key barrier for (a) less risky and (b) customer-specific SLA-based CC service provisioning.

I. Chrisment et al. (Eds.): AIMS 2011, LNCS 6734, pp. 53–56, 2011.

As far as known today, there is no past or current work that addresses this problem of mapping low-level measures of interdependent resources into SLOs inherent to typical Cloud services. Moreover, solutions like SLA assessments [5] and SLA monitoring [2] that provide an approach of SLA assessment, do not take into consideration the CC infrastructure as whole, but just very specific network parameters.

Therefore, this paper proposes the *SLA Support System for Cloud Computing* (SLACC) which aims to design, build, and evaluate a Decision Support System (DSS) for CC in order to estimate in a formalized methodology (*e.g.*, statistical analysis, machine learning) — based on available CC infrastructure parameters — what CPs will be able to offer/accept as SLOs or KPIs and, as a consequence, which increasing levels of SLA specificity for their customers can be reached. Furthermore, SLACC will handle specific knowledge about the CC infrastructure in support of the negotiation of dedicated SLA contracts. Thus, SLACC's main objectives include: (1) CPs will benefit from SLACC to propose accurate SLA parameters and SLOs/KPIs beforehand and (2) once CPs receive CU requests for dedicated SLOs/KPIs, the CP can evaluate, if such values can be guaranteed in his CC infrastructure. In both cases SLACC will take into consideration inter-dependencies of resources inside the CC infrastructure, since SLA parameters of high-level Cloud applications are composed by the sum of multiple low-level factors.

2   Approach

The SLACC decision support system will estimate SLA parameters (*e.g.*, KPIs based on SLOs) to enable the design of more specific SLA documents. The system will map high-level requirements into low-level factors that, combined together in a balanced manner, form an estimation. Thus, the following key steps should be undertaken and are described in the remainder of this section: an integrated architecture, a well-defined Cloud IT Infrastructure Model, and an estimation algorithm.

The SLACC must be based on a scalable and fully interoperable architecture. Fig. 1 shows the abstract view of this architecture, which will serve as the starting point for SLACC development. The SLACC interacts with the Accounting Records Repository, the SLAs Repository, and the Infrastructure Model. The Infrastructure Model component enables an updated view of all inter-dependencies of the Cloud IT Infrastructure. It is important to reflect exactly the organization of the physical IT environment, otherwise the SLA DSS will be based on erroneous and not up-to-date data. The CP Operator interacts with the SLA Designer in order to build a well-defined SLA, using an SLA model/language. The SLA DSS can be split in many sub components such as the estimation engine (implementing an estimation algorithm). Such sub components' interface should be defined using an API (Application Programming Interface) to interact, in a standardized manner, with other components of a common SLA management architecture. This API will serve as the CPs openness factor as well as the supporting interface for any inter-domain interactions.

The key mechanism within the SLACC decision support systems is the design and development of the algorithm estimating with a defined level of confidence — may be in a configured manner — SLA parameters, such as the "minimum database query time" for a given application. Based on an example, the principle operation of the estimation algorithm is described as follows. The CU proposes an SLA with a specific SLO, which is the

"RTO of Virtual Machines under 3 minutes". It is known that the Return Time to Operation can be measured in different ways, but the KPI associated to this SLO is measured by a composition of low-level values inherent to the bootstrap of virtual machines. The SLACC decision support system will consult the CC IT Infrastructure knowledge base to check "what are the factors (time-wise) that matter for a successful bootstrap of a virtual machine?". Based on relations defined in an CC IT Infrastructure Model, a set of factors will be determined. In this case, as an example, it can be assumed that the following factors were mapped: (1) network bandwidth from the virtual machine's template repository to the physical server, which the virtual machine will be hosted on — assuming a transfer from the repository to the assigned physical server; (2) processing capacity from the physical server, which hosts the virtual server; (3) average workload of the physical server in an interval period of time; (4) time to deploy and configure the specific requested virtual machine template in the virtual server; and (5) time to (re)configure the deployed virtual machine in the load balancing front-end of the CP. The estimation algorithm will consider a viable distribution to compose and balance these factors to estimate the final result. Statistical methods such as non-linear Regression Analysis can be employed. At the last step, the CP can evaluate based on known facts, if the SLO "RTO of Virtual Machines under 3 minutes" proposed by the CU can be guaranteed by the CP, or if the CP has to negotiate, in this case, this parameter's value to a higher value, or if the CP has to offer different parameter(s).

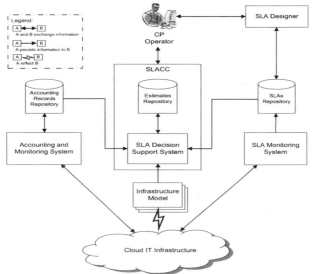

Fig. 1. SLACC architecture

In the process to estimate a certain SLA parameter, the CP operator can intervene within the SLACC system if there is a lack of available information provided by the Accounting Records Repository. Therefore, the operator can manually point some other factors that he judges that has an influence. For example, if the "processing capacity from the physical server (holding the virtual server)" is not measured/specified, the operator can leave it or point an other variable with the same unit (*e.g.*, processing capacity from an other physical server with the same characteristics) to be included in the estimation process.

Existent SLA management solutions like [6], [4], and [7], take into consideration the use of historical data that is collected through SLA monitoring processes or by accounting means. However, SLACC estimation algorithm will consider a wider range of parameters inside the CC IT infrastructure, balancing historical information, current IT infrastructure status (*e.g.*, server's load, network bandwidth at a given moment), and how the Cloud is organized internally, including its IT inter-dependencies.

In order to evaluate SLACC's benefits and advantages, it must be shown that the system can provide accurate estimates to CPs in order to better enhance its SLAs. For this to be proven, it is planned to test the functionality of SLACC by using different CC IT infrastructure's scenarios in a test-bed. Based on the estimates for some SLA parameters, these will be monitored in order to evaluate the confidence level of such generated values. Moreover, comparisons between estimates generated by humans and by SLACC should be observed.

3   Conclusions

This paper sketches a new approach for estimating accurate SLA parameters in order to evaluate what CPs will be able to offer/accept as SLOs or KPIs. The solution proposed and partially outlined in terms of key aspects will increase the level of SLA specificity, not just handling service's availability but also aiming to embrace a wider range of specific performance parameters. The respective and general architecture of the new system termed SLACC was described. An example concerning the estimation algorithm were discussed, also presenting key differences from other approaches in the area of SLA management. Furthermore, for the upcoming fine design, refined solution, and implementation of SLACC (future work), this paper also briefly presented a possible evaluation.

References

1. Amazon.com Web Services: Amazon Elastic Compute Cloud (EC2) Service Level Agreement, http://aws.amazon.com/ec2-sla (last visited on February 2011)
2. Comuzzi, M., Kotsokalis, C., Spanoudakis, G., Yahyapour, R.: Establishing and Monitoring SLAs in Complex Service Based Systems. In: IEEE International Conference on Web Services (ICWS 2009), July 6-10, pp. 783–790. IEEE Computer Society, Washington, DC, USA (2009), doi:10.1109/ICWS.2009.47
3. Google.com Apps: Google App Service Level Agreement, http://www.google.com/apps/intl/en/terms/sla.html (last visited on February 2011)
4. Padgett, J., Gourlay, I., Djemame, K. (eds.) AssessGrid Deliverable 1.3: System Architecture Specification and Developed Scenarios, Version 0.30 (December 2006)
5. Serral-Gracià, R., Labit, Y., Domingo-Pascual, J., Owezarski, P.: Towards an Efficient Service Level Agreement Assessment. In: IEEE Infocom, Rio de Janeiro, Brazil, April 19-25 (2009)
6. RESERVOIR Project Website: Service Manager Scientific Report, http://www.reservoir-fp7.eu/fileadmin/reservoir/delivarables/A4_ServiceManager_ScientificReport_V1.0.pdf (last visited on February 2011)
7. SLA@SOI Project Website: Empowering the service industry with SLA-aware infrastructures, http://sla-at-soi.eu (last visited on February 2011)
8. SalesForce.com Website: The Leader of Customer Relationship Management (CRM) and Cloud Computing, http://www.salesforce.com (last visited on February 2011)

Autonomic Management for Personalized Handover Decisions in Heterogeneous Wireless Networks

Joon-Myung Kang[1,*] and James Won-Ki Hong[2]

[1] Dept. of Computer Science and Engineering
[2] Div. of IT Convergence Engineering,
Pohang University of Science and Technology (POSTECH), Republic of Korea
{eliot,jwkhong}@postech.ac.kr

Abstract. The computation of good and optimal handover decisions is a significant problem in a heterogeneous network environment. This is exacerbated when the goal is to provide personalized services for mobile users as opposed to generic device metrics such as received signal strength. Personalized handover decisions should not only consider received signal strength, but also context information, user preferences, and other non-functional requirements. In this paper, we propose a novel autonomic management method for personalized handover decisions to satisfy end users' demands in heterogeneous wireless networks. We define two objective metrics for evaluating specific access points: access point acceptance value and access point satisfaction value.

Keywords: Personalized Handover Decision, Autonomic Management.

1 Introduction

Growth in ubiquitous and mobile computing systems has led to the early introduction of a wide variety of new access networks and Internet-capable devices [1]. As a result, multiple heterogeneous wireless access networks can be used at the same place and a mobile device can access them simultaneously [2]. A foreseen feature of these networks and mobile devices is the support of flexible and personalized handover decisions by dedicated devices to satisfy the demands of the end user using context information [3,4].

The current handover decision methods based on *Received Signal Strength (RSS)* or pre-defined simple policies do not provide good solutions because they do not take into account services that satisfy the preferences of a user at a given time, location, and/or application context. Therefore, handover decisions should

---

* This research was supported by the WCU program through National Research Foundation of Korea funded by the Ministry of Education, Science and Technology (R31-2010-000-10100-0) and by the IT R&D program of MKE/KEIT(KI003594 , Novel Study on Highly Manageable Network and Service Architecture for New Generation).

I. Chrisment et al. (Eds.): AIMS 2011, LNCS 6734, pp. 57–60, 2011.
© IFIP International Federation for Information Processing 2011

be based on additional considerations, such as the capacity of each network link, usage charge of each network connection, power consumption of each network interface, battery status of the mobile device, and user preferences. We call these and similar data *context* information.

In this paper, we propose an autonomic handover decision method for satisfying the end user's demand for different types of services in heterogeneous wireless networks by using fuzzy logic and utility functions as part of the decision-making process. We call this method *AUHO*, which is an abbreviation for **A**Utonomic **H**and**O**ver. We define two objective metrics for evaluating the performance of *Access Points (APs)*: a) *Access Point Acceptance Value (APAV)* and b) *Access Point Satisfaction Value (APSV)*. Our algorithm supports the selection of the best AP (horizontal handover) as well as the best access network (vertical handover) using current user preferences and profile data, application requirements, and context information. The novelty of our approach is in using a combination of functional and non-functional requirements, filtered by the particular context.

2   Related Work

We present previous approaches for handover decision strategies proposed in the literature. We divide these studies into six categories based on the metrics or techniques used for handover decisions [5]: 1) RSS-based, 2) cost function-based, 3) user-centric, 4) Artificial Intelligence (AI)-based, 5) Multiple-Criteria Decision Making (MCDM), and 6) context-aware approaches. In summary, compared to our AUHO approach, none of these approaches provide sufficient flexibility in satisfying user needs, and most cannot adapt to a changing context. Additional details on each algorithm are provided in the following sub-sections.

RSS-based approaches cannot be applied to vertical handover decisions because of different characteristics of the heterogeneous wireless networks. Cost function-based approaches use a pre-defined cost function which is a measurement of the benefit obtained by handing over to a particular network [6]. Among the different criteria that a vertical handover decision takes into account, user preferences such as cost and QoS, are the most interesting policy parameter for a user-centric strategy [7]. The handover decision problem selects among a limited number of candidate networks from various service providers and technologies with respect to different criteria. This is a typical MCDM problem, which deals with choosing from a set of alternatives which are characterized by their attributes [8]. The concepts of *Fuzzy Logic (FL)*, *Neural Networks (NN)*, Expert Systems, and *Genetic Algorithms (GA)* from AI can be used to decide when handover should occur and which network to should be chosen among different available access networks [9]. The context-aware handover concept is based on knowledge of the context information of the mobile terminal and networks in order to make intelligent and better decisions [10]. Our comparative study shows different issues related to the handover decision problem: network performance, user satisfaction, flexibility, efficiency, and multi-criteria solution [5].

3   Proposed Approach

Our research hypothesis is that our AUHO algorithm always *maximizes end user satisfaction* by computing the optimal handover decision for different types of mobile services in heterogeneous wireless networks based on user preferences. Our approach is as follows. First, we define and categorize context information for handover decisions by surveying available information from mobile devices, networks, applications, and users. Second, we construct an information model to represent different data models of mobile devices, access networks, applications, policies, users, and contexts, because data from each of these entities come from different sources and are defined using different languages. Third, we develop a decision making algorithm by evaluating each access network using a *weighted* combination of context information, user preferences, and service requirements. Note that the weighting enables the decision method to be adjusted to better suit the needs of the end user. We define how to measure and evaluate the quality of each AP and then calculate the end user satisfaction for achieving our hypothesis. We define the concept of an *"acceptance value"* using a fuzzy logic-based classifier to process all relevant context information, regardless of whether different languages and formats are used. We then define the concept of a *"satisfaction value"* using a utility function based on user preferences. We then select the *"best satisfying"* AP for supporting *Context-aware Always-Best-Satisfying (CABS)* mobility based on a utility function that maximizes user preferences. Fourth, we evaluate the performance of the proposed method using a network simulator that we developed for testing handover decisions in heterogeneous wireless networks. Finally, we compare our method with other decision making algorithms, and show that our algorithm supports a CABS service, which other methods do not support.

We defined two objective metrics for handover decisions: an APAV and an APSV. The former represents the suitability of a particular AP for an end user based on a given set of user preferences. The latter represents how well a particular AP satisfies the needs of the end user based on his or her user profile, as used in this context. We calculate the APAVs and APSVs for all candidate APs, and determine the AP that best satisfies the current application and context requirements. If the new candidate AP is the same as the old AP, no handover is performed. In addition, if the APSV of the new AP is higher than that of the current AP, we must consider handover overheads such as latency. Otherwise, handover to the new AP is performed. This process is continuously repeated within a pre-defined timeout that is defined by profiling. This is a our algorithm's feedback control loop to achieve autonomic management. After connecting the best satisfying AP, we repeat a maintenance loop by evaluating the current connected AP. If a connected AP exists, the network selection task is stopped. We then calculate the APAVs of the current AP and calculate the APSV based on them. If the APSV of the current AP is lower than the pre-defined threshold, the handover decision task is started again and all candidate APs are evaluated to select the best satisfying AP.

Currently, we have evaluated our AUHO with two case studies: a) the same application using different user profiles, and b) different applications using the same user profile. The former tests different weighting factors for each user preference, while the latter tests different application requirements for the same user profile. We showed that our AUHO provides the best satisfying AP compared to other handover decision making algorithms [5].

4 Conclusions

Seamless mobility and roaming in next-generation networks is an important issue. In particular, a handover should support not only *Always-Best-Connect* mobility, but also *Always-Best-Satisfying (ABS)* mobility for providing personalized mobile services. In this paper, we have proposed a novel handover decision method for supporting ABS mobility based on the end user's preferences and context information. Our method determines the access network and the AP that can best satisfy the requirements of the end user for a particular context. We showed how autonomic management can be used for handover decisions.

For future work, we will optimize our algorithm to calculate APAVs and APSVs. We will find the optimized timeout value for periodic decisions. Finally, we will perform more tests and optimize by considering handover overhead and network performance.

References

1. Weiser, M.: Ubiquitous Computing. Computer 26, 71–72 (1993)
2. Eastwood, L., Migaldi, S., Xie, Q., Gupta, V.: Mobility using IEEE 802.21 in a heterogeneous IEEE 802.16/802.11-based, IMT-advanced (4G) network. IEEE Wireless Communications 15(2), 27–34 (2008)
3. Kang, J.M., Ju, H.T., Hong, J.W.K.: Towards Autonomic Handover Decision Management in 4G Networks. In: Helmy, A., Jennings, B., Murphy, L., Pfeifer, T. (eds.) MMNS 2006. LNCS, vol. 4267, pp. 145–157. Springer, Heidelberg (2006)
4. Kassar, M., Kervella, B., Pujolle, G.: An overview of vertical handover decision strategies in heterogeneous wireless networks. Computer Communications 31(10), 2607–2620 (2008)
5. Kang, J.M.: Autonomic Management for Personalized Handover Decisions in Heterogeneous Wireless Networks, Ph.D. Thesis, POSTECH (2011)
6. McNair, J., Zhu, F.: Vertical handoffs in fourth-generation multinetwork environments. IEEE Wireless Communications 11(3), 8–15 (2004)
7. McNair, J., Zhu, F.: A user-centric analysis of vertical handovers, In: Proc. of the WMASH 2004, pp. 137–146 (2004)
8. Song, Q., Jamalipour, A.: A network selection mechanism for next generation networks, In: Proc. of the ICC 2005, pp. 1418–1422 (2005)
9. Alkhawlani, M., Ayesh, A.: Access network selection based on fuzzy logic and genetic algorithms. Advances in Artificial Intelligence 8(1), 1–12 (2008)
10. Wei, Q., Farkas, K., Prehofer, C., Mendes, P., Plattner, B.: Context-aware handover using active network technology. Computer Networks 50(15), 2855–2872 (2006)

Optimising P2P Overlays for Pervasive Environments

Fei Peng and Apostolos Malatras

PAI Group, University of Fribourg, 1700 Fribourg, Switzerland
name.surname@unifr.ch

Abstract. In this paper we propose a topology optimisation algorithm for multi-layer P2P overlays on top of pervasive computing environments based on ant algorithms for the distributed network-wide collection of information. Our goal is to construct a robust and responsive overlay with low overhead so that it suits the highly dynamic and heterogeneous characteristics of pervasive environments.

1   Introduction

Pervasive computing environments are built over highly dynamic heterogeneous networks. Moreover, diversity exists in all aspects of such environments, including computing performance, network connections, mobility, etc. In order to reduce the perceived complexity of the underlying network, P2P overlays are usually adopted by large-scale network applications for resource discovery and network management [3]. However, the robustness of P2P overlays can be adversely affected under dynamic conditions. Existing works have made attempts to optimise overlay topologies in different ways, e.g. by considering superpeer architectures [5] or self-organised approaches [1] inspired by sophisticated and robust solutions found in nature. Nonetheless, these approaches consider environments with low dynamicity.

The responsiveness and overhead traffic of P2P overlays are critical concerns in pervasive computing. We propose a topology optimisation algorithm called X-Ant that is based on the theory of Ant Colony Optimisation (ACO) [2]. By developing different families of artificial ants with unique features, network information can be collected rapidly with low overhead traffic, hence supporting responsive overlay topology optimisation over dynamic underlying networks. Moreover, considering the wide range of information collected by ants, overlay layers with different links of diverse quality features can be simultaneously maintained, therefore increasing the overall robustness. A similar approach was used by the CAN [4] overlay on top of a low dynamicity underlying network.

The rest of this paper is as follows. Section 2 presents the research problem by describing the goal of this project and the proposed methodology. In section 3 we discuss our proposed X-Ant algorithm by describing its multi-layer overlay design, the ant families used for network parameter collection, and the corresponding topology optimisation. Section 4 concludes this paper by presenting our current work as well as giving insight to future plans.

I. Chrisment et al. (Eds.): AIMS 2011, LNCS 6734, pp. 61–64, 2011.

2   Research Problem

Our goal is to promote the responsiveness, efficiency and robustness of P2P overlay networks built on top of pervasive environments by employing bio-inspired methods. Although no special restriction is imposed on the type of applications, those for semi-public urban spaces, supporting socialization by enabling people to meet, work, learn and have fun, will be considered with high priority.

Our research is based on the theory of ACO, which has shown fruitful outcomes utilising artificial ants to optimise overlays, e.g. the BlatAnt algorithm [1] that effectively bounds the diameter of grid overlays. However, the characteristics of our considered underlying networks are essentially different from grids in that the dynamicity and device heterogeneity are much higher. To address these unique features, we first aim at reducing the overhead traffic by creating new ant families and new types of pheromones to optimise information collection. This information will then be used to restructure and optimise overlay topology. Additionally, maintaining a multi-layer overlay composed of diverse types of virtual links according to different quality criteria, complemented by an adaptive layer switching mechanism, are expected to increase the overall overlay robustness.

3   X-Ant Algorithm

3.1   Multi-layer Overlay

To tackle the multifold requirements of different pervasive applications, we propose an overlay structure composed of different layers each of which being optimised in terms of different network parameters, such as bandwidth, latency, packet loss rate, link type (wired or wireless), etc.

According to the requirements from pervasive applications, these layers can be maintained with identical or near identical priority so that all of them can simultaneously serve different applications' needs. Alternatively, as illustrated in Fig.1, a selected layer can be given the highest priority (active), while other layers are maintained in the background (standby). The latter mode generates less overhead traffic, making it particularly suitable for networks with restrained bandwidth. An advantage shared by both modes of operation is that the topology of one layer is not likely to overlap with another, thus increasing the overall robustness by means of available backup paths for recovery.

Layer switching is triggered by applications. Whenever an overlay optimised for a different parameter is needed, the corresponding standby layer will become the active one. Furthermore, standby layers also serve as backup layers. In case of link disconnections in the active layer, links in backup layers can be temporarily exploited as alternatives to ensure connectivity. Therefore backup layers can help the recovery of the active layer.

3.2   Ant Families

For the collection of multiple network parameters, we propose a bio-inspired, lightweight and responsive information collection mechanism. We draw inspira-

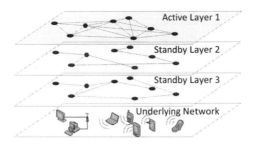

Fig. 1. Multi-layer overlay deployment scenario

tion from ant algorithms and plan to expoit three families of ants. Ants migrate from node to node and gather new information regarding the node and its neighbourhood, while also exchanging their stored information with the node they are visiting, leading thus to information dissemination across the network. Ants indirectly interact with each other via several types of pheromones.

Long-range Ants are responsible for network-wide information collection and exchange. They have a large TTL (Time-To-Live) and are capable of collecting multiple parameters during their life time. Migration of ants is biased by the pheromone concentration of the node's outgoing links. During migration, long-range ants reinforce outgoing and incoming pheromone concentration on the two connected nodes to reflect the latest status of the link. High pheromone concentration indicates links with relatively optimal quality characteristics in regard to the aforementioned network parameters. Pheromones evaporate at a constant rate; complete evaporation implies that a link is no longer active. The overhead traffic generated by long-range ants is composed of a standard 384 bits IPv6 (UDP) packet header, 96 bits ant header (ID, timing) and data payload. The payload contains information of visited nodes and their neighbours. Each visited node contributes 272 bits, plus 192 bits for every neighour.

Short-range Ants monitor the mobility of neighbouring nodes by frequently collecting relevant information. They differ from long-range ants in three aspects, i.e. the ant size, the activity frequency, and their migration behaviour. Their activity range is restricted to 2 hops, effectively leading to the collection of fewer information. This limits the short-range ants size to around 1/9 of the average size of long-range ants, and therefore we can increase their dispatch frequency without incurring too much additional overhead. The migration of short-range ants differs from that of long-range ants in that they leave pheromone trails labeled with their nest IDs, i.e. the dispatching node, to ensure that ants always return to the nest.

Messenger Ants are responsible for enforcing management decisions such as layer switching as instructed by higher-level applications. Messenger ants are in charge of propagating the decisions across the network, i.e. they do not collect information. This means that messenger ants should avoid following the footsteps of others. In this respect, we use a negative pheromone to guide the messenger ants to visit less explored links and nodes.

3.3   Topology Optimisation

Based on parameter information collected by ants, each node periodically optimises its overlay links to other nodes by initiating connections and disconnections and maintaining its neighbours. Each node keeps a local view of the network topology based on the information provided by long-range and short-range ants. This helps nodes to optimise their neighbour sets by comparing properties of the links to their current neighbours to those of other nodes in the local view. Better qualified nodes replace existing neighbours by setting up new overlay links to remote nodes and removing existing links to old neighbours, while additionally ensuring that all neighbours of the requesting node are kept connected. Although any change to a node's neighbour set can eventually be detected by ants, it is more efficient for the node to directly notify its neighbours via a simple message when a new neighbour has been detected. These messages do not flood the whole network and only affect the routing table of direct neighbours. Long-range ants will eventually propagate the change to other nodes.

4   Conclusion and Future Works

We report here the key concepts of our ongoing research work. Currently, the algorithm including the long-range and short-range ants have been implemented, while messenger ants are under development. Initial simulations using OM-NeT++ in low dynamicity environments have shown promising results in constructing P2P overlays with desired characteristics and with low overhead. Our future work mainly focuses on three aspects. First, the model of ants needs to be further improved to eliminate any unnecessary information. Second, a better topology optimising algorithm utilising the information collected by all ants and taking into account the different layers is necessary. Last, balancing the performance of the algorithm and its overhead traffic is also an open issue.

Acknowledgements

This work was conducted in the context of the BioMPE project financially supported by the Swiss National Science Foundation (SNF), grant 200021_130132.

References

1. Brocco, A., Frapolli, F., Hirsbrunner, B.: Bounded diameter overlay construction: A self organized approach. In: IEEE SIS 2009. pp. 114–121 (April 2009)
2. Dorigo, M., Birattari, M., Stutzle, T.: Ant colony optimization. IEEE Computational Intelligence Magazine 1(4), 28–39 (2006)
3. Lua, E.K., Crowcroft, J., Pias, M., Sharma, R., Lim, S.: A survey and comparison of peer-to-peer overlay network schemes. IEEE Comm. Surveys 7(2), 72–93 (2005)
4. Ratnasamy, S., Francis, P., Handley, M., Karp, R., Shenker, S.: A scalable content-addressable network. In: ACM SIGCOMM, pp. 161–172 (2001)
5. Snyder, P.L., Greenstadt, R., Valetto, G.: Myconet: A fungi-inspired model for superpeer-based peer-to-peer overlay topologies. In: IEEE SASO, pp. 40–50 (2009)

Towards Vulnerability Prevention in Autonomic Networks and Systems

Martín Barrère, Rémi Badonnel, and Olivier Festor

LORIA - INRIA Nancy Grand Est, France
{barrere,badonnel,festor}@inria.fr

Abstract. The autonomic paradigm has been introduced in order to cope with the growing complexity of management. In that context, autonomic networks and systems are in charge of their own configuration. However, the changes that are operated by these environments may generate vulnerable configurations. In the meantime, a strong standardization effort has been done for specifying the description of configuration vulnerabilities. We propose in this paper an approach for integrating these descriptions into the management plane of autonomic systems in order to ensure safe configurations. We describe the underlying architecture and a set of preliminary results based on the Cfengine configuration tool.

1 Introduction and Challenges

The continuous growth and dynamics of networks, as well as the diversification of their services in the context of Future Internet has considerably increased the complexity of their management. In order to face this problem, *autonomic computing* [5], [4], has been introduced providing new perspectives. Highly inspired on the central nervous system, this approach aims to define a strong basis for automated systems capable of managing themselves in an autonomous manner, identifying four major properties, namely, self-configuration, self-optimization, self-healing and self-protection. Despite numerous benefits have been already obtained from this new paradigm, several challenges must be addressed in order to introduce this approach into current systems and networks.

When autonomic related tasks are performed, the environment is modified in order to achieve specific objectives. Such changes may lead to potential vulnerable states, thus change management techniques for assessing change associated risks are required [8]. The vulnerability management activity usually consists in checking the configurations of the system components, identifying the presence of vulnerable states and performing the required maintenance operations (typically, modification of configuration parameters and/or application of security patches). Vulnerability detection and prevention techniques not also increase systems security but also complement the change management process by providing useful information for risk assessment mechanisms.

Even though vulnerability detection techniques have been proposed [7], [3], [6], and mechanisms for uniformly describing vulnerabilities and exchanging related

I. Chrisment et al. (Eds.): AIMS 2011, LNCS 6734, pp. 65–68, 2011.
© IFIP International Federation for Information Processing 2011

information have been provided [2], there is no integration of such mechanisms within the framework of autonomic networks and systems. Such integration constitutes the target of our work as we consider that autonomic environments should exploit the knowledge provided by vulnerability repositories in order to increase their security, stability and sustainability.

In this paper we present our approach for integrating vulnerability descriptions in the autonomic management plane, considering the OVAL [2] process and the autonomic maintenance system Cfengine [1]. The remainder of this paper is organized as follows. Section 2 presents the proposed approach for increasing vulnerability awareness within autonomic environments, whereas the results achieved to date are outlined in Section 3. Section 4 presents conclusions and perspectives.

2 Self-Configuration with Vulnerability Prevention

Within the autonomic computing field, the self-configuration property refers to the ability of networks and systems for automatically configuring themselves according to high-level policies. When autonomous networks and systems perform changes in order to be compliant with the specified policies, collateral effects can be introduced without explicit knowledge. Such unexpected effects can vary from internal malfunction to the exposure of vulnerable states.

We propose to support the self-configuration of autonomic systems with vulnerability management mechanisms. These mechanisms can ensure safe configurations and also reduce the probability of potential attacks and failures of the involved self-managed entities. Autonomic systems must be able to perform retro-inspection, identify required changes and execute the appropriate tasks. As happens in the real world, autonomic elements coexist within dynamic environments, interacting with other autonomic and non-autonomic elements. Nevertheless, such scenarios present continuous threats that may compromise autonomic elements safety. If an autonomic element is violated in some way, its functions and abilities become untrustworthy and eventually disabled; thus autonomic elements that use services of the former become compromised as well. This inevitably leads to distrust and the failure of the autonomic system. Autonomic systems must be able to manage their own state and perform the required activities to achieve secure configurations. Autonomic elements unable to support this capability will age with time, becoming more vulnerable, insecure and useless. Automation is really possible only if autonomic networks and systems are capable of ensuring safe configurations.

We therefore argue in favor of the integration of vulnerability descriptions into the management plane of autonomic systems. Our objective is to translate these vulnerability descriptions into policies that are interpretable by an autonomic system. In particular, we propose to translate standardized OVAL[1] vulnerability descriptions into Cfengine policy rules. In this manner, the vulnerability prevention process associated to OVAL can be integrated into Cfengine

---

[1] Open Vulnerability Assessment Language.

devices when maintenance operations are performed as depicted in Figure 1. The OVAL language is a standard XML-based language used by vendors and security organizations for publishing security related information warning about current threats and system vulnerabilities. OVAL repositories offer a wide range of security advisories that can be used for avoiding vulnerable states as well as augmenting networks and systems security considering best practices recommendations. Autonomic maintenance systems such as Cfengine provides support for automating the management of large-scale environments based on high level-policies. Cfengine offers a powerful distributed agent framework that combined with the OVAL vulnerability language, provides an efficient strategy for aligning security aspects on autonomic environments.

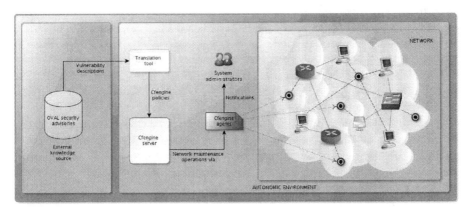

Fig. 1. Self-configuration with vulnerability prevention

In that context, we consider a translation module, identified on Figure 1, responsible for the generation of Cfengine rules corresponding to the vulnerability descriptions defined in the OVAL repository. Generated policies are deployed by the Cfengine server into its several Cfengine agents (points in the cloud) which are in charge of managing the devices present in the target network, in order to detect and prevent vulnerable configurations when self-management activities are performed.

3   Preliminary Results

We have formalized our approach by designing an intermediate formal language that provides mathematical tools for supporting the translation between OVAL advisories and Cfengine policies. In order to provide a computable infrastructure for the proposed approach, we have developed a first implementation prototype of the translation engine. At this early stage we have focused on dealing with IOS vulnerabilities over Cisco devices, nevertheless we aim to provide support for managing other platforms as well. The implementation prototype has been designed over a plugin-based architecture with the purpose of enabling easy means for extending its translation capabilities. Current plugins provide a large variety of IOS vulnerability descriptions available within the official OVAL repository. The logical data model used by the translator is automatically generated based on the OVAL specification, thus enabling a seamless declarative evolution with the OVAL language and providing support for existing and future security related knowledge. We are currently finalizing the proposed prototype and performing several experiments over a simulated environment for evaluating factors such as functionality, performance, and quality of the generated Cfengine code.

4   Conclusions and Perspectives

Vulnerability awareness is a key challenge in autonomic networks and systems. The autonomy of such dynamic environments will really be made possible when they fully integrate support mechanisms for preventing vulnerabilities and maintaining safe configurations. In that context, we propose an approach for integrating vulnerability descriptions into the autonomic management plane. We have formalized how these descriptions can be translated into policy rules that are interpretable by an autonomic configuration tool. We have developed a first prototype based on the Cfengine configuration tool, that covers a subset of OVAL definitions and permits to generate vulnerability alerts during the self-configuration activity. For future work, we are interested in extending the coverage of our solution to a larger variety of OVAL definitions, and in investigating further the execution of treatments by the autonomic network, when a vulnerable configuration is observed.

References

[1] Cfengine, http://www.cfengine.org/ (last visited on February 14, 2011)
[2] OVAL Language, http://oval.mitre.org/ (last visited on February 14, 2011)
[3] Achi, H., Hellany, A., Nagrial, M.: Network Security Approach For Digital Forensics Analysis. In: Proceedings of the International Conference on Computer Engineering and Systems (CCES 2008), pp. 263–267 (November 2008)
[4] Autonomic Computing. An Architectural Blueprint For Autonomic Computing. IBM White Paper (2006)
[5] Kephart, J.O., Chess, D.M.: The Vision of Autonomic Computing. Computer 36(1), 41–50 (2003)
[6] Khan, M.J., Awais, M.M., Shamail, S.: Enabling Self-Configuration in Autonomic Systems Using Case-Based Reasoning with Improved Efficiency. In: Proceedings of the 4th International Conference on Autonomic and Autonomous Systems (ICAS 2008), pp. 112–117 (March 2008)
[7] Wang, T., Wei, T., Gu, G., Zou, W.: TaintScope: A Checksum-Aware Directed Fuzzing Tool for Automatic Software Vulnerability Detection. In: Proceedings of the IEEE Symposium on Security and Privacy, pp. 497–512 (May 2010)
[8] Wickboldt, J.A., Bianchin, L.A., Lunardi, R.C.: Improving IT Change Management Processes with Automated Risk Assessment. In: Proceedings of the IEEE International Workshop on Distributed Systems: Operations and Management (DSOM 2009), pp. 71–84 (2009)

Autonomous Platform for Life-Critical Decision Support in the ICU

Kristof Steurbaut and Filip De Turck

Department of Information Technology (INTEC), Ghent University - IBBT,
Gaston Crommenlaan 8 Bus 201, 9050 Gent, Belgium
Kristof.Steurbaut@intec.UGent.be

Abstract. The Intensive Care Unit is a complex, data-intensive and critical environment in which the adoption of Information Technology is growing. As physicians become more dependent on the computing technology to support decisions, raise real-time alerts and notifications of patient-specific conditions, this software has strong dependability requirements. The dependability challenges are expressed in terms of availability, reliability, performance, usability and maintenance of the system. Our research focuses on the design and development of a generic autonomous ICU service platform. COSARA is a computer-based platform for infection surveillance and antibiotic management in ICU. During its design, development and evaluation, we identified both technological and human factors that affect robustness. We presented the identified research questions that will be addressed in detail during PhD research.

Keywords: Dependability, services, ICU.

1 Introduction

The computerization of medical decision support processes and clinical guidelines contributes to better quality of care [1]. Decisions can be based on large amounts of patient-specific data and computing power is used to execute complex clinical guidelines. The aim of our Intensive Care Unit (ICU) service platform is to provide Computer-based Surveillance and Alerting of Nosocomial Infections, Antimicrobial Resistance and Antibiotic Consumption (COSARA) [2]. The COSARA platform collects and combines data from existing clinical sources such as laboratory database, Picture Archiving and Communication System (PACS), Intensive Care Information System (ICIS) and antibiotics registrations [3]. COSARA offers an overview of all antibiotic prescriptions, infection registrations, microbiology and related clinical parameters in one single application. Even information which was not present in the originating systems is registered, for example by requesting physicians' motivation for starting an antibiotic therapy. Advanced decision support services can be created on the platform, to notify about antibiotic dosage or organ failure. As the application is entirely integrated in the physicians' daily workflow, physicians become more dependent on this patient-specific visualisation and decision support functionality.

I. Chrisment et al. (Eds.): AIMS 2011, LNCS 6734, pp. 69–72, 2011.
© IFIP International Federation for Information Processing 2011

2   Motivation

The dependability of the ICU platform is investigated. Dependability of the software system is the ability to deliver service that can justifiably be trusted. It encompasses a combination of reliability, availability, confidentiality, integrity, maintainability, safety. The alternate definition is to avoid service failures that are more frequent and more severe than acceptable [4]. With the introduction of advanced clinical decision support services, healthcare is becoming more dependent on software. Most of the quality attributes were not directly measurable, but were expressed as perceived by the end users. Our aim is to provide a platform which can autonomously react on unexpected failures, while ensuring the high level of dependability. As physicians do not have the technical expertise to reconfigure or redeploy the system, the system should autonomously detect failures and self-configure or self-manage the services, even without the intervention of the IT developer. The development has been a continuous interative process since the start in 2007 [2]. In Fig.1 we identified the impact of issues that occured in the COSARA evaluation: (i) data inaccuracy, (ii) integration mismatches, (iii) human registration inaccuracy, (iv) slow system response, (v) link failures, (vi) software server crash, (vii) hardware and power failures. Data inaccuracy is the result of unavailable data, missing data or invalid data. Integration mismatches occur when wrong or different patient identifications are used.

3   Automomous Service Platform

Unlike traditional approaches, such as logging system failures and keeping an audit trail of all interactions, the system should anticipate on unexpected failures by reconfiguring, recovering the services. In order to obtain a fully autonomous computer-based ICU service platform, we formulated our research questions:

– *How can the COSARA software platform support dependability in the best possible way?*

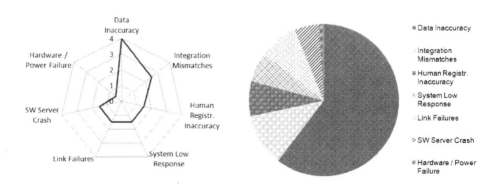

Fig. 1. Evaluation of COSARA reliability: importance of the observed issues by the physicians (left) and the relative number of issue reports (right)

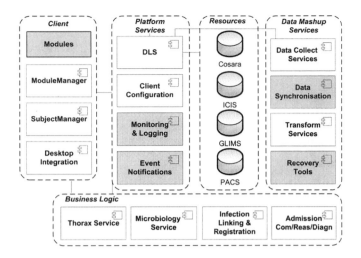

Fig. 2. COSARA Platform Architecture

– *What platform components are necessary in the platform design?*
The architecture consists of Data Mashup Services, Platform Services, Business Logic Services and Client Modules. Fig. 2 highlights the necessary components to achieve an autonomous service platform.
– *How to monitor the system health and service performance?*
A monitoring component allows to track the system health and status of all running bedside clients. Database performance is measurable because the execution time of each query is logged. The client can be restarted if it appears in off-line status. From the physicians' perspective, time delays, for example to display large images, were associated with a complete malfunctioning of the application. The user was unaware of the delay and expected a failure of the system. Usability and notications about the system behavior are crucial.
– *How to realize autonomous synchronisation with external resources?*
The physician and developer are notified of detected fault states by tracking service variables. The availability of the communication links between the data sources (such as lab or PACS) must be high. When a link breaks, the ICU administrator is notified about this failure. In case of other failures (such as server restart), a flexible recovery mechanism can restart all services.
– *How to ensure high level of data quality?*
In the resources (ICIS, GLIMS-Lab, PACS), data might not be available in a well-structured format, might be missing or become available at a later moment. The data quality is of major importance and has to be up-to-date and display the same information as the existing systems. Human factors can influence the data accuracy. For example, registering different patient-identifications across systems, can cause mismatches of data. Registrations should be correctly entered in the system. Inaccurate data could result in wrong decisions and offering only valid data creates trust among its users. Therefore a data synchronisation mechanism is needed between the existing

clinical data sources and the COSARA database. The data collection process and synchronisation use the Data Lookup Service (DLS) to query the databases. This DLS is monitored and in case of low performance, the load has to be spread across different DLSs.

- *How to adapt the platform to changes in business logic and data persistence?* Some assumptions about the presence of clinical values and identifications were made in the initial design. However, during operation, it was noticed that some parameters could be missing and were added after the patient was admitted a couple of days.

4   Validation

The COSARA application, which has been deployed on 56 bedside PCs in the Intensive Care Unit of Ghent University Hospital since April 2010, was evaluated during a 5-month period. The prototype was evaluated by a study nurse and the data quality was validated by all ICU researchers. We are now planning to further apply dependability mechanisms to the platform.

Acknowledgments. This research has been done within the context of the COSARA project, which was supported by the Institute for the Promotion of Innovation through Science and Technology in Flanders (IWT).

References

1. Damiani, G., Pinnarelli, L., Colosimo, S., Almiento, R., Sicuro, L., Galasso, R., Sommella, L., Ricciardi, W.: The effectiveness of computerized clinical guidelines in the process of care: a systematic review. BMC Health Services Research 10, 2 (2010)
2. Steurbaut, K., Van Hoecke, S., Colpaert, K., Lamont, K., Taveirne, K., Depuydt, P., Benoit, D., Decruyenaere, J., De Turck, F.: Use of web services for computerized medical decision support, including infection control and antibiotic management, in the intensive care unit. J. Telemed Telecare 16, 25–29 (2010)
3. Steurbaut, K., Van Hoecke, S., Taveirne, K., Lamont, K., De Turck, F., Colpaert, K., Depuydt, P., Benoit, D., Danneels, C., Decruyenaere, J.: Design of Software Services for Computer-Based Infection Control and Antibiotic Management in the Intensive Care Unit. In: International Conference on eHealth, Telemedicine, and Social Medicine (2009)
4. Avizienis, A., Laprie, J., Randell, B., Landwehr, C.: Basic Concepts and Taxonomy of Dependable and Secure Computing. IEEE Transactions on Dependable and Secure Computing 1(1) (2004)

Policy-Based Pricing for Heterogeneous Wireless Access Networks

Javier Baliosian[1], Joan Serrat[2], Matias Richart[1], Juan Saavedra[1],
Mariela Borba[1], and Jose Luis Melus[2]

[1] School of Engineering, University of the Republic, Montevideo, Uruguay
javierba@fing.edu.uy
[2] Polytechnic University of Catalonia (UPC), Barcelona, Spain
serrat@tsc.upc.edu

Abstract. Our cities are already covered by a myriad of diverse wireless
access networks. The most ubiquitous access networks are the well organized homogeneous and centralized operator-based cellular networks
that sustain their business model on a captive client basis. However, a
new billing paradigm is rising, where a client can choose to connect to the
provider that best comply with his/her current requirements and context. Inside this paradigm, this paper presents a distributed, rule-based
pricing strategy aimed to improve the quality of service and to increase
the global income of a service provider. The performance and reliability
of the rule-based decisions is supported by a Finite State Transducers-
based inference machine specially designed to manage networking systems. We show, with simulations, that, using our strategy, the operators
can make the new billing paradigm profitable while the clients benefit
from the economic advantages of competition and of the quality given
by a pricing–based network balance mechanism.

1 Introduction

Our cities are already covered by a myriad of diverse wireless access networks.
The most ubiquitous are the well organized homogeneous and centralized
operator-based cellular networks that base their business on a captive client
model. However, a more heterogeneous and free network of WiFi, WiMAX and
3G access-providers has appeared and it is starting to challenge the dominant
billing paradigm. In this new world, clients can choose the best or the cheapest
provider for the time and place they are trying to connect from, setting the
grounds of a future free market of Internet connectivity-providers. In this context, pricing will have a fundamental role. Using the right pricing strategy, an
operator will try to obtain the highest possible revenue while the users will try
to get a service that fits their requirements at the minimum possible price. As
stated in [1] "From an economic point of view, pricing plays an important role
in trading any resource or service. The most important objective of trading is
to provide benefits to both the sellers and the buyers. Therefore, the price must
be chosen so that the revenue of the sellers is maximized while the highest satisfaction is achieved by the buyers. There are two main factors influencing the

I. Chrisment et al. (Eds.): AIMS 2011, LNCS 6734, pp. 73–85, 2011.

price setting, namely, user demand and competition among service providers. Price and demand are functions of each other." Following these ideas, if demand is high the service provider can charge a high price in order to earn more. However, if demand is low, the price must be reduced to attract more mobile users. Competition between service providers also impacts on the price of the service. Typically, if the services are substitutable (even though different), users buy a service that provides the highest satisfaction at the lowest price.

As explained by Courcoubetis and Weber in [2] the communication services that we are considering in this work can be considered simply as means for the transport of data with a given quality, characterized as a certain error rate, delay and jitter. Obviously, the network access providers will want to recover their investment charging a price for their services, but that is not the only reason for which pricing is important. The price of simple goods it is often determined by only one parameter such as the number of copies, their weight or the length of a lease. However, communication services are specified by several parameters such as peak rate, average bandwidth or loss rate. Moreover, multimedia service contracts are specified with additional parameters such as tolerance to bursts and adaptability to network changes. Since connectivity services can be specified in terms of so many variables, the number of different possible contracts is enormous and complicates the design of a reasonable and coherent pricing strategy. On the other hand, contracts are more than simple price agreements. For example, a contract may be an incentive for the user to produce traffic conforming to the agreed parameters. This, at time, will impact positively on the service quality and the price paid by the clients in general. All this motivates an effort to develop a pricing technique simple enough to be implemented by the operators, but, at the same time, sophisticated enough to compete successfully with other strategies and work as a scalable feedback mechanism to control how the network is used. A provider can reduce the price of a service during off-peak hours to incentive the use of idle resources or charge an extra price to a user that exceeds the agreed traffic. Additionally, pricing may be seen as an alternative to TCP for congestion control. Thus, in a similar manner to TCP and its signaling, a higher price may induce users to reduce the packet transmission rate or to stop it completely. However, to be useful as a congestion-control mechanism, a pricing technique must be very dynamic. It should be able to change the price of a particular service in real time and in a particular region of the network, for example in a particular access point that is suffering of congestion.

This paper presents a distributed, rule-based pricing system that implements exactly the same intuitive ideas in the shape of policy-rules to be enforced on the price charged by each provider. Those rules are aimed to improve the quality of service and to increase the global income of a service provider in that world in which users are free to choose every time they connect.

The paper is organized as follows: in §2 we introduce the rationale of our solution and and overview of its architecture. In section 2.2 and 2.3 we present the set of rules governing our system and the kind of conflicts that arise using them. In §3 we present details of the system design and the manner in which policy conflicts are solved. Finally, in §4 we depict a simulation-based evaluation and we conclude and present some future work in §5.

2   A Policy-Based Pricing Solution

The rationale behind the proposal of this paper is twofold: first, it tries to offer an autonomic, scalable pricing system that provides the operators with simple and business-understandable means to set prices. In the examples presented in this paper, we follow the principles of demand and competition mentioned above. Second, our proposal is aimed to demonstrate that the process of solving the conflicts between the pricing policies constitutes an optimization procedure that is capable of, for example, balance an access network using the price of the access service as an incentive-based tool to drive the users choices. The following sections describe the overall scenario and the design of the proposed system.

2.1   Overall System Architecture

We envisage scenarios where three types of actors coexist on a geographical area: users, providers and a regulator (see Figure 1). Users are persons in possession of some wireless-capable device that are willing to establish a connection to the Internet with some quality of service requirements and at the minimum possible cost. As we envision it, users are not attached to a provider by a contract. Instead, they pay for the provider's service on demand, by, for example, a credit card or pre-paid means, as it is common in current cellular 3G services. In our model, in front of equal or similar services, users will always choose the services of less expensive provider. The providers have an access network conformed

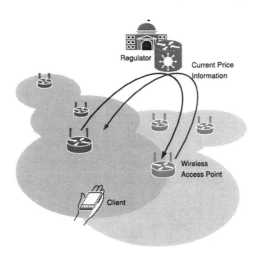

Fig. 1. Scenario

for a set of access devices that we will call generically Access Points (AP). A provider's objective is to sell access services to users while maximizing their revenue. The third entity, the regulator, is a neutral entity, probably played by a governmental agency in a real setup, with the objective of enforcing the sharing of pricing information between the providers to allow pure market competition.

In our scenario, there are two different providers offering their connectivity services through a network of APs over the overlapping geographical regions. This means that at any point of this region, a user has network coverage from one or more APs of each provider. In the particular world we are envisioning, each AP has its own price for a connectivity service of a given bandwidth and duration. Those prices may vary from one AP to another even if they are operated by the same provider and from time to time. In this manner, an AP in a popular part of the city may have a higher price than another in a neighborhood with few users or the same AP can diminish the service price during the low-usage parts of the day. The mobile user's terminal can connect to any of those APs and run an agent that is able to communicate with an AP and get information about the current price for a certain service the AP provides (later we will discuss about the technical solutions for this issue). Once it has the price from different APs, the agent connects to the AP with the lowest price, with or without human assistance (another possible criteria will be discussed bellow in §5). The established connection will last for the contracted time or until the connection is lost, for example, because the user moved out of the AP's coverage region. For this paper, the manner in which the regulator collects and shares price information between APs is not relevant but it may be made with a standard publish-subscribe mechanism with some integrity and no-repudiation guaranties.

2.2   Governing Policies

Policies are intended to allow each AP to decide which is the most advantageous price for its own connectivity service, having into account its context, user's demand and potential competitors. These decisions are made by a Policy Decision Point [3] installed in the same AP, independently from the others regardless whether they belong to the same or competing providers, following a set of policy-rules modeling the economic criteria of demand and competition mentioned in §1. It is worthy to mention that these sets of policies can be freely established by each provider according to best practices founded on past experience, forecasts based on economic models, etc and that by no means are imposed by the regulator. Even more, a provider could participate without making use of pricing policies, just fixing a flat rate for its services. Nevertheless, for the sake of illustrating the approach, and also to allow a quantitative evaluation we present hereafter specific sets of policies; one concerning demand and the other competition.

The set of rules driving the decisions regarding demand is presented in Table 1. The rationale behind this set of rules is simple; the price of the service is increased, kept constant or decreased depending on the number of users served and its gradient of change. In this way, the price will be adapted to stimulate or inhibit service

Table 1. Set of rules driving an access point behavior on demand bases

Rule 1: **if** few_users and users_steady **then** decrease_price_slow
Rule 2: **if** few_users and users_decreasing_slow **then** decrease_price_slow
Rule 3: **if** few_users and users_decreasing_fast **then** decrease_price_fast
Rule 4: **if** few_users and users_increasing_slow **then** keep_price
Rule 5: **if** few_users and users_increasing_fast **then** keep_price
Rule 6: **if** mid_users and users_steady **then** increase_price_slow
Rule 7: **if** mid_users and users_decreasing_slow **then** decrease_price_slow
Rule 8: **if** mid_users and users_decreasing_fast **then** decrease_price_fast
Rule 9: **if** mid_users and users_increasing_slow **then** keep_price
Rule 10: **if** mid_users and users_increasing_fast **then** increase_price_slow
Rule 11: **if** lots_users and users_steady **then** keep_price
Rule 12: **if** lots_users and users_decreasing_slow **then** decrease_price_slow
Rule 13: **if** lots_users and users_decreasing_fast **then** decrease_price_fast
Rule 14: **if** lots_users and users_increasing_slow **then** increase_price_slow
Rule 15: **if** lots_users and users_increasing_fast **then** increase_price_fast

Table 2. Set of rules driving an access point behavior on competitors' bases

Rule 16: **if** competitor_price_lower and competitor_price_decreasing_slow **then** decrease_price_slow
Rule 17: **if** competitor_price_lower and competitor_price_decreasing_fast **then** decrease_price_fast
Rule 18: **if** competitor_price_lower and competitor_price_steady **then** decrease_price_fast
Rule 19: **if** competitor_price_lower and competitor_price_increasing_slow **then** decrease_price_slow
Rule 20: **if** competitor_price_lower and competitor_price_increasing_fast **then** decrease_price_fast
Rule 21: **if** competitor_price_higher and competitor_price_decreasing_fast **then** decrease_price_slow
Rule 22: **if** competitor_price_higher and competitor_price_steady **then** increase_price_slow
Rule 23: **if** competitor_price_higher and competitor_price_increasing_slow **then** increase_price_fast
Rule 24: **if** competitor_price_higher and competitor_price_increasing_fast **then** increase_price_fast

demand and its adaptation rate will track the evolution of such demand. In practice we accomplish it by classifying the number of users in three categories (few, mid and lots), the gradient of change in two (slow and fast) and also allowing two rates of price change (slow and fast).

On the other hand, the set of rules facing the competition is presented in Table 2. Here the global objective is to accommodate the price to the evolution of the competitors to avoid users' migration. In particular we have classified the price of the competition in two categories (lower and higher) and considered two adaptation rates (slow and fast). In this context, a competitor is an individual AP and two APs are competitors between them when their coverage regions overlap and they belong to different providers.

2.3   Conflicting Policies

Conflicts, or logic contradictions, are an intrinsic phenomenon of the policy-based management. The process to solve those conflicts is the way that policy-based network management has so as to optimize the configuration of the services and devices of a communications network.

In the particular case of the this work, conflicts arise mainly because the diversity of objectives of our system. For example, lets consider the following simple –and quite intuitive– version of the rules presented above:

Rule 1: if few_users then decrease_price_slow

Rule 2: if competitor_price_higher then increase_price_fast

Rule 1 models a pricing policy based on demand, and Rule 2 models a pricing policy based on competition. Although in a simple manner, they are the most patent case in which our previous set of rules may present a conflict: which action has the system to trigger if there are a small number of users connected to an AP but the price of the competitor is higher than the local price?

The process that our system uses to decide in front of this kind of situations is described bellow in §3.1.

3 A Policy-Based System Design

Our solution combines centralized, hierarchical and fully-distributed management
structures to address different challenges with the most appropriate approach. Our basic design criteria is to maximize the distribution of tasks over the nodes as much as possible. Only the tasks that inherently require a centralized organization, such as global optimizations, or those tasks which perform better on a weakly-distributed structure, are carried out using hierarchical structures. Management tasks such as local optimizations follow a fully distributed approach.

The system can be seen as mainly composed by independent units or nodes that work as peers deployed at each managed network device (a wireless access point). From a high level architectural point of view those nodes follow a classical policy-based architecture constituted by a Policy Decision Point (PDP), a Policy Enforcement Point (PEP) and an agent that monitors the state of the device and the behavior of the network. Policies follow the Event Condition Action (ECA) model, where the condition may be the occurrence of some event (e.g., an alarm or a service request) or certain network state, and the action is the desired response when the condition is true or just it occurs. The monitoring agent of any of the nodes of the network generates notifications, which are the source of events for the PDP of the same or any other node. All the communications between nodes, including control messages, notifications and request for actions are carried out by a content-routed asynchronous communication bus that organizes the nodes in a hierarchical overlay. The communications bus' design is inspired by existent notification services such as Siena [4]. Finally, a centralized management station is in charge of the edition, optimization and distribution of rules into the nodes.

The reconfiguration actions decided by the PDP may also involve other network elements, in which case the node may be the manager of the activity and delegate responsibility for some actions to other nodes. As it will be described in the next section, policies have to be managed as finite state transducers (FST). The translation from policy rules expressed in natural language into the FSTs implementing those rules is currently made by programmer assisted algorithms

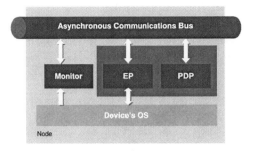

Fig. 2. Architecture of a Node

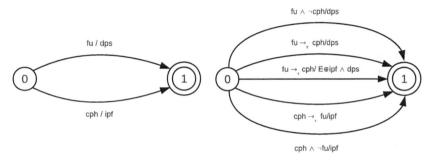

(a) TFFST Modeling two Conflicting Pricing (b) TFFST Modeling two Pricing Rules with
Rules   their Conflicts Solved

Fig. 3. Finite State Transducers for Conflict Resolution

presented in [5]. Despite the fact of being a software assisted process, it is still a complex and work-intensive task.

3.1 The Logic behind the Pricing Management System. Finite State Transducers for Conflict Resolution

To better understand how the FST-based conflict-resolution process works, we will describe it with the help of the rules presented above in §2.3.

As stated above, Rule 1 models a pricing policy based on demand, and Rule 2 models a pricing policy based on competition. The FST in Figure 3(a) models both rules at once. In the figure, the TF few_users is depicted as fu, the TF competitor_price_higher as cph, action decrease_price_slow is depicted as dps and increase_price_fast as ipf.

For simplicity, we are considering the case in which a single notification arrives, then the PDP makes a decision based on it, and nothing else happens. (This makes the FST simpler because only has to accept strings made of a single symbol).

Now, consider the case in which a notification arrives stating that the price of a competitor has changed. At that time the PDP evaluates the FST in

Figure 3(a) as follows: starting in the initial state "0" it evaluates the TFs on the input label of each of the state's outgoing edges. This is, the PDP evaluates `few_users` and `competitor_price_higher`. In the case that there are few users connected to the local AP and that the price of the competitor is lower or equal to the price charged by the local node, `few_users` is a positive number and `competitor_price_higher` a negative number. Therefore, the PDP chooses the upper edge of the FST, which produces `decrease_price_slow` as an output, causing local EP to decrease the price slowly. However, in the case that the price of the competitor is higher than the local price, we have two edges going out of state "0" with positive TFs and not a straightforward choice to be made. To solve this problem, before being deployed to the AP's PDP, the FST is determinised and the FST in Figure 3(b) is computed using the algorithm mentioned before. Now, when the PDP evaluates the determinised transducer, at each state it has only one possible edge to follow. Let us assume that, when the PDP evaluates it, the TF `few_users` takes a value of 0.3 and `competitor_price_higher` a value of 0.5. We are in the case in which `few_users` is "tauter than" `competitor_price_higher`, expressed in Figure 3(b) as $fu \rightarrow_\lambda cph$, therefore, the transducer produces a single output, in this case the order to decrease the price charged by the local AP slowly (action decrease_price_slow).

4   Evaluation

The simulation platform presented hereafter was designed with the aim to evaluate the viability of the proposed solution and, above all, the viability of the new pricing paradigm. In this section we present the result of two sets of experiments in which we compare the behavior of our proposal against the most popular pricing strategy for WiFi and 3G access networks.

4.1   Evaluation Setup

In order to evaluate our solution we simulated an environment with two competing providers offering access services on the same geographical region and with identical networking infrastructure resources. However, one of the providers follows our pricing strategy and the other follows the prevailing fixed-rate pricing structure presented in §2.2. Although it will not happen in a real deployment, to ensure a fair comparison between competitors in our experiments, both providers have identical sets of APs installed on the same coordinates and with identical coverage areas. A large number of clients move along the area covered by both providers choosing to connect to the AP with the lower price for a randomly specified service. To perform the experiments in this section we developed a simple discrete events simulator based on the JavaSimulation library.

For each experiment, each provider has nine APs deployed in a 1200x1200m region. Those APs are distributed in a mesh at approximately 400m of each other (see Figure 4). As said before, APs are by pairs, one owned by the provider

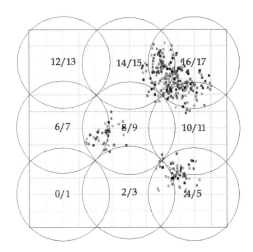

Fig. 4. Position of APs and Users (RPGM Mobility)

following our strategy and the other owned by the competitor provider following a fixed-rate strategy. The price charged by each AP is a random variable that follows a uniform distribution with values between 50 and 60 units. Each AP has an available bandwidth of 3.5 Mbps, and a homogeneous circular coverage area with a radius of 285m. For the experiments, there are 450 mobile users. Each user tries to hire a connectivity service with a random bandwidth of between 50 and 150 Kbps with any of the APs in its connectivity range. These users move inside the square area mentioned above following one of two mobility models. In the first set of experiments we assume an urban environment and use the Manhattan mobility model [6] to capture the movements of the users. Following this model, each user moves along a mesh of parallel, perpendicular streets placed every 100m. For all the experiments using the Manhattan model, the speed of a terminal varies randomly with a pedestrian mean of 1m/s and a standard deviation of 0.2. At each intersection, a terminal decides whether to turn left, right or keep the direction with a probability of 0.2.

The second set of experiments were made to study the balancing capabilities of our strategy assuming that the clients move following the Reference Point Group Mobility (RPGM) model [7]. The RPGM models a set of clients moving in groups but with some individual freedom to move inside and between groups. Each group has a logic center (group leader) that determines the behavior of the rest of the group. At the beginning of the simulation each client is uniformly distributed in the vicinity of the leader, then, each client moves with random speed and direction. All the experiments run during a simulated time of 120 minutes.

The metric used to compare the behavior of both providers is the total amount of money made by each provider (adding the money made by all its APs) within the simulation time.

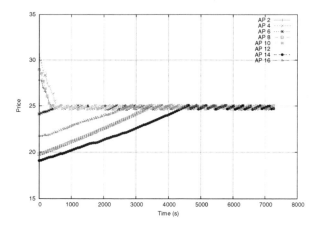

Fig. 5. Prices by AP for the Provider using our Strategy (Manhattan Mobility)

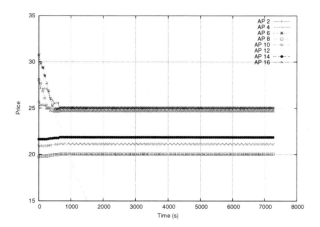

Fig. 6. Prices by AP for the Provider using our Strategy (RPGM Mobility)

4.2 Evaluation Results

Figure 5 shows the price evolution for the 9 APs of the provider implementing our pricing strategy. In this experiment the users move following the Manhattan model. In the figure, it is possible to see how the prices change getting similar to the competitor price but slightly below. This makes the clients to prefer our provider. The higher number of clients connected to APs owned by our provider explains the bigger revenue despite charging lower prices for the same service.

The Reference Point Group Mobility left regions of the geography without users and regions with high concentrations of them. This situation makes more visible the price dependence on the number of users trying to connect to an APIn this experiment, APs 0 and 12 have no users in their coverage regions (see Figure 4), consequently, the price charged by those APs decreases until it reaches

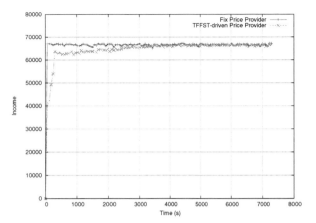

Fig. 7. Revenue by Provider(Manhattan Mobility)

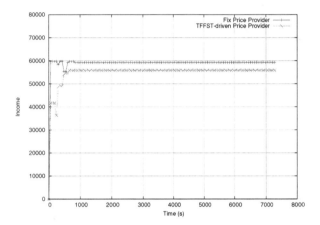

Fig. 8. Revenue by Provider (RPG Mobility)

the minimum possible cost defined by the provider. The APs 2, 6, and 8 have a small number of users in range, therefore, they moderately reduce the price. Finally, those APs with most clients in their coverage area maintain their price close to the price charged by the competitor provider. This divergence between the prices charges by different APs of the same provider causes that some clients migrate from their closest APs to an AP with a lower price. In this manner, the pricing strategy works as a network balancing tool. We can see that the global earnings made by our provider are also higher than the earnings of the competitor (see Figure 8).

This experiment also shows how rule-based pricing can be used as a congestion control tool. As more users start connecting to a given AP, the price rises following for example Rule 15, naturally pushing some users out to other APs. Finally, an accessory, hard access-control prevents the connection of too many users to an AP in case the pricing mechanism is not enough.

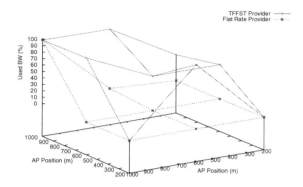

Fig. 9. Distribution of BW usage per Provider (RPGM Mobility)

The stability of the connections is related with the users' movement and ve-
locity. When a user that is connected to a given AP is informed of the existence
of a lower price AP in its current position, it terminates its current connection
and tries to connect to the AP with the lower price. However, a high percentage of users are connected along the simulation to any of the AP with the only
exceptions of the intervals in which the users are switching from one AP to
another.

5   Conclusions and Future Work

In this work we present a distributed, rule-based pricing system that improves
the quality of service –by means of a smart access control and dynamic network
balance– while increasing the global income of a service provider. This pricing
mechanism assumes a business model, not yet existing today, where users can
freely select any service provider with radio coverage at their location. However, we believe that this work supports the thesis of the plausibility of such a
model. The depicted simulations encourage the idea that operators can make
the new billing paradigm profitable while the clients benefit from the economic
advantages of competition and of the quality given by a pricing–based network
balance mechanism. First, a solution must be designed to let the mobile nodes
and the access point to communicate the price between the AP and the mobile
node, even if there is no established connection between them. There are several possible solutions for this issue, for example, in the case of WiFi APs the
price information can be transmitted as part of the AP beacon, we have made
experiments that support this solution, however, using this method it is at least
difficult to offer different prices to different clients but other solutions may be
envisioned. Another issue to address is the stability of the solution. As can be
seen in the graphs, even if the dynamic price of the rule-based APs converges
to a region near an optimum, it keeps fluctuating above and below it. This issue can be alleviated with a proper study on the functions representing fuzzy
concepts such as "decrease price slowly´´. This fine kind of tuning is a whole

research issue that will be part of our future work. Finally, another future work issue is the inclusion of additional AP selection criteria such as signal strength, preferred provider or handover reduction.

Acknowledgments

This work has been done in the context of the MICINN project TEC2009-14598-C02-02.

References

1. Niyato, D., Hossain, E.: Competitive Pricing in Heterogeneous Wireless Access Networks: Issues and Approaches. IEEE Network 22(6), 4–11 (2008)
2. Courcoubetis, C., Weber, R.: Pricing Communication Networks: Economics, Technology and Modelling. John Wiley & Sons, Ltd, Chichester (2003) ISBN: 0-470-85130-9
3. Moore, B., Ellesson, E., Strassner, J., Westerinen, A.: Policy Core Information Model Version 1 Specification, RFC 3060 (Proposed Standard), updated by RFC 3460 (February 2001),
   http://www.ietf.org/rfc/rfc3060.txt
4. Caporuscio, Carzaniga, A., Wolf, A.L.: Design and evaluation of a support service for mobile, wireless publish/subscribe applications, Department of Computer Science, University of Colorado, Tech. Rep. CU-CS-944-03 (January 2003),
   http://www.inf.unisi.ch/carzaniga/papers/
5. Baliosian, J., Serrat, J.: Finite State Transducers for Policy Evaluation and Conflict Resolution. In: Proceedings of the Fifth IEEE International Workshop on Policies for Distributed Systems and Networks (POLICY 2004), pp. 250–259 (June 2004)
6. ETSI, Universal Mobile Telecommunication System (UMTS), Selection procedures for the choice of radio transmission technologies of the umts, UMTS 30.03 Version 3.2.0 (1998-2004), http://www.3gpp.org/ftp/Specs/html-info/3003U.htm
7. Hong, X., Gerla, M., Pei, G., Chiang, C.-C.: A Group Mobility Model for Ad Hoc Wireless Networks. In: ACM International Workshop on Modeling, Analysis, and Simulation of Wireless and Mobile System (MSWiM) (1999)

Decision Engine for SIP Based Dynamic Call Routing

Sajjad Ali Musthaq, Christophe Lohr, and Annie Gravey

Department of Computer Science TELECOM Bretagne Brest, France,
Technopôle Brest-Iroise - CS 83818 - 29238 Brest Cedex 3 - France
http://www.telecom-bretagne.eu

Abstract. Enterprises nowadays are subscribing access to several Internet Service Providers (ISPs) for reliability, redundancy and better revenues underlying the service extension, while providing good Quality of Service (QoS). In this paper, a dynamic decision-making framework is presented for Session Initiation Protocol (SIP) based voice/video call routing in multihomed network. The decision engine takes multiple criteria into account while computing the routing decision (attributes from context of the request, platform's latest conditional parameters, business objectives of the company, etc.). Two Multi-Criteria Decision Making (MCDM) methods, namely Grey Relational Analysis (GRA) and an extended version of Technique for Order Preference by Similarity to Ideal Solution (TOPSIS) are used for decision calculation in outsourcing and provisioning enforcement modes respectively. The proposed solution gives higher throughput and lower call dropping probability while fulfilling the desired goals, taking into account the multiple attributes for choosing the best alternative.

Keywords: Decision Engine, Multi-Criteria Decision Making (MCDM), Grey Relation Analysis (GRA), Call Dropping Probability, Throughput.

1 Introduction

Companies use Internet to deliver data, applications and services. Traditionally, multihoming to multiple Internet Service Providers (ISPs) has been employed to ensure performance, availability and reliability. However, over the past few years, multihoming has been increasingly leveraged for improving wide-area network performance, lowering bandwidth costs and optimizing the way in which upstream links are used. The correct link selection can optimize resource utilization by ensuring the required Quality of Service (QoS). With the advent of economical and high-bandwidth broadband connection technologies, multihoming is poised to emerge from a niche technique for large businesses and has become a dominant technology that underlies Internet connectivity solutions for small to mid-sized businesses. Although the main focus in multihoming is primarily on reliability, it is also being used for Load Balancing and latency reduction. A straightforward method, that is being used widely is to perform Round Trip

I. Chrisment et al. (Eds.): AIMS 2011, LNCS 6734, pp. 86–99, 2011.

Time (RTT) measurements and take the decision in favor of the destination with minimum RTT value. However, this method is not scalable and cannot take into account the platform-local preferences (business objectives, routing rules and Service Level Agreement (SLA), QoS for voice, video, etc). To address the reliability and scalability issues, businesses typically use Border Gateway Protocol (BGP). However, BGP deployment is costly and requires lots of administration effort and hence does not suit small-to-medium business. Autonomous System Number, range of IP address prefixes, netmasks address assignment and allocation policies are required to configure the BGP. Stream Control Transport Protocol (SCTP) was launched to overcome the shortcomings of TCP and UDP. It provides multihoming support, offering failover and fault tolerance options only. There are two main factors involved in the design and development of multihoming load balancing systems: calculation of the decision for link selection among the available choices and the mechanism involving the enforcement of the calculated decision.

Multihoming Load Balancing systems being developed and deployed are examined from the functionality (algorithmic) and performance implications view points. Decision-making, i.e., the choice of link in these systems is usually static and/or semi-dynamic. Moreover, these systems take into account few attributes among the set of available parameters over the platform, while calculating the decision (service profile, Service Level Agreement (SLA) reliability information, time of the day, business objectives of the company, latest state of the links and user profiles). A system capable of taking into account Service Level Specifications (SLS), e.g. susceptible delay, jitter and packet loss may not accommodate the technology specific information. Systems considering user, service and QoS profiles do not compensate for dynamic context of the request. The first challenge is to utilize the available information over the platform maximally, which comes from different sources with different dimensions so that the final decision for link selection reflects dynamic control and effective resource utilization with good QoS. Another objective is to enforce the calculated decision using existing technologies (e.g NAT, DNS cycling hashing, etc.) so that we do not have to revamp the existing protocol stack. Both these issues (decision calculation and its enforcement) are addressed in this paper by taking into account the static and dynamic information available over the platform alongside the multihomed link data.

The rest of this paper is organized as follows: Section 2 describes the proposed architecture. Section 3 elaborates the MCDM theory and its application with two distinct methods. In section 4, the test bed for the validity of the proposed solution is presented. Section 5 outlines related work. Finally, in section 6, concluding remarks are made while outlining our future work.

2   Proposed Architecture

The architecture shown in Fig. 1 is proposed in the Companym@ges [1] project, which provides a platform where companies are linked to the rest of the world via

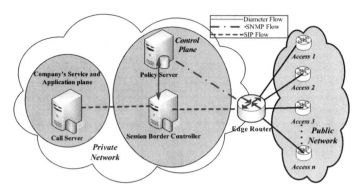

Fig. 1. Proposed Architecture

two or more network accesses offering multimedia services. QoS-centered architecture integrates devices and modules from different vendors over a single platform while offering multimedia services for public and private(local) networks. The global objective is the accommodation of dynamic modifications/variations into the decision-making criteria for request routing to different links by using enhanced general methods/techniques and protocols. Service, control and routing issues posing a multi-criteria problem are handled together without affecting the standard mechanisms and classical layered approach.

Policy Server (PS) is the main controller in the proposed architecture. It acts as a Policy Decision Point (PDP). It computes all the decisions by taking into account the static configurations and dynamics taking place over the platform, in addition to the policy enforcement supervision. The proposed dynamic decision engine partly constitutes the core of PS. Session Border Controller (SBC) in the offered framework is primarily dedicated to multimedia communication. It provides a number of vendor specific functionalities depending on the requirements and its deployment. More details are available in [2,3]. In addition to SBC's standard functionalities, it is tweaked to act as a Policy Enforcement Point (PEP) in the proposed architecture. Call Server (CS) is an important component of IP-based PBX/Softswitch. It supports proxy, registrar, redirect and location services. CS here provide registration, user profile management and service control mechanism. It is modified to handle the user profile based Call Admission Control (CAC) functionality. It is worthwhile to mention here that we are targeting the Session Initiation Protocol (SIP) based multimedia communication over the platform while focussing on decision making and its enforcement. SIP is a Hypertext Transfer Protocol (HTTP) like request response signaling protocol used for creating, modifying and tearing down sessions [4]. Components of this platform (Fig. 1) are provided by partners: the platform's service and application plane is realized by modules from Alcatel-Lucent whereas SBC and PS are/will be developed and tweaked by two different teams at TELECOM Bretagne Brest. For detailed functionality, information sharing and communication between different devices over the presented architecture, the reader is referred to [2,3].

The protocol chosen to communicate the information/decisions between PDP and PEP is Diameter with newly defined and developed Attribute Value Pairs (AVPs). Diameter is natively an Authentication Authorization Accounting (AAA) protocol. Due to its AAA characteristics, its enhancement orientations are becoming natural for decision-based network management. It has large AVP space and supports large number of pending requests. Common Open Policy Service (COPS) [6], a strong candidate for Policy Based Network Management (PBNM) [5] has not been chosen for decision(policy) provisioning and dissemination, as it is specifically designed for device-level configuration and management. However, dynamic session/call/data-connection management is required while taking into account the variations and latest dynamics. SNMP has sometimes been proposed in the literature to be a candidate for PBNM [7]. SNMP-based information in our system is exploited to gauge the QoS parameters of access router interfaces. This paper addresses the private-public border traffic management issues for request routing decisions at the application layer (OSI) while taking multiple criteria into consideration. It supports dymamicity by using Multi-Criteria Decision Making (MCDM) theory. The calculated decisions are enforced during the signaling phase of SIP-based multimedia communication using existing mechanisms (NAT, Back-2-Back User Agent (B2BUA), Proxying etc.).

3   Multi-Criteria Decision Making Theory and its Application

The process of decision making involves choosing the best alternative, given a set of alternatives (available links in our case) and a set of criteria (context of the request and predefined configurations/settings over the proposed platform). These alternatives can also be ranked on the basis of multiple criteria using some specific MCDM method. MCDM methods have been used to help solve a wide variety of problems in many different applications such as telecommunications, manufacturing, transportation and software engineering [8],[9]. Experiences show that there is not a single MCDM technique to deal with all multi-criteria problems. Indeed each situation requires a specific MCDM technique. The choice of the technique and its impact on the decision making is not within the scope of this work and reader is referred to [10] for an overview of this particular domain. The targeted objectives in the multi-criteria decision making problems might sometimes be conflicting and/or overlapping. In the posed problem, SLA includes Delay, Jitter and Packet Loss (DJPL) which falls under the business objectives of the company when they sign the direct or reciprocal agreements with partners or companies. However, the same set of parameters (DJPL) are used to grade the QoS of the available links (a link has to be chosen). The triplet (DJPL) can be used to gauge the authorization and authentication of a particular user class (e.g., Gold user must have the best QoS profile, while Silver can be assigned either a good or a satisfactory QoS profile) while executing the context of the request. There are various approaches to deal with such sort of problems each having its pros and cons but we will not address this issue due to space limitations. Two MCDM methods have been chosen to address the problem of SIP-based multimedia traffic routing on the basis of multiple criteria, while making decision for the best link. Each MCDM problem is associated with multiple attributes. These attributes are linked to the goals and are referred as decision criteria. Since different criteria represent different dimensions of alternatives, they may conflict with each other (e.g., Cumulative Bandwidth may be confused with Total Bandwidth, traffic measurements, granularity (connection/session level) obsession, cost etc.). The criteria are assigned different weights according to context of the request and the rules defined over the platform. Conventional algorithms used for link selection in multihomed networks are either user-centric or motivated for efficient resource utilization over the platform and/or they are centered towards application optimization for desired QoS. However, to cope with all these multi-criteria goals and objectives, the choice of MCDM is indispensable. Hence we picked GRA among the number of available MCDM methods to be applied to our problem of decision making in outsourcing decision enforcement mode. The reader is referred to [2] for detailed mechanism and information sharing (among different modules especially between PDP and PEP) about outsourcing decision enforcement mode. This mode takes latest platform conditions and network information into account and computes the decision on the fly, in accordance with the context of the request.

3.1 Grey Relational Analysis (GRA)

GRA is a decision-making technique that is based on grey system theory. Originally developed by Deng [11], Grey theory is widely applied in fields such as systems analysis, data processing, modeling and prediction, as well as control and decision-making. It is an effective mathematical means to deal with systems characterized by conflicting and partial information. Grey relation refers to the uncertain relations among things, among elements of systems, or among elements and behaviors. Due of its ability to use reference attribute vector, it is being applied in the proposed decision-making system in outsourcing mode. Moreover, the platform's latest conditions and the context of the request are taken into account while constructing the reference vector.

3.2 Problem Formulation and GRA Application

For brevity and to avoid the complexity of stringent mathematics, 6 attributes are chosen for the application of MCDM methods on 4 alternative links for routing the multimedia sessions. Fig. 2 illustrates the hierarchy of the desired goal, the criteria and the available alternative links. As mentioned before, we are focusing on SIP based multimedia communication, so let us have the QoS requirements for these services as follows:

Video Call: It requires a higher bandwidth than voice so the available bandwidth, transport cost and current utilization are important factors. Its ability to buffer a longer duration data before playback makes it less vulnerable to delay and jitter than voice.

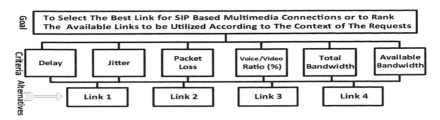

Fig. 2. Candidate Links, Attributes and Objectives Hierarchy

Voice Call: It is very sensitive to delay and jitter, requiring low bandwidth but this service is susceptible to packet losses to some extent. Because of its low bandwidth usage, the transport cost factor is considered negligible. Total bandwidth and available bandwidth are not significant factors due to low bandwidth requirements. Since there is some correlation of utilization with jitter and delay, it is preferred to have a low utilization for the selected network.

There are four links L_1, L_2, L_3 and L_4 and for the sake of simplicity, we assume that the reference constituted contains 6 attributes denoted by UR, D, J, PL, TB and AB represents the voice/video Utilization Ratio of a link (UR), with Delay (D), Jitter (J), Packet Loss (PL), Total Bandwidth (TB) and Available Bandwidth (AB) respectively. Two user Alice (local) and Bob (remote) are supposed to communicate (outgoing SIP communication) with each other by using the available resources on the platform as shown in Fig.1. Alice initiates the communication and sends an initial INVITE to the SBC at the border of the platform to start a voice call with Bob. SBC extracts the information from the request and constructs the reference for decision making by taking into account the platform's pre-defined set of objectives for different services and users. At minimum, user and communication types (more details available in [3]) have to be known. This information is sent to the PS and the corresponding user, application and QoS profiles are loaded from the profile base. The information from the context of the request is bundled with the link latest information to construct the reference vector as follows:

$$Ref(L) = \begin{bmatrix} UR & D & J & PL & TB & AB \end{bmatrix} \tag{1}$$

The candidate link attributes constituting the Decision Matrix (DM) is given as follows:

$$DM = \begin{bmatrix} UR_1 & D_1 & J_1 & PL_1 & TB_1 & AB_1 \\ UR_2 & D_2 & J_2 & PL_2 & TB_2 & AB_2 \\ UR_3 & D_3 & J_3 & PL_3 & TB_3 & AB_3 \\ UR_4 & D_4 & J_4 & PL_4 & TB_4 & AB_4 \end{bmatrix} \begin{matrix} L_1 \\ L_2 \\ L_3 \\ L_4 \end{matrix} \tag{2}$$

The values of these attributes are obtained from the SNMP traps and the Service Level Agreements (SLAs) of the corresponding links over the platform. As the parameters involved in the Decision Matrix come from different sources, the units representing the values are different. We need to normalize these parameters in order to make them unit-less. The attributes having bigger values (e.g., TB is in Mega) are divided by the largest value in the corresponding column vector while the smaller range attribute (e.g., D, which is in milliseconds) is divided by the smallest value in the corresponding column vector. The normalized Decision Matrix is given by

$$
\widetilde{DM} = \begin{bmatrix} \widetilde{UR_1} & \widetilde{D}_1 & \widetilde{J}_1 & \widetilde{PL}_1 & T\widetilde{B}_1 & A\widetilde{B}_1 \\ \widetilde{UR_2} & \widetilde{D}_2 & \widetilde{J}_2 & \widetilde{PL}_2 & T\widetilde{B}_2 & A\widetilde{B}_2 \\ \widetilde{UR_3} & \widetilde{D}_3 & \widetilde{J}_2 & \widetilde{PL}_3 & T\widetilde{B}_3 & A\widetilde{B}_3 \\ \widetilde{UR_4} & \widetilde{D}_4 & \widetilde{J}_4 & \widetilde{PL}_4 & T\widetilde{B}_4 & A\widetilde{B}_4 \end{bmatrix} \begin{matrix} L_1 \\ L_2 \\ L_3 \\ L_4 \end{matrix} \tag{3}
$$

The normalized reference vector is given by

$$
Ref\left(\widetilde{L}\right) = \begin{bmatrix} \widetilde{UR} & \widetilde{D} & \widetilde{J} & \widetilde{PL} & T\widetilde{B} & A\widetilde{B} \end{bmatrix} \tag{4}
$$

Now the distance between the corresponding normalized reference vector entities and the normalized Decision Matrix entities is calculated as follows:

$$
\Delta_{UR_i} = \left| \widetilde{UR} - \widetilde{UR_i} \right|, i = 1, 2, 3, 4 \tag{5}
$$

The Δ Decision Matrix is obtained by applying Eq. 5 to the corresponding entities in the normalized Decision Matrix and the normalized reference vector:

$$
\Delta_{DM} = \begin{bmatrix} \Delta_{UR_1} & \Delta_{D_1} & \Delta_{J_1} & \Delta_{PL_1} & \Delta_{TB_1} & \Delta_{AB_1} \\ \Delta_{UR_2} & \Delta_{D_2} & \Delta_{J_2} & \Delta_{PL_2} & \Delta_{TB_2} & \Delta_{AB_2} \\ \Delta_{UR_3} & \Delta_{D_3} & \Delta_{J_3} & \Delta_{PL_3} & \Delta_{TB_3} & \Delta_{AB_3} \\ \Delta_{UR_4} & \Delta_{D_4} & \Delta_{J_4} & \Delta_{PL_4} & \Delta_{TB_4} & \Delta_{AB_4} \end{bmatrix} \begin{matrix} L_1 \\ L_2 \\ L_3 \\ L_4 \end{matrix} \tag{6}
$$

Grey Relation Coefficients (GRCs) representing the measurement of similarity of an attribute to its reference are calculated (e.g. for voice/video Utilization Ratio of a link UR) as follows:

$$
GRC_{UR_i} = \frac{\Delta_{\min} + \alpha\Delta_{\max}}{\Delta_{UR_i} + \alpha\Delta_{\max}}, i = 1, 2, 3, 4 \tag{7}
$$

where $\alpha \in [0, 1]$ and $\Delta_{\min}$ and $\Delta_{\max}$ are calculated as follows:

$$
\Delta_{\max} = \max_i \left(\Delta_{UR_i} + \Delta_{D_i} + \Delta_{J_i} + \Delta_{PL_i} + \Delta_{TB_i} + \Delta_{AB_i} \right) \tag{8}
$$

$$
\Delta_{\min} = \min_i \left(\Delta_{UR_i} + \Delta_{D_i} + \Delta_{J_i} + \Delta_{PL_i} + \Delta_{TB_i} + \Delta_{AB_i} \right) \tag{9}
$$

As we are emphasizing on voice communication (outbound calls) and to meet the QoS requirements of voice, (Delay and Jitter are given more weight), we choose the weights corresponding to each attribute in the Decision Matrix. The available bandwidth is coupled with user profile loaded from the profile base (in case of gold profile, it is highly desirable to choose the link with good available bandwidth so AB and U will also be given suitable weight values). These assigned weights illustrate the relative importance of each attribute in Decision Matrix such that:

$$
W = W_{UR} + W_D + W_J + W_{PL} + W_{TB} + W_{AB} = 1 \tag{10}
$$

The weighted GRC coefficient representing an attribute column is given by:

$$GRC_{wUR_i} = W_{UR} * GRC_{UR_i}, i = 1, 2, 3, 4 \tag{11}$$

The resulting weighted GRC matrix is given by:

$$GRC_{wDM} = \begin{bmatrix} GRC_{wUR_1} & GRC_{wD_1} & GRC_{wJ_1} & GRC_{wPL_1} & GRC_{wTB_1} & GRC_{wAB_1} \\ GRC_{wUR_2} & GRC_{wD_2} & GRC_{wJ_2} & GRC_{wPL_2} & GRC_{wTB_2} & GRC_{wAB_2} \\ GRC_{wUR_3} & GRC_{wD_3} & GRC_{wJ_3} & GRC_{wPL_3} & GRC_{wTB_3} & GRC_{wAB_3} \\ GRC_{wUR_4} & GRC_{wD_4} & GRC_{wJ_4} & GRC_{wPL_4} & GRC_{wTB_4} & GRC_{wAB_4} \end{bmatrix} \begin{matrix} L_1 \\ L_2 \\ L_3 \\ L_4 \end{matrix} \tag{12}$$

The GRC value for individual link is calculated as follows:

$$Coef(GRC)_i = GRC_{wUR_i} + GRC_{wD_i} + GRC_{wJ_i} + GRC_{wPL_i} + GRC_{wTB_i}$$
$$+GRC_{wABi}, i = 1, 2, 3, 4. \tag{13}$$

The Candidate Link with the highest GRC coefficient value is the final decision, i.e., the best link for the request. There are two possibilities for calculat-
ing/declaring the reference attribute vector: the first is to compute the reference
attribute vector before the request arrives and the second is to calculate it on
the fly (discussed above in the GRA method). The susceptible QoS set of parameters are well defined and known for voice and video. The range of required
bandwidth for different codecs (used by the end points during the multimedia
communication) is also well documented. The attribute, available bandwidth is
calculated by keeping the track of number of ongoing calls/requests on a particular link (i.e., Available Bandwidth=Total Bandwidth - Used Bandwidth). It
is important to mention that the presented GRA includes the simplest possible
case. Embedding the reference vector beforehand can be tedious and complex
as the number of links and attributes increases. The business objectives of an
enterprise might change (e.g., voice might be given priority over video, the silver profile might use gold profile service during night (free hours), etc.), the
user profile priorities/authentication/authorization parameter (QoS profile corresponding to a user profile) may go through modification, or the link resources
might go through up-gradation/downgrading. Although this complexity can be
handled but it requires extensive administrative efforts. The objective however,
is to minimize these efforts at minimal while taking into account the dynamicity
that the manual system is not able to accommodate.

3.3 Technique for Order Preference by Similarity to Ideal Solution (TOPSIS) MCDM Method

TOPSIS was developed by Yoon and Hwang [12]. It is an alternative to ELEC-
TRE [13] and is considered to be one of its variants. It is known as a double
standard method that evaluates alternatives through two basic criteria. First,
the chosen alternative should have the shortest distance from the positive ideal
solution and secondly it must be farthest from the negative-ideal solution for a
MCDM problem. The perceived positive and negative ideal solutions are based

on the range of attribute values available for the alternatives. The distances are measured in Euclidean terms. The Euclidean distance approach is proposed to evaluate the relative closeness of the alternatives to the ideal solution. The reason for choosing TOPSIS in provisioning enforcement mode (i.e., pre-computed decisions are available at PEP in this mode, which is described in detail in [2]) is that it will rank/grade the available alternatives (links) whenever applied. Moreover, TOPSIS is extended to be applied on interval data (i.e. lower and upper values of an attribute) for the provisioning enforcement mode over the proposed architecture. In provisioning mode, the decision engine is not very much interactive with the platform's variations especially at the arrival of a new request so it provides half hearted dynamicity. Hence if the exact value of an attribute is not known, then these bounds (upper and lower) are used for the application of an extended TOPSIS. The best link among the available alternative links (ranked by the application of an extended TOPSIS) is assigned to request by following the predefined set of criteria. Due to space limitations and to avoid the complexity, only the Decision Matrix (equation 14) is expressed with lower and upper bounds while considering the same set of 6 attributes and 4 links as follows:

$$DM = \begin{bmatrix} (UR_1^L, UR_1^U) & (D_1^L, D_1^U) & (J_1^L, J_1^U) & (PL_1^L, PL_1^U) & (TB_1^L, TB_1^U) & (AB_1^L, AB_1^U) \\ (UR_2^L, UR_2^U) & (D_2^L, D_2^U) & (J_2^L, J_2^U) & (PL_2^L, PL_2^U) & (TB_2^L, TB_2^U) & (AB_2^L, AB_2^U) \\ (UR_3^L, UR_3^U) & (D_3^L, D_3^U) & (J_3^L, J_3^U) & (PL_3^L, PL_3^U) & (TB_3^L, TB_3^U) & (AB_3^L, AB_3^U) \\ (UR_4^L, UR_4^U) & (D_4^L, D_4^U) & (J_4^L, J_4^U) & (PL_4^L, PL_4^U) & (TB_4^L, TB_4^U) & (AB_4^L, AB_4^U) \end{bmatrix} \begin{matrix} L_1 \\ L_2 \\ L_3 \\ L_4 \end{matrix}$$

(14)

3.4   TOPSIS MCDM Method Application Steps

TOPSIS method is explained and applied here by using the standard approach to avoid rigorous mathematics in the following steps.

1. Normalize the Decision Matrix containing the link attributes: the process is to transform different scales and units among various criteria into common measurable units in order to allow comparisons across the criteria. The normalization procedure is the same as described in section 3.2.
2. Construct the weighted normalized Decision Matrix: it cannot be assumed that each evaluation criterion is of equal importance because the evaluation criteria have various meanings. The decision engine in provisioning mode calculates the weight of the corresponding column vector representing an attribute by using the environmental conditions and administrative rules/conditions at the time of TOPSIS execution. The context of the request is not taken into account, as opposed to GRA.
3. Determine positive and negative ideal solutions for each attribute: the positive ideal solution indicates the most preferable alternative, and the negative ideal solution indicates the least preferable alternative as follows (e.g. for voice/video link Utilization ratio, U)

$$UR^+ = (Max\,(UR_{w-norm})_i)\,\|\,(Min\,(UR_{w-norm})_i)\,, i = 1, 2, 3, 4 \qquad (15)$$

and

$$UR^- = (Min\,(UR_{w-norm})_i)\,\|\,(Max\,(UR_{w-norm})_i)\,, i = 1, 2, 3, 4 \qquad (16)$$

4. The Euclidean distance method is applied to measure the separation from the positive and negative ideal for each alternative

$$S_i^+ = \sqrt{\begin{array}{l} ((UR_{w-norm})_i - UR^+)^2 + ((D_{w-norm})_i - D^+)^2 + ((J_{w-norm})_i - J^+)^2 + \\ ((PL_{w-norm})_i - PL^+)^2 ((TB_{w-norm})_i - TB^+)^2 + ((AB_{w-norm})_i - AB^+)^2 \end{array}}$$

(17)

and

$$S_i^- = \sqrt{\begin{array}{l} ((UR_{w-norm})_i - UR^-)^2 + ((D_{w-norm})_i - D^-)^2 + ((J_{w-norm})_i - J^-)^2 + \\ ((PL_{w-norm})_i - PL^-)^2 + ((TB_{w-norm})_i - TB^-)^2 + ((AB_{w-norm})_i - AB^-)^2 \end{array}}$$

(18)

5. Finally, the candidate links are ranked by measuring the relative closeness of an alternative (candidate links L_1, L_2, L_3 and L_4 under consideration represented by a row vector in the Decision Matrix) to the ideal solution S^+ as follows:

$$R_i = \frac{S_i^+}{S_i^+ + S_i^-}$$

(19)

Table 1. Links With Corresponding Parametric Values

	UR	D	J	PL	TB	AB
	%	Milliseconds(ms)	ms	%	Megabits per second(Mbps)	Mbps
L_1	66.65	300	50	100	100	65
L_2	53.84	200	25	25	100	71
L_3	81.81	100	15	10	100	81
L_4	25.00	150	30	30	100	46

The links L_1, L_2, L_3 and L_4 characterized by attributes voice/video Utilization ratio UR, Delay (D), Jitter (J) Packet Loss (PL), Total Bandwidth (TB) and Available Bandwidth (AB) respectively are represented by the values shown in Table 1. D, J and L are given higher weights (step 2) due to voice call (outgoing) while keeping in view the required bandwidth judged from the codec negotiated during the call setup. For the application of TOPSIS on the links represented by the corresponding row vectors in Table 1, all 5 steps are gone through in the order stated above in this section. The links are ranked with R values as mentioned in Table 2.

Table 2. R Values and the Corresponding Grading of Links

	L_1	L_2	L_3	L_4
R Value	0.0788	0.6852	0.7805	0.7186
Rank	4	3	1	2

4 Test Bed and Experimental Setup

OpenSIPS [14], an open source SIP server is tweaked to act as SBC and Load Balancer (LB). It is built around the core that is responsible for the basic

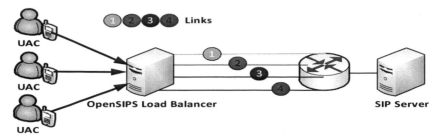

Fig. 3. Test Bed With 4 Links

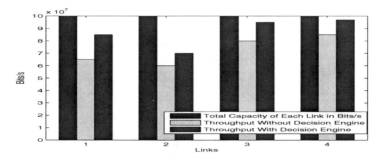

Fig. 4. Throughput of Each Link With and Without Decision Engine

processing and handling of SIP messages. The modules developed around its core are responsible for the majority of OpenSIPS functionalities. Its scalable and modular design provides a number of functionalities (registrar, router/proxy (LCR, dynamic routing, dialplan features), redirect server, B2BUA etc). It enforces the calculated decision and forwards the outgoing SIP request to different links for the experimental setup as shown in Fig. 3. SIPp [15] is used to generate extensive SIP requests (INVITE). It is a configurable traffic generator and is extensible via a simple XML configuration language. Call model with User Agent Client (UAC) sends an INVITE to OpenSIPS, and it is analyzed to judge its communication type. It is important to mention here that a random number is generated to send the codec information along with the SIP message. The bandwidth requirement of the call is judged from the codec information and the request is forwarded to an appropriate link (already ranked by using TOPSIS) by following the predefined criteria. Network Address Translation (NAT) is enabled on OpenSIPS and the decision is enforced during NAT implementation in provisioning mode. Details about the design and development of the parser for embedding the calculated decisions during NATing are avoided due to space limitations. The SIP server responds with 100 TRYING, 180 RINGING and 200 OK. UAC then sends an ACK and the call is established. The UAC closes the communication after variable pause by sending a BYE which is acknowledged by the SIP server with 200 OK. Wireshark is used to capture the traffic at different interfaces (links).

OriginLab [16] is used for data analysis from the captured file. Throughput of each link is plotted with and without decision engine (i.e. using built-in LB

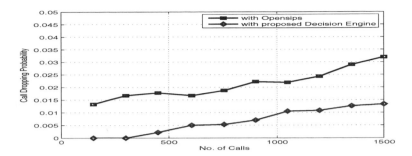

Fig. 5. Call Dropping Probability With and Without Decision Engine

in OpenSIPS) as shown in Fig. 4. It is observed that there is a significant improvement in the throughput for each link with decision engine while performing SIP call routing. The retransmission mechanism within SIPp is turned off when INVITE messages are sent in order to know that a call has been dropped. The aggregated call dropping probability (for the 4 links shown in Fig. 3) with the proposed decision engine has lower value than the ordinary Opensips's LB as shown in Fig. 5. The performance may improve by decision computation in outsourcing mode (on the fly) alongside attribute space enlargement as the present tests are performed in simplest possible scenario.

5   Related Work

There are commercial and proprietary solutions available for SIP-based call routing at application layer. Publicly available information does not reveal the decision making mechanism and the LB algorithms. The core design and lower-level functionality are hidden because of commercial implications. However some vendors provide Software Development Kit (SDK) for customization of the specific solution with limited interaction and access to the core [17,18]. Some products offer partial dynamicity with limited controls, while others are enforcing static decisions/rules. F5 networks [19] uses NAT for Load Balancing the SIP traffic to multiple links with static configurations. The proposed solution in this work accommodates the dynamic behavior of the platform and the context of the request with the provision of off-line (provisioning mode) and on the fly (outsourcing mode) decision making using MCDM theory. This theory is used for access network technology (UMTS, GSM, WLAN, etc.) selection during the handoff based on user preferences [20]. A user priority scheme for admission control using Analytic Hierarchy Process (AHP) is proposed in [21]. The proposed solution here uses GRA and an extended TOPSIS for online (on the fly) and off-line decision making respectively.

6   Conclusions and Future Work

Context of the request, state of the links and variations over the platform constitutes a multidisciplinary problem. This multi-criteria issue outlines more complexity when a single decision is required for routing a SIP request in a multihomed network. Traditional algorithms used for link selection in multihomed setups are either user-centric or service-oriented. Nevertheless, these solutions either focus on performance optimization or they are technology specific. To cope with all these multi-disciplinary objectives, Multi Criteria Decision Making (MCDM) theory is chosen. A dynamic decision engine for SIP-based call routing has been presented. It is capable of handling dynamicity and fluctuations over the platform by taking into account a large number of attributes with corresponding weights. Two MCDM methods, namely GRA and TOPSIS are used in outsourcing (on the fly) and provisioning (off-line) enforcement modes respectively. A test bed is developed to validate the proposed solution. Few calls are dropped with the proposed decision engine giving lower aggregated call dropping probability than the ordinary Load Balancer. The throughput of the individual multihomed links is improved significantly. Decision and enforcement modules can be integrated in a single box but the solutions are developed by partners/teams independently so it might be an emerging step. Future work includes development of an automated linguistics to specify goals, criteria and alternatives along with their translation. This landmark will connect MCDM to conventional Policy Based Network Management (PBNM), but with dynamicity. Introduction of parallelism while handling the user and network-based information constitutes another dimension of our future work.

References

1. http://www.images-et-reseaux.com/en (last Visited (LV), 12/01/2011)
2. Mushtaq, S.A., Salem, O., Lohr, C., Gravey, A.: Policy-based QoS Management for Multimedia Communication 14th EUNICE Open European Conference (2008)
3. Mushtaq, S.A., Salem, O., Lohr, C., Gravey, A.: Distributed Call Admission Control in SIP Based Multimedia Communication, NEM Summit (2008)
4. Rosenberg, J., et al.: Session Initiation Protocol, RFC 3261 (June 2002)
5. Brenner, M.: Diameter Policy Processing Application, RFC 5224 (March 2008)
6. Durham, D., et al.: The COPS (Common Open Policy Service) Protocol, RFC 2748
7. Boros, S.: Policy-based network management with SNMP (October 2000)
8. Önüt, S., Kara, S.S., Isik, E.: Long term supplier selection using a combined fuzzy MCDM approach: A case study for a telecommunication company (2008)
9. Bonissone, P.P., Subbu, R., Lizzi, J.: MCDM: A framework for research and applications. IEEE Computational Intelligence Magazine (August 2009)
10. Kornyshova, E., Salinesi, C.: MCDM Techniques Selection Approaches; State of the Art. In: IEEE Symposium on Computational Intelligence in MCDM (2007)
11. Deng, J.L.: Introduction to Grey System. J. Gerry Syst. 1(1), 1–24 (1989)
12. Hwang, C.L., Yoon, K.: Multiple Attribute Decision Making Mehtods and Applications. Springer, New York (1981)
13. Benayoun, R., Roy, B., Sussmann, N.: Manual de reference du programme electre, Note de Sythese et Formation Direction Scietifique SEMA (25) (1966)
14. Goncalves, F.E.: Building Telephony Systems with OpenSIPS 1.6 (2010)
15. SIPp: Test Tool Traffic Generator for the SIP Protocol, http://sipp.sourceforge.net

16. OriginLab, `http://www.originlab.com` (December 26, 2010, LV)
17. `http://www.metaswitch.com/sbc-session-border-controller`
    (05/01/2011, LV)
18. `http://www.acmepacket.com` (05/01/2011, LV)
19. `http://f5.com/products/big-ip/local-traffic-manager.html`
    (05/01/2011, LV)
20. Seghal, A., Agrawal, R.: QoS Based Netwrok Selection Scheme for 4G Systems.
    IEEE Transactions on Consumer Electronics (2010)
21. Pervaiz, H.: A Multi-Criteria Decision Making (MCDM) Network Selection Model
    providing enhanced QoS differentiation to customers. In: MCIT 2010 (2010)

Evaluation of the Resource Requirements of SNMP Agents on Constrained Devices

Siarhei Kuryla and Jürgen Schönwälder

Computer Science, Jacobs University Bremen, Germany
{s.kuryla,j.schoenwaelder}@jacobs-university.de

Abstract. Constrained devices equipped with a microcontroller and a low-power low-bitrate wireless interface are becoming part of the Internet. We investigate whether the monitoring and configuration of such constrained devices can be performed by adapting the Simple Network Management Protocol (SNMP) to the capabilities of these devices. To this end, we have implemented an SNMP agent under the Contiki operating system. We provide an analysis of its resource requirements and its runtime behaviour on an 8-bit AVR Raven platform.

Keywords: SNMP, 6LoWPAN, Contiki, Internet of Things.

1 Introduction

The Simple Network Management Protocol (SNMP) [1] is widely deployed to monitor, control, and sometimes also configure network elements. Even though the SNMP technology is well documented and well understood, it remains unclear what the exact resource requirements are of running SNMP on constrained devices, such as an 8-bit microcontroller with 16 kB of RAM connected to the Internet via an IEEE 802.15.4 transceiver. The origins of SNMP date back to the late 1980s when computers had much less resources compared to what we are used to today. In fact, one of the stated goals was that "the impact of adding network management to managed nodes must be minimal, reflecting a lowest common denominator" [2]. From this historic perspective, SNMP seems to be a reasonable fit for managing today's constrained devices. However, it must be noted that SNMP did evolve during the 1990s and in particular security mechanisms present in SNMP version 3 (SNMPv3) add significant complexity, increasing the code size and impacting runtime performance. Hence, we were approached with question such as the following:

- What are the resource requirements of a minimal SNMPv3 implementation running on constrained devices?
- Which parts of an SNMP protocol engine are most expensive?
- What is the cost of adding instrumentation (additional MIB objects)?
- What is the runtime behaviour of SNMP over an IPv6 link using an IEEE 802.15.4 radio and the 6LoWPAN adaptation layer?

I. Chrisment et al. (Eds.): AIMS 2011, LNCS 6734, pp. 100–111, 2011.

The answers to these questions are crucial in order to understand whether it is feasible to run multiple protocols concurrently on constrained devices providing end-to-end interoperability with deployed systems or whether it is necessary to adopt architectures, where interoperability with deployed systems is achieved via gateways translating between standard Internet protocols and a single protocol (e.g., CoAP [3]) interfacing constrained devices.

The rest of the paper is structured as follows. We first discuss some architectural options for using SNMP in constrained networks in Section 2 before we review related work in Section 3. The design choices behind our SNMP implementation running on the Contiki [4] operating system are summarized in Section 4. In Section 5, we describe our experimental setup in. We present an analysis of the memory requirements in Section 6, which is followed by a discussion of the observed latency in Section 7. We conclude the paper in Section 8.

2   Architectural Considerations

Low-Power Wireless Personal Area Networks (LoWPANs) typically consist of a (potentially large) number of constrained devices embedded into everyday objects. Unlike conventional networks, nodes in such networks should need minimal configuration, they should preferably work "out of the box", they should be easy to bootstrap, and they should be largely self-healing [5]. However, even the best automated mechanisms may fail and require explicit management once in a while. As such, a certain amount of explicit management can never be completely removed. Since the goal of IPv6 over LoWPANs (6LoWPAN) is to reuse existing protocols as much as possible, it makes sense to look at the question how SNMP can be used to manage 6LoWPAN networks consisting of constrained devices. Figure 1 outlines four architectural options for the common scenario where a network management system residing in the normal Internet manages constrained devices connected via a 6LoWPAN network.

Figure 1(a) assumes direct end-to-end SNMP communication. This option provides straight forward access to individual 6LoWPAN nodes. Reuse of existing deployed SNMP-based tools is easy and end-to-end security can be provided. The downsides of this option are related to message sizes and fragmentation issues, the requirement to embed a full SNMP engine into constrained devices, and the trap-directed polling nature of SNMP if energy consumption is a concern.

By utilizing an SNMP proxy (see Figure 1(b)), it is possible to optimize the transport of SNMP messages on the 6LoWPAN network, e.g., by using an alternate encoding or by using different security mechanisms. Since SNMP proxies are well defined in the SNMP specifications, management applications supporting SNMP proxies should need no modifications. Note that this approach still requires an SNMP agent on the constrained devices and that it does not overcome the trap-directed polling nature of SNMP.

Figure 1(c) outlines the usage of SNMP subagent technology where a single SNMP agent, typically running on an edge router, provides access to management information, utilizing a special purpose subagent protocol to interact with

(a) End-to-end SMP communication with agents on constrained devices

(b) Communication via an SNMP proxy with agents on constrained devices

(c) Communication via an SNMP agent with subagents on constrained devices

(d) Communication via an SNMP agent utilizing a new data fusion protocol

Fig. 1. Architectural options for using SNMP in 6LoWPAN networks

subagents residing on constrained devices. By tailoring the subagent protocol to the constraints of the link and the devices, it is possible to improve efficiency in the 6LoWPAN network and some amount of caching of data in the SNMP agent becomes feasible. However, this approach is not transparent to the management system since management applications need to address management information by using specific SNMP contexts. The fact that SNMP security ends at the SNMP agent residing at the edge router may be considered a feature or a problem, depending on the deployment scenario. The subagent option only has a clear advantage if the implementation costs of subagents is significantly lower than the costs for implementing an SNMP agent.

Finally, Figure 1(d) develops the subagent approach further by introducing a new protocol enabling data fusion in the 6LoWPAN network, e.g., in-network data aggregation. This approach requires not only new protocols, but also new management applications that are able to properly address management information and that understand the semantics of aggregated management data. On the other hand, communication in the 6LoWPAN network can be optimized and in particular tree-like routing structures can be exploited by aggregating data as it travels towards the edge router.

3   Related Work

During the past decade, a large number of papers discussing various performance aspects of SNMP have been published [6]. The majority of these papers assume high bandwidth network links and PC-like end devices. In this section, we focus solely on recent work dealing with 6LoWPAN networks and constrained devices.

In 2008, Hamid Mukhtar et al. [7] proposed a LoWPAN Network Management Protocol (LNMP). Their approach aims at a reduction of communication cost in order to increase the network lifetime and to avoid congestion. In the proposed

architecture, SNMP is supported on the native IPv6 network side only and a
6LoWPAN gateway acts as a subagent proxy, translating between the SNMP
protocol and the protocol used on the 6LoWPAN network. Their work therefore
follows the subagent model shown in Figure 1(c). Whenever an SNMP request
arrives at the gateway, it is translated from SNMP to a simplified query format.
The gateway sends a query (via UDP) that contains identifiers of the objects to
be retrieved from the agent residing on the destination device. Similarly, when a
reply from the device arrives at the gateway, it is translated back into the SNMP
protocol format and an SNMP response packet is sent back to the SNMP engine
that requested the object. The gateway is also responsible for responding to requests for objects whose values are constant for the whole network. The proposed
LNMP protocol was implemented for the Atmel ATmega 128L microcontroller.
Unfortunately, the query protocol between the gateway is not further detailed
and no details are given concerning the code size or the memory requirements.
Furthermore, the proposal appears to be incomplete since protocol security has
not been considered nor has the addressing through SNMP contexts and the
OID mapping been fully worked out.

Haksoo Choi et al. describe two modifications of SNMP in order to optimize
SNMP for resource-constrained low-power and low data-rate wireless networks
[8]. The first change is the introduction of compressed SNMPv1 and SNMPv2c
message headers and the usage of SNMP delta compression [9]. The second modification is the introduction of new protocol operations to push management information periodically from an SNMP agent towards an SNMP manager and the
usage of UDP multicasts. In order to interface existing SNMP applications with
their extended version of SNMP, they introduce an SNMP proxy that performs
the necessary translations. From an architectural viewpoint, this work follows
the proxy model shown in Figure 1(b). The work by Haksoo Choi et al. has two
major limitations: (i) The work is limited to SNMPv1 and SNMPv2c and does
not consider protocol security. In fact, the elimination of community strings on
the 6LoWPAN network causes SNMP agents to respond to any request. (ii) The
push mechanism only works for non-dynamic MIB objects since it relies on Get-
operations. Periodic retrieval of data in dynamically changing tables is thus not
optimized. Multicasting has the same limitations and becomes rather complex if
protocol security mechanisms would be considered. The modified SNMP protocol was implemented using the TinyOS operating system [10] on the Tmote Sky
platform featuring the 16-bit TI MSP430 microcontroller with 10 kB of RAM
and 48 kB of flash memory.

4   Implementation

Our Contiki SNMP implementation supports the SNMPv1 and SNMPv2 message processing models and the Get, GetNext and Set protocol operations. The
USM security model has been implemented. It supports the HMAC-MD5-96 authentication and CFB128-AES-128 symmetric encryption protocols. The standard specifies that SNMP entities must accept messages up to at least 484 bytes
in size, which is the maximum message size supported by our implementation.

One of the goals of our implementation is memory efficiency. However, whenever a choice had to be made between easily readable and maintainable source code and memory efficient but hard to understand programming constructs, we gave preference to the readable code. Due to the small amount of available RAM memory, necessary data structures were optimized and designed very carefully. Since the amount of ROM memory provided by the hardware platform is significantly larger than the amount of RAM, ROM memory has been preferred for storing read-only data.

```
typedef struct {                        typedef struct varbind_list_item_t {
    u8t      version;                       varbind_t                     varbind;
    pdu_t pdu;                              struct varbind_list_item_t*   next_ptr;
} message_t;                            } varbind_list_item_t;

typedef struct {                        typedef struct varbind_t {
    u8t              request_type;          ptr_t*             oid_ptr;
    u8t              response_type;         u8t                value_type;
    s32t             request_id;            varbind_value_t    value;
    u8t              error_status;      } varbind_t;
    u8t              error_index;
    varbind_list_item_t *varbind_first_ptr;  typedef union {
    u16t             varbind_index;         s32t        i_value;
} pdu_t;                                    u32t        u_value;
                                            ptr_t       p_value;
                                        } varbind_value_t;
```

Fig. 2. Key data structures representing SNMP messages

Some key data structures are shown in Figure 2. In the implementation, OID values are never decoded but instead natively stored in ASN.1/BER format. This not only enables a memory efficient representation of OID values, it also allows to refer to the OID of a varbind by pointing inside the received packet, thus reducing the need for runtime memory allocations.

MIB objects are internally represented by instances of the mib_object_t structure shown in Figure 3. The attrs member specifies the attributes of the object. The varbind member holds the OID of the object and its value. The get_fnc_ptr and set_fnc_ptr members are pointers to the user-defined getter and setter functions respectively. In case of enabled tabular objects, two additional bytes are required for the get_next_oid_fnc_ptr pointer for every managed object. Tabular objects are an optional feature and they can be disabled by changing the value of the ENABLE_MIB_TABLE macro definition.

The OID of a managed object is an array of bytes which does not change its value over time. By default, such arrays are handled as all other initialized variables: they occupy RAM and they occupy the same amount of flash ROM so they can be initialized to the actual value by startup code. This is a waste of RAM, which is the most critical resource of today's constrained devices. Of course, such data can be moved to flash ROM. However, to access the data stored in the flash ROM special functions have to be used, which results in additional complexity. The implementation allows to store OIDs either in RAM or flash ROM. This can be defined at compile time, by switching the value of the ENABLE_PROGMEM macro definition between 0 and 1.

```
struct mib_object_t {
  u8t attrs;
  varbind_t varbind;
  get_value_t get_fnc_ptr;
#if ENABLE_MIB_TABLE
  get_next_oid_t get_next_oid_fnc_ptr;
#endif
  set_value_t set_fnc_ptr;
#ifndef MIB_SIZE
  struct mib_object_t* next_ptr;
#endif
};
```

Fig. 3. MIB data structures representing MIB objects

Our SNMP implementation supports two ways to organize the storage of managed objects by using either an array or a linked list. In the first case, the number of objects has to be predefined at compile time by using the MIB_SIZE macro definition, otherwise a linked list is used. In the latter case, every managed object requires two extra bytes for the next_ptr member.

Several objects of the SNMPv2-MIB [11], IF-MIB [12] and ENTITY-SENSOR-MIB [13] have been implemented. The SNMPv2-MIB defines managed objects describing the identity and the capabilities of an SNMP entity. The IF-MIB provides access to information related to network interfaces. It exposes counters of packets received on and transmitted out an interface. In order to obtain such statistical data, the Contiki radio driver has been instrumented. The managed objects of the ENTITY-SENSOR-MIB provide access to physical sensors. The readings of the temperature sensor can be obtained via the objects of this module.

5   Hardware Platform and Experimental Setup

The AVR Raven board includes two microcontrollers (MCUs), a radio transceiver chip and an LCD display. The ATmega1284PV MCU runs the communication while the LCD display is driven by the ATmega3290PV. The wireless communication is enabled by the AT86RF230 transceiver. Both the ATmega1284PV and the ATmega3290PV are modified Harvard architecture 8-bit RISC single chip MCUs. The ATmega1284PV runs at 20 MHz and has 16 kB of SRAM, 128 kB of flash program memory and 4 kB of EEPROM. It embeds two 16-bit timers, two 8-bit timers and one real time counter. The ATmega3290PV runs at 16 MHz and has 2 kB of SRAM, 32 kB of flash memory and 1 kB of EEPROM. The AT86RF230 is a 2.4 GHz radio transceiver targeted for IEEE 802.15.4 and 6LoWPAN applications. It supports automatic frame acknowledgement and retransmission, automatic CSMA-CA and data transfer speeds of up to 250 kbps.

The network setup used consists of a PC equipped with an 802.15.4 interface connected via the USB bus. The AVR RZUSBstick, a USB stick with a 2.4 GHz IEEE 802.15.4 transceiver, is used to provide the PC with an 802.15.4 interface. The software running on the MCU on the USB stick is doing the 6LoWPAN adaptation and hence no software changes are needed on the PC.

The Contiki SNMP implementation has been tested for interoperability with the snmpget, snmpgetnext, snmpset and snmpwalk applications from the

Net-SNMP[1] suite. All measurements reported in this paper were made with Contiki 2.4 using the IPHC header compression mechanism.

6   Memory and Code Footprint

Due to the limited memory resources of constrained devices, the RAM and flash ROM used by the agent are important parameters that have to be evaluated. However, RAM usage is hard to measure because of the variable size of the stack and the heap used for dynamic memory allocation. In this section, we present memory usage estimations obtained by using three different approaches.

6.1   Flash ROM and Static Memory Usage

In the first step, the `avr-size` utility was employed to determine the flash ROM and static memory usage. We are interested in measuring the memory used only by the agent and not by the whole program that also includes the Contiki operating system. To achieve this, we first compile the source code of Contiki with the agent and measure the size of the output object file using the `avr-size` utility. Then, the same procedure is repeated for Contiki without the agent. The total memory used by the agent is obtained by a simple subtraction. The full implementation uses 31220 bytes of ROM, which is around 24% of the available ROM on the targeted platform, and 235 bytes of statically allocated RAM. In case SNMPv1 is only enabled, the agent uses 8860 bytes of ROM (about 7% of available ROM) and 43 bytes of statically allocated RAM. In a similar way, we measured the code and memory footprint of each module of the agent. Table 1 shows the detailed breakdown of the measurements.

As can be seen from the table, the cryptographic primitives occupy a significant amount of flash ROM. The AES and MD5 implementations constitute around 31% and 33% respectively of the agent code size. Almost half of the ROM occupied by the AES implementation is used to store constants. The MD5 implementation intensively uses macro definitions for transformations, which results in the large code size. Using functions instead of macros could reduce the code size, but would negatively impact the performance. It is worth to mention that the cryptographic primitives were ported from the OpenSSL library and that they are not optimized for the instruction set of the MCU.

The USM security model occupies almost half of the agent's statically allocated RAM. This RAM is mostly used to store localized keys and OIDs of the error indication counters.

6.2   Stack Usage

An experimental approach has been taken to estimate the stack size used by the agent while processing a request. Upon receipt of an incoming SNMP message,the memory region allocated to the program stack is filled with a specific

---

[1] http://www.net-snmp.org/

Table 1. Flash ROM and static RAM memory usage of the agent (bytes)

Module	Flash ROM	RAM (static)
snmpd.c	172	2
dispatch.c	1076	26
msg-proc-v1.c	634	6
msg-proc-v3.c	1184	30
cmd-responder.c	302	0
mib.c	1996	6
ber.c	4264	3
usm.c	1160	122
aes_cfb.c	9752	40
md5.c	10264	0
utils.c	416	0

Table 2. Maximum runtime stack size usage (bytes)

Version	Security level	Max. stack size
v1	–	688
v3	noAuthNoPriv	708
v3	authNoPriv	1140
v3	authPriv	1144

bit pattern. When the processing has been finished, the stack is examined to see how much of it is overwritten.

Table 2 presents the maximum stack size observed during experiments for different versions of SNMP and different selected security levels. Most of the stack is occupied by the response message buffer of 484 bytes. The SNMPv1 and SNMPv3 protocol versions with the **noAuthNoPriv** security level use approximately the same stack size, which constitutes around 4% of the available RAM. When authentication and privacy are enabled, the stack grows up to 1144 bytes, which is about 7% of RAM on the targeted platform.

6.3 Heap Usage

Memory for the data structures used to store the fields of an SNMP message (see Section 4) is allocated from the heap using the **malloc()** function. Table 3(a) provides a memory estimation for the **message_t** structure.

Each variable binding is stored in a linked list using an instance of the **varbind_list_item_t** structure. In addition to the memory calculation shown in Table 3(c), a variable binding uses 4 additional bytes for an instance of the **ptr_t** structure, which points to the OID stored in the message buffer.

The overall memory utilized to store an SNMPv1 message with N variable bindings is given by the formula $13 + N(9+4) = 13(N+1)$. The SNMP message size is limited in the implementation to 484 bytes. Each variable binding encoded in the BER format requires at least 7 bytes, therefore, in the worst (albeit

Table 3. Memory usage of key data structures

(a) Memory estimation for the message_t structure (13 bytes)

Member	Size (bytes)
version	1
pdu.request_type	1
pdu.response_type	1
pdu.request_id	4
pdu.error_status	1
pdu.error_index	1
pdu.varbind_first_ptr	2
pdu.varbind_index	2

(b) Memory estimation for the mib_object_t structure (16 bytes)

Member	Size (bytes)
attrs	1
get_fnc_ptr	2
set_fnc_ptr	2
get_next_oid_fnc_ptr	2
next_ptr	2
varbind.oid_ptr	2
varbind.value_type	1
varbind.value	4

(c) Memory estimation for a variable binding (9 bytes)

Member	Size (bytes)
next_ptr	2
varbind.oid_ptr	2
varbind.value_type	1
varbind.value	4

unrealistic) case an SNMPv1 message may carry $484/7 = 69$ variable bindings, which would require $13(69 + 1) = 910$ bytes of the heap to store such a message.

6.4   Managed Objects

As discussed in Section 4, each managed object is stored in memory as an instance of the mib_object_t structure. Table 3(b) presents a memory estimation for the members of this structure. A managed object uses additional $4 + L$ bytes for the OID, where L is the length in bytes of the OID encoded in the BER format. In case a managed object is of a string-based type, S extra bytes are required to store its value, where S is the length of the value. The total RAM usage for a managed object is given by the formula $16 + (4 + L) + S$. Using flash ROM to store OIDs allows to save $4 + L$ bytes of RAM for every managed object. In this case, the formula changes to $16 + S$, which would require 1600 bytes of RAM for 100 managed objects of an integer-based type.

7   Response Latency

A simple udp-echo application has been developed for Contiki, which allows to obtain a round-trip time estimation for a UDP datagram of a certain size. Table 4 provides some experimental results obtained using udp-echo. The results reveal that the transmission time of an 802.15.4 frame depends significantly on the amount of data being sent. For example, the difference between the round-trip time for datagrams with a payload of 1 byte and 90 bytes, both of which fit into one 802.15.4 frame, is around 8 ms. The delay is caused by the low speed

Table 4. Round-trip time (RTT) measured with `udp-echo`

Payload (bytes)	802.15.4 frames	RTT (ms)	Variance
1	1	30.75	2.07
90	1	38.87	6.58
91	2	49.90	6.54
175	2	58.93	6.63

Table 5. Experimental results obtained by measuring the response latency (presented in the latency and variance columns) for SNMP requests. The round-trip time (RTT) is estimated using `udp-echo`. The last column is the processing time taken by the agent. All time measurements are given in milliseconds

Version	Operation	Security level	Latency	Variance	RTT	Δ
v1	Get	–	37.05	5.69	34.70	2.35
v1	GetNext	–	36.98	6.58	34.70	2.28
v1	Set	–	37.14	4.39	34.70	2.44
v3	Get	noAuthNoPriv	56.64	4.05	52.62	4.02
v3	GetNext	noAuthNoPriv	56.58	2.72	52.62	3.96
v3	Set	noAuthNoPriv	56.78	3.00	52.62	4.16
v3	Get	authNoPriv	91.41	3.45	53.02	38.39
v3	GetNext	authNoPriv	91.95	3.75	53.02	38.93
v3	Set	authNoPriv	92.41	3.22	53.02	39.39
v3	Get	authPriv	105.70	5.38	55.03	50.67
v3	GetNext	authPriv	106.46	2.59	55.03	51.43
v3	Set	authPriv	106.73	3.59	55.03	51.70

of the radio transceiver. When sending a UDP packet with a 91 byte payload, 6LoWPAN fragmentation is used and, as expected, we observe an abrupt increase in the round-trip time compared to the 90 byte payload packet.

In order to estimate the SNMP request processing time taken by the agent, the request-response latency for individual messages was measured at the gateway by noting the delay between sending of the message and receiving of the response. In addition to the actual processing time, the measured delay also includes the time to transmit messages over the air between the gateway and the agent. If a message does not fit into a single 802.15.4 frame, the 6LoWPAN fragmentation takes place, which causes additional overhead as explained above. The SNMP request processing time can be found as the difference between the the SNMP request-response latency and the round-trip time estimated with `udp-echo` for datagrams with the same payload length.

Table 5 and Figure 4(a) present latency measurements for SNMPv1 and SN-MPv3 with three different security levels. All measurements were obtained for requests with one variable binding referring to the same MIB object. The first observation is that the time spent in the SNMP request processing is small relative to that spent in data transfer for SNMPv1 and SNMPv3 in the `noAuthNoPriv` security level. The SNMP processing constitutes only around 6-7% of the total latency. As expected, the usage of the authentication protocol results in a sig-

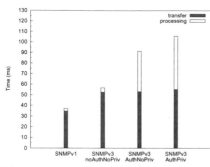

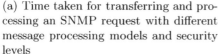

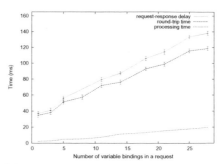

(a) Time taken for transferring and processing an SNMP request with different message processing models and security levels

(b) Time spent in transferring and processing SNMPv1 requests and responses as a function of the number of variable bindings in a request

Fig. 4.

nificant increase of this metric. The results also reveal that encryption does not have that much impact on the processing time as the authentication does. It is important to mention that the measurements for SNMPv3 do not include the discovery procedure, which would result in an additional message exchange.

Figure 4(b) shows changes in the processing time by varying the number of variable bindings in a request. These measurements were accomplished for the SNMPv1 protocol and the `Get` operation. The processing time varies from 2 to 19 ms, which is not significant when compared to the transfer time. Even though the object lookup time depends on its position in the MIB, for this targeted platform, it is unlikely that the MIB will contain that many objects to change the results considerably.

8 Conclusions

An implementation of the Simple Network Management Protocol for resource constrained devices under the Contiki embedded operating system has been presented. The implementation is modular and extensible by design. It supports the `Get`, `GetNext` and `Set` operations, the SNMPv1 and SNMPv3 message processing models and the User-based Security Model (with the HMAC-MD5-96 authentication and the CFB128-AES-128 symmetric encryption protocols). The implementation provides an interface to define and configure accessible managed objects. A couple of the existing MIB modules have been implemented as part of the agent.

The evaluation of the implementation has been carried out on the AVR Raven hardware platform. The experimental results reveal that the request processing time for SNMPv1 and SNMPv3 with the `noAuthNoPriv` security level is relatively small compared to the transfer time. Using the authentication protocol results in a significant increase of this metric, while the encryption protocol does not have that much impact on it. The RAM and flash ROM usage has been estimated by using three different approaches.

Possible further work would be to implement the GetBulk operation, notifications (Trap and Inform), and the SNMPv2c message processing model. It is also possible to use this platform to develop and prototype additional MIB objects for 6LoWPAN networks and related protocols.

References

1. Case, J., Mundy, R., Partain, D., Stewart, B.: Introduction and Applicability Statements for Internet Standard Management Framework. RFC 3410 (December 2002)
2. Rose, M.T.: The Simple Book – An Introduction to Management of TCP/IP based Internets. Prentice Hall, Englewood Cliffs (1991)
3. Shelby, Z., Hartke, K., Bormann, C., Frank, B.: Constrained Application Protocol (CoAP). Internet-Draft <draft-ietf-core-coap-05> (March 2011)
4. Dunkels, A., Gronvall, B., Voigt, T.: Contiki – A Lightweight and Flexible Operating System for Tiny Networked Sensors. In: Proc. 29th IEEE International Conference on Local Computer Networks (LCN 2004) (2004)
5. Kushalnagar, N., Montenegro, G., Schumacher, C.: IPv6 over Low-Power Wireless Personal Area Networks (6LoWPANs): Overview, Assumptions, Problem Statement, and Goals. RFC 4919 (August 2007)
6. Andrey, L., Festor, O., Lahmadi, A., Pras, A., Schönwälder, J.: Survey of SNMP Performance Analysis Studies. International Journal of Network Management 19(6), 527–548 (2009)
7. Mukhtar, H., Kang-Myo, K., Chaudhry, S.A., Akbar, A.H., Ki-Hyung, K., Yoo, S.W.: LNMP - Management architecture for IPv6 based low-power Wireless Personal Area Networks (6LoWPAN). In: Proc. 11th IEEE/IFIP Network Operations and Management Symposium (NOMS 2008), pp. 417–424. IEEE, Los Alamitos (April 2008)
8. Choi, H., Kim, N., Cha, H.: 6LoWPAN-SNMP: Simple Network Management Protocol for 6LoWPAN. In: Proc. 11th IEEE International Conference on High Performance Computing and Communications, pp. 305–313. IEEE, Los Alamitos (2009)
9. Schönwälder, J.: SNMP Payload Compression. Internet Draft <draft-irtf-nmrg-snmp-compression-01.txt> (April 2001)
10. Gay, D., Levis, P., von Behren, R., Welsh, M., Brewer, E., Culler, D.: The nesC Language: A Holistic Approach to Networked Embedded Systems. In: Proc. of the ACM Conference on Programming Language Design and Implementation (PLDI 2003). ACM, New York (June 2003)
11. Presuhn, R.: Version 2 of the Protocol Operations for the Simple Network Management Protocol (SNMP). RFC 3418 (December 2002)
12. McCloghrie, K., Kastenholz, F.: The Interfaces Group MIB. RFC 2863 (June 2000)
13. Bierman, A., Romascanu, D., Norseth, K.C.: Entity Sensor Management Information Base. RFC 3433 (December 2002)

Carrier Ethernet OAM:
An Overview and Comparison to IP OAM

Rick Hofstede, Idilio Drago, Giovane C.M. Moura, Aiko Pras

University of Twente, The Netherlands
r.j.hofstede@student.utwente.nl, {i.drago,g.c.m.moura,a.pras}@utwente.nl

Abstract. Ethernet has evolved from a local area to a wide area network technology. When it is used in a service provider environment, it has more complex requirements, which demand a set of management techniques for the Ethernet layer. Ethernet OAM comprises a set of management techniques for Carrier (or Metropolitan) Ethernet networks. Carrier Ethernet devices often have IP connectivity for management purposes, which might be used for IP OAM as an alternative management solution to Ethernet OAM. This paper provides an overview of Carrier Ethernet technology and evaluates whether, and until which extent, IP-based protocols can replace Ethernet OAM in Carrier Ethernet networks.

Keywords: Network Management, Carrier Ethernet, Metropolitan Ethernet, Provider Backbone Bridging, Ethernet OAM, IP OAM.

1   Introduction

Ethernet has been the number one link-layer technology in local area networks (LANs) for a long time [1]. To make Ethernet suitable to be used in larger networks, such as metropolitan and wide area networks (MANs and WANs respectively), it was extended to provide high availability, quality of service, secure communication, and superior scalability [1]. Carrier Ethernet[1] allows service providers to offer connectivity at the Ethernet level, in contrast to the IP level. Some backbone network operators are already considering a deployment of Ethernet in their Next-Generation Network [2].

With the deployment of Carrier Ethernet services it is required to manage Ethernet in an end-to-end manner, besides managing it on the link-layer. To achieve this, IEEE and ITU-T have standardized two Operations, Administration & Maintenance (OAM) protocol suites by means of IEEE 802.1ag [3] and ITU-T T.1731 [4], respectively. Ethernet OAM offers end-to-end fault and performance management over Ethernet Virtual Connections (EVCs), which are logical connections between various customer sites [5].

From a functional point of view, the Ethernet OAM standards seem to be very similar to IP OAM protocols, such as Ping and Traceroute. Assuming that most

---

[1] When Ethernet technology is used in large-scale (*e.g.* service provider) networks, it is commonly referred to as 'Carrier Ethernet' or 'Metropolitan Ethernet'.

I. Chrisment et al. (Eds.): AIMS 2011, LNCS 6734, pp. 112–123, 2011.

Carrier Ethernet devices support IP OAM, one could wonder whether OAM functionality is now duplicated at both the link and network layer. Moreover, if this is the case, could IP OAM functionality be used as a replacement for Ethernet OAM? Since IP OAM has been used already for a long time, operators have more experience with it than with Ethernet OAM. This lead us to the following research questions:

1. *What exactly is Carrier Ethernet and which functionality does it provide?*
2. *How does Ethernet OAM functionality compare to IP OAM, and, more specifically, can IP-based protocols in Carrier Ethernet networks provide the same functionality as comparable Ethernet OAM management techniques?*

Since many papers have already been published on the topic of Ethernet OAM, we will first review those that focus on using alternative solutions for Ethernet OAM in Section 2. Section 3 describes the evolution of Ethernet towards a WAN protocol, especially for deployment in service provider environments. The Ethernet OAM standards for managing Carrier Ethernet networks are discussed in Section 4. Although several works state that IP OAM is not (entirely) suited to manage a Carrier Ethernet [1] [5], a clear explanation or motivation is not provided. Section 5 will fill this gap by defining an Ethernet OAM deployment scenario, by means of which an IP-based approach will be analyzed. Finally, we close this paper in Section 6, where we draw our conclusions and future work.

2   Related Work

Many studies have already been performed on the usage of Ethernet OAM for WANs. McFarland *et al.* [1] state that enterprise networks typically have straightforward topologies and that IP-based protocols such as SNMP, ICMP, Ping and Traceroute will suffice for management. However, it will not be suitable for managing service provider networks, carrying thousands of services for different customers. Motivations for the unsuitability of IP are not given.

Indukuri goes beyond IP-based protocols for managing Ethernet networks [6], by outlining the use of IP Ping, MPLS LSP Ping, Bidirectional Forwarding Detection (BFD) and especially Ethernet OAM for Virtual Circuit Connectivity Verification (VCCV). It is desirable for metropolitan and especially critical networks to have a fast and accurate fault detection mechanism. Such a sub-50 ms detection and restoration facility is provided by BFD and Ethernet OAM. The author concludes, however, that the choice for a VCCV mechanism should not only depend on technical decisions, but also on the underlying transport infrastructure. In the case that a virtual circuit is constructed on top of an Ethernet network (*e.g.* an Ethernet Virtual Connection (EVC)) and end-to-end management should be performed, it is wise to use Ethernet OAM in order to avoid the need for translation layers between different network layers. However, this work does not outline why IP-based management techniques do not suffice for the management of Carrier Ethernet networks.

3 Carrier Ethernet Evolution

During its evolution from a LAN technology to a MAN and WAN technology, Ethernet was extended to support customer traffic separation, quality of service (QoS) and, most importantly, a greater number of MAC addresses (of customers, among others) in the forwarding tables of switches [7]. The frames of the various Ethernet standards are depicted in Figure 1. 'Ethertype' and 'Frame Check Sequence' fields are left out for the sake of space. The evolution of Ethernet has been standardized by the IEEE in several standards, starting with IEEE 802.1Q [8]. This standard adds a VLAN tag to an Ethernet frame, right after the source and destination MAC addresses, by means of which the forwarding plane can be partitioned into logical segments.

In the same year as IEEE 802.1Q was standardized, an amendment was defined in IEEE 802.1ad [9], also known as Provider Bridging (PB). We assume this standard and all following ones to be Carrier Ethernet standards. The IEEE 802.1Q VLAN tag contains VLAN IDs of 12 bits, supporting up to 4094 VLANs. Although this number of VLANs will be enough for most LANs, it will not suffice for large service provider environments. To overcome this scalability problem [7], IEEE 802.1ad defines VLAN tag stacking, allowing service providers to insert an additional VLAN tag of 12 bits in an already tagged frame. This 'S-VID' VLAN tag is only used inside the service provider domain and is inserted in front of the initial VLAN tag, which is now referred to 'Customer VID' (C-VID).

IEEE 802.1ah [10], also known as Provider Backbone Bridging (PBB), allows a strict separation between customer and service provider domains by encapsulating customer traffic. This is achieved by inserting a new Ethernet header in front of the existing one, including a new backbone VLAN tag (B-VID) and a new 'Service Instance ID' (I-SID) field. The latter can be considered an extended VLAN ID, used to identify customer instances inside the operator network. By considering the entire PB frame as payload and inserting a new Ethernet header in front of it, a completely isolated address space is used inside the Ethernet backbone network. The result is a drastically reduced complexity/size of the forwarding tables in backbone nodes, since only backbone node addresses and backbone VIDs are needed for switching.

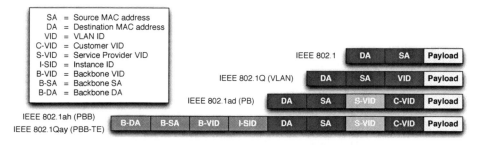

Fig. 1. Evolution of Ethernet frames

The most recent Carrier Ethernet standard is IEEE 802.1Qay [11]. It uses the same frames as IEEE 801.ah (PBB), but it adds traffic engineering capabilities and related rapid protection against failures [12]. IEEE 802.1Qay is therefore referred to as Provider Backbone Bridging with Traffic Engineering (PBB-TE). It adds support for static, traffic-engineered paths by replacing the use of the spanning tree protocol (STP) by an external method. Besides disabling STP, also broadcasting and MAC address learning are disabled [13]. Broadcast traffic and traffic for unknown destinations are discarded by the edge nodes of the network.

In the next section we present Ethernet OAM, by means of which fault and performance management have been added to Ethernet.

4   Ethernet OAM

End-to-end OAM has been added to Ethernet by means of IEEE 802.1ag & ITU-T Y.1731. While these standards had different focal areas when work on them started, IEEE 802.1ag is nowadays considered a subset of ITU-T Y.1731. Both standards cover fault management, while performance management is solely covered by ITU-T Y.1731. Fault management can be used for detecting and isolating faults in a network, just as notifying about faults. Performance management allows to measure throughput, delay, etc. This will help to verify and prove service performance against a Service-Level Agreement (SLA) [14], for instance.

Before the Ethernet OAM management techniques can be discussed, some terminology needs to be described. *Maintenance End-Points* (MEPs) are actively managed components, which are positioned at *Maintenance Domain* (MD) boundaries. Interconnected MEPs are called a *Maintenance Entity* (ME). A *Maintenance Entity Group* (MEG)[2] can include several MEs, depending on the topology: for point-to-point Ethernet connections, a MEG contains a single ME. In a multipoint setup, a MEG consists of several MEs. Inside a ME, and thus between MEPs, one or more *Maintenance Intermediate-Points* (MIPs) can be placed. MIPs only react to OAM flows, while MEPs initiate and terminate them. In order to have management hierarchies, OAM levels can be defined to run OAM mechanisms completely separated. These concepts will be highlighted again in Section 5.1, where a deployment scenario for Ethernet OAM will be discussed.

The remainder of this section will focus on the most commonly known/used Ethernet OAM management techniques.

4.1   Continuity Check

Continuity Check (CC) can be used to detect interruptions in connectivity (and thus continuity) between end points (MEPs) in an Ethernet network. This is accomplished by transmitting 'heart-beat' messages between MEPs, which are forwarded by MIPs. By doing so in a periodic manner, connectivity can be verified. MEPs exchange CC messages with the other MEP inside the same ME, and at each administrative OAM level.

---

[2] This terminology is based on ITU-T Y.1731. In IEEE 802.1ag, a MEG is called a Maintenance Association (MA).

4.2 Loopback

Loopback (LB) provides a way to transmit request/response messages, in order to verify bi-directional connectivity with another MEP or MIP. Upon reception of a LB message, a response message is returned towards the requester. In contrast to Continuity Check, which sends messages in a periodic fashion, LB messages are typically initiated by operator command, although nodes can be configured to transmit LB messages in a periodic fashion as well.

4.3 Link Trace

Link Trace (LT) can be used to isolate faults in Ethernet networks. MEPs send out LT messages on a particular ME, in order to identify the connectivity and relationships with remote MEPs and MIPs. While a LT can only be initiated by a MEP, all MIPs and MEPs downstream the path towards a destination MEP at the same OAM level will respond to it.

4.4 Alarm Indication Signal

Alarm Indication Signal (AIS) provides a method for notifying operators about a network anomaly. As soon as a MIP detects a failure at its OAM level, it will send out an AIS message towards the reachable peer MEPs of the same ME. After the MEPs receive the AIS from the MIPs, they will send out a multicast AIS message in the upstream direction of a fault, at the next most superior OAM level and on every service provider VLAN affected by the failure. AIS is not supported by IEEE 802.1ag.

4.5 Loss Measurement

Loss Measurement (LM) offers a way for operators to determine the amount of frame loss in an Ethernet network, over an EVC for instance. More precisely, it is the ratio between undelivered OAM frames and the total number of OAM frames transmitted during a specific time interval.

ITU-T Y.1731 defines two types of LM:

1. *Single-Ended.* LM messages are transmitted to another MEP, which includes transmission and reception frame counts in its response message. In this case, only the LM initiator is able to derive frame loss from the counters (since it does not include its local counters in the initial LM message).
2. *Dual-Ended.* Continuity Check messages are used to carry frame transmission and reception counters. In contrast to the single-ended approach, this approach allows all MEPs inside a ME to derive frame loss, instead of only the initiating node.

4.6 Delay Measurement

Delay Measurement (DM) can be used for measuring delay in a Carrier Ethernet network. The unit of measurement is the round trip delay of a frame, measured from its first transmitted bit, until the reception of its last bit. Since a DM frame needs to be sent back to its originating node, LB messages are used.

Two types of DM can be identified:

1. *One-way measurement.* An initiating MEP includes a transmission timestamp in the Ethernet frame. The destination node will capture the frame
   reception timestamp, and compare both timestamps. As a consequence, the
   clocks of the sending and receiving nodes need to be synchronized.
2. *Two-way measurement.* In contrast to the one-way measurement, this DM
   type does not require clock synchronization. The initiating node still includes
   a timestamp in the Ethernet frame. After the destination node performs
   a loopback on the frame, the initiating node will receive the frame again.
   On reception, this node will capture the reception timestamp. Finally, the
   difference between the timestamps can be calculated.

5   Comparison to an IP-Based Approach

The Ethernet OAM management techniques discussed in the previous section
are, from a functional point of view, very similar to IP-based management techniques. A few examples:

- *Ethernet OAM Continuity Check* resembles a uni-directional IP Ping.
- *Ethernet OAM Loopback* verifies connectivity with a MEP or MIP, by per-
  forming a loopback on a frame. This is similar to IP Ping.
- *Ethernet OAM Link Trace* offers comparable functionality as IP Traceroute.
  Both techniques allow to trace a path between nodes through a network.
  Instead of using a 'time-to-live' (TTL) field in a frame header, MEPs/MIPs
  pass LT messages downstream the path towards a destination node.
- *Ethernet OAM Alarm Indication Signal* is able to send out notifications to
  the reachable MEPs of Maintenance Entity (ME). SNMP allows the trans-
  mission of traps/notifications to a SNMP manager as well.
- *Ethernet OAM Loss Measurement* & *Delay Measurement* offer similar features as certain SNMP Management Information Bases (MIBs) do.

As we outlined in the Introduction, we would like to verify whether it is
possible at all, or until which extent, to manage Carrier Ethernet networks with
IP-based protocols. In order to do so, IP needs to be supported on top of the
Ethernet infrastructure. Although this seems to contrast the principle of having
a pure Ethernet network, most network devices already have an IP interface
for management purposes, in order to support a Web interface, Telnet, SSH,
syslog or SNMP, for instance. Since it might not be desirable to have a full IP
infrastructure on top of an Ethernet backbone network, we assume that IP will
not be used for routing purposes and that all managed devices take part in a
management VLAN. This has the following consequences:

1. *Only devices inside the same management VLAN and IP domain are reachable.* However, it can be advantageous for end-to-end EVC management to
   have nodes reachable from outside a specific domain, for instance.
2. *The IP TTL field value is not lowered on Ethernet network hop transition.*

3. *Since frames destined to a node (identified by a B-MAC and B-VID) for which no path has been defined will be discarded by ingress Backbone Edge Bridges (BEBs), paths from a management node to all managed devices need to be defined.*

In order to verify whether an IP-based approach could be used to manage a Carrier Ethernet network, we defined a typical deployment scenario for a Carrier Ethernet, in which Ethernet OAM could be deployed. It will be used to analyze an IP-based approach for managing a Carrier Ethernet network.

5.1   Deployment Scenario

Figure 2 shows our deployment scenario for a Carrier Ethernet network. Four customer sites are shown, belonging to two different customers (A and B). Customers can be end customers, service providers, operators, and access or aggregation networks [15]. Both customers acquired an EVC between their two sites. The result is a (virtual) one-hop connection between the customer-facing switch ports of the edge devices. The transport network considered here is based on IEEE 802.1Qay (PBB-TE).

A customer site is connected to a BEB, which consists of two components [15]:

1. *I-Component*: maps S-VIDs to I-SIDs (Instance IDs) and adds a PBB header with/without[3] a B-VID.
2. *B-Component*: maps I-SIDs to B-VIDs and adds a B-VID to the PBB header (or the whole PBB header in case the I-Component has not done so).

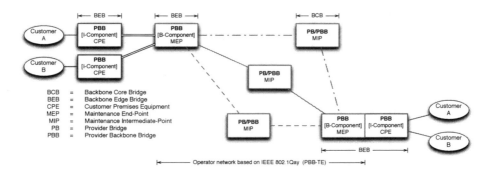

Fig. 2. Deployment scenario of a PBB-TE network with Ethernet OAM

I-Components are used for bridging in the customer space, based on customer MAC addresses and S-VIDs. B-Components are used for bridging in the provider domain based on B-MAC addresses and B-VIDs [15]. The I-Component is often called Customer Premises Equipment (CPE). A CPE is the last hop between a

---

[3] Whether an I-Component inserts PBB header or not depends on vendor implementation.

service provider network and a customer's equipment [16]. The two components of a BEB can be either in one or in two devices. In Figure 2, the components of the left BEB are in separate devices. EVCs are established between two CPEs.

The next hop after the first BEB is one of the Backbone Core Bridges (BCB), depending on the B-VID onto which the frame's I-SID (Instance ID) got mapped. Although a PBB network is considered here, the BCBs consider the frames as normal (VLAN-tagged) Ethernet frames. This is because the first three fields of the Ethernet header are the same for PB, PBB and IEEE 802.1Q, as shown in Figure 1. After the BCBs, the (BEB) egress switch of the backbone network is the next hop. The I-Component and B-Component are now packed into one device and perform the same tasks as the first BEB, but in reverse order.

Section 4 discussed how Carrier Ethernet networks could be managed by using either IEEE 802.1ag or ITU-T Y.1731. These standards require managed nodes to be either a Maintenance End-Point (MEP) or Maintenance Intermediate-Point (MIP). In our deployment scenario, (B-Components of the) BEBs are assigned the role of MEP and BCBs the role of MIP. Three Maintenance Entities (MEs) can be identified, one for each path through the network, so that each MEP is taking part in three MEs. In this work we consider only the operator's OAM mechanisms and a single OAM level.

The remainder of this section discusses the use of IP-based protocols in place of Ethernet OAM management techniques.

5.2   Continuity Check & Loopback

To automate Ping message transmission and to make it easier for an operator to handle this, a 'Remote Ping' MIB, which is part of the DISMAN (short for 'Distributed Management') framework, could be used. It lets a 'Local host' command a 'Remote host' to perform a Ping to a 'Target host'. Assuming that all nodes are reachable by the 'Remote host' and have a 'Remote Ping' implementation, a network operator could issue a Ping request from and to each node inside the same VLAN.

Compared to Ethernet OAM, the following advantages can be identified when using IP Ping:

- *When using IP Ping, both source and destination nodes can detect a failure.* Request messages can be sent in a periodic fashion, and a destination node must be configured to expect them in that fashion as well. When a reception timeout occurs, a faulty link or device can be assumed. This is not possible with Ethernet OAM CC, which is uni-directional by definition.
- *All nodes between which a path exists in a PBB-TE network, can exchange IP Ping messages by means of the DISMAN framework.* If such a path does not exist, frames will be dropped by the edge switches. The same is done for broadcast traffic [13]. Ethernet OAM CC and LB can only be initiated and terminated by MEPs. Therefore, the set of nodes reachable by IP Ping can be larger than the amount of nodes reachable by Ethernet OAM.

Besides these advantages, also several disadvantages can be identified:

- *Without network-layer routing, the set of manageable nodes is restricted to a single IP/management domain.* In contrast, Ethernet OAM can be performed in an end-to-end manner over an EVC for monitoring a single service, spanning multiple domains. It is not possible for a service provider to inject (IP) packets into an EVC to verify its functioning in an end-to-end manner.
- *It is hard to ensure that IP Ping takes the path of a particular EVC, to ensure its connectivity.* When customer data arrives at an ingress BEB, it is mapped onto a B-VID, which takes a predefined path through the network. It is hard to ensure that the management VLAN uses exactly the same path.
- *A per-customer/EVC granularity requires several translation steps.* Since Ethernet OAM allows the verification of an EVC, it is immediately clear which customers are affected by a fault. More knowledge about the network is required with IP-based protocols, in order to derive the same information. Operators will need to know onto which VLAN the customer traffic is mapped. This involves active cooperation with other parties, since operators normally do not know how others mapped customer traffic onto the VLANs.

Customers can also be involved in monitoring an EVC by using IP Ping. They will, however, see the EVC service as a one-hop path. As such, they will be able to detect a problem on the EVC, but without being able to isolate it.

The deployment scenario discussed before can also be made more complex, by considering multiple operator networks between the customer sites. Customers will still see the provider domain as a one-hop connection. As soon as a customer detects a problem without Ethernet OAM, it is up to the service provider[4] to find out which operator network causes the fault. Assuming that the path of the operator's management VLAN is the same as the customer's EVC, fault isolation with IP Ping is possible. With Ethernet OAM however, several (external) nodes could be configured as MIPs, so that a service provider could isolate a fault directly, even if it is located in another administrative domain.

5.3   Link Trace

In a similar way as we discussed the replacement of Continuity Check and Loopback by IP Ping, we assume the use of IP Traceroute as a replacement for Link Trace (LT). By adjusting the value in the 'time-to-live' (TTL) field of the IP header, the path through the network can be traced. Since IP is only used inside the management VLAN and not used for routing purposes, intermediate nodes towards a destination will never modify the TTL field value. All traces will then consist of one-hop connections and link tracing by using IP Traceroute will therefore never work in our deployment scenario.

---

[4] We assume the service provider network here to consist of at least two operator networks.

5.4   Alarm Indication Signal

Ethernet OAM allows the transmission of fault notifications by means of an Alarm Indication Signal (AIS). In IP-based networks, SNMP traps can be used for the transmission of notifications from agents to managers. Several default traps have been defined, such as 'linkup' and 'linkdown'. When a node inside the network detects a failure, it could send out a trap to an SNMP manager.

SNMP as a replacement for AIS offers several advantages:

- *SNMP traps can be sent out to an arbitrary set of SNMP managers inside the management VLAN, while AIS can only be sent out to MEPs.*
- *SNMP offers more flexibility in defining trap structures, by allowing the definition of custom ('enterprise-specific') traps.* An arbitrary set of variables can be included in a SNMP trap. Also different traps can be sent for different purposes, while Ethernet OAM AIS has a fixed structure.

Besides these advantages, several disadvantages can be identified. At first, AIS can be multicasted on each S-VLAN affected by the failure automatically. This is also possible with IP-based solutions, but this requires more overhead in deriving the EVCs/customers affected by a failure. Second, SNMP traps can only be sent out inside a single IP/management domain.

5.5   Loss Measurement

Ethernet OAM Loss Measurement (LM) calculates the frame loss between two MEPs, by comparing the difference between OAM frame transmission and reception counters at the MEPs of a particular ME. By means of the RMON-MIB [17], SNMP manages Ethernet interface counters, such as 'etherStatsPkts'. Although this counter keeps track of the sum of ingoing and outgoing frames, it is possible to define an 'enterprise-specific' MIB which manages these counters individually. Some MIBs exist for this purpose, such as a 'Round Trip Time Monitoring' (RTTMON) MIB and 'Service Assurance Agent' of Cisco.

The use of SNMP for LM offers several advantages:

- *Arbitrary values can be retrieved, depending on the used MIB.* The IF-MIB and RMON-MIB offer a rich set of counters and other interface statistics. Ethernet OAM LM only allows OAM frame counters to be retrieved.
- *SNMP PDUs can be sent to an arbitrary set of SNMP managers inside the management VLAN.* If all nodes have the IF-MIB/RMON-MIB deployed, a SNMP manager can retrieve the counter values from each of these nodes. Ethernet OAM LM only allows MEPs to calculate loss on a path.

Ethernet OAM LM measures OAM frame loss between MEPs inside a single ME. As such, frames coming from nodes outside the ME are not considered. To do the same with SNMP, an 'enterprise-specific' MIB would be needed to differentiate between frame sources or types for measuring frame loss between two network end points. Besides that, SNMP PDUs can only transmitted inside a single management/IP domain. This has been discussed in Section 5.2.

5.6   Delay Measurement

The use of IP Ping for managing Ethernet networks has been discussed before. This protocol provides round trip delay measurements together with its results. Although Ethernet OAM DM offers some sophisticated ways to compensate for processing times at end nodes, round trip delays can be measured by using IP Ping inside the management VLAN as well. This results in the same advantages and disadvantages as described before in Section 5.2. Besides that, several SNMP MIBs have been defined for the purpose of delay measurement, such as Cisco's RTTMON MIB, as discussed in the previous subsection.

6   Conclusions

This paper presented an overview of the various Carrier Ethernet standards and the related Ethernet OAM mechanisms. By considering a specific deployment scenario for a Carrier Ethernet operator network, an IP-based approach for managing these networks has been analyzed.

In the first section of this paper, two research questions were addressed:

1. *What exactly is Carrier Ethernet and which functionality does it provide?* Compared to the initial Ethernet standard for LANs, especially scalability improvements have been added to Ethernet. This allowed Ethernet to deal better with a greater number of MAC address in wide area networks. Due to this network scale increase, management of Ethernet became much more important than before. As a result, a set of management techniques was defined, in order to manage Ethernet on the Ethernet layer. When Ethernet is used in large-scale networks and manageable by using Ethernet OAM, it is commonly referred to as 'Carrier Ethernet' or 'Metropolitan Ethernet'.

2. *How does Ethernet OAM functionality compare to IP OAM, and, more specifically, can IP-based protocols in Carrier Ethernet networks provide the same functionality as comparable Ethernet OAM management techniques?* From a functional point of view, the various Ethernet OAM management techniques appeared to be very similar to IP OAM protocols, such as Ping, Traceroute and SNMP. For a single operator domain, most IP-based protocols discussed in this paper are able to provide similar functionality, as their Ethernet OAM 'counterparts'. IP Traceroute is the only protocol that turned out not to be functional at all. Besides that, the scope of an IP-based approach is limited to a single management/IP domain, since network layer routing was not considered in our deployment scenario. Consequently, IP-based protocols are not deployable in an end-end-end fashion over an Ethernet Virtual Connection, which makes it impossible to verify the end-to-end service offered to a customer. IP-based protocols are therefore not a suitable replacement for Ethernet OAM in operator environments.

As future work, a multi-domain Carrier Ethernet deployment could be investigated. Besides that, the use of other OAM techniques for Carrier Ethernet networks, such as MPLS OAM or SDH OAM, could be investigated.

Acknowledgements

This research work has been supported by SURFnet's GigaPort3 project for Next-Generation Networks and the EU FP7-257513 UniverSelf Collaborative Project. Special thanks to Mark Prins from TNO-ICT for his valuable contribution to the research.

References

1. McFarland, M., Salam, S., Checker, R.: Ethernet OAM: Key Enabler for Carrier Class Metro Ethernet Services. IEEE Communications Magazine 43(11), 152–157 (2005)
2. SURFnet: GigaPort3 and SURFnet7 (April 2011), http://www.surfnet.nl/en/innovatie/giga-port3/Pages/Default.aspx
3. IEEE: 802.1ag: Connectivity Fault Management (December 2007)
4. ITU-T: Y.1731: OAM functions and mechanisms for Ethernet based networks (February 2008)
5. Chiruvolu, G., Ge, A., Elie-Dit-Cosaque, D., Ali, M., Rouyer, J.: Issues and Approaches on Extending Ethernet Beyond LANs. IEEE Communications Magazine 42(3), 80–86 (2004)
6. Indukuri, N.: Pseudowire VCCV - BFD vs Ethernet OAM. In: 2nd International Symposium on Advanced Networks and Telecommunication Systems, pp. 1–3 (2008)
7. Allan, D., Bragg, N., McGuire, A., Reid, A.: Ethernet as Carrier Transport Infrastructure. IEEE Communications Magazine 44(2), 95–101 (2006)
8. IEEE: 802.1Q: Virtual Bridged Local Area Networks (May 2006)
9. IEEE: 802.1ad: Virtual Bridged Local Area Networks - Amendment 4: Provider Bridges (May 2006)
10. IEEE: 802.1ah: Virtual Bridged Local Area Networks - Amendment 7: Provider Backbone Bridges (August 2008)
11. IEEE: 802.1Qay: Virtual Bridged Local Area Networks - Amendment 10: Provider Backbone Bridge Traffic Engineering (August 2009)
12. Bottorff, P., Saltsidis, P.: Scaling Provider Ethernet. IEEE Communications Magazine 46(9), 104–109 (2008)
13. Lee, W., Kim, D., Song, H.: Autonomous Client Discovery in Backbone Edge Bridges for Multipoint PBB-TE Networks. In: 12th International Conference on Advanced Communication Technology (ICACT), pp. 712–716. IEEE, Los Alamitos (April 2010)
14. Ryoo, J., Song, J., Park, J., Joo, B.: OAM and Its Performance Monitoring Mechanisms for Carrier Ethernet Transport Networks. IEEE Communications Magazine 46(3), 97–103 (2008)
15. Luyuan, F., Zhang, R., Taylor, M.: The Evolution of Carrier Ethernet Services — Requirements and Deployment Case Studies. IEEE Communications Magazine 46(3), 69–76 (2008)
16. Sofia, R.: A Survey of Advanced Ethernet Forwarding Approaches. IEEE Communications Surveys & Tutorials 11(1), 92–115 (2009)
17. Waldbusser, S.: Remote Network Monitoring Management Information Base. RFC 2819 (Informational) (May 2000)

Using Diffusive Load Balancing to Improve Performance of Peer-to-Peer Systems for Hosting Services

Ying Qiao and Gregor v. Bochmann

School of Information Technology and Engineering
University of Ottawa
Ottawa, Canada
{yqiao074,bochmann}@site.uottawa.ca

Abstract. This paper presents a diffusive load balancing algorithm for peer-to-peer systems. The algorithm reduces the differences of the available capacities of the nodes in the system using service migrations between nodes in order to obtain similar performance for all nodes. We propose algorithms for handling homogeneous services, i.e., services with equal resource requirements, and for heterogeneous services, i.e., services with diverse resource requirements. We have investigated the effect of load balancing in a simulated peer-to-peer system with a skip-list overlay network. Our simulation results indicate that in case that the churn (nodes joining or leaving) is negligible, a system that hosts services with small resource requirements can maintain equal performance for all nodes with a small variance. In case that churn is high, a system that hosts homogeneous services with large resource requirements can maintain equal node performance within a reasonable variance requiring only few service migrations.

Keywords: Load balancing; diffusive load balancing; peer-to-peer systems; distributed resource management.

1   Introduction

Peer-to-peer nodes are different by their resource capacities, geographic region, or on-line time (i.e., time of being part of the peer-to-peer system). This diversity could cause performance issues. For example, some peer-to-peer requests are delayed or even lost by some nodes while other nodes are idle. Load balancing schemes, such as [2], [5], [7] and [8], are proposed to dynamically reallocate nodes or shared objects in the system. Therefore, the services accessing shared object could have a short mean response time.

We propose two different algorithms in this paper. They are for a diffusive load balancing scheme to decide load movements between nodes in a peer-to-peer system. These two algorithms are the variations of an algorithm proposed in [9], where tasks with the same unit of resource requirements are considered. Our algorithms implement a directory-initiated policy; they consider the amount of resource requirements of services instead of the number of services on nodes. They are intended for systems with homogeneous services (i.e., all services have the same

I. Chrisment et al. (Eds.): AIMS 2011, LNCS 6734, pp. 124–135, 2011.
© IFIP International Federation for Information Processing 2011

resource requirements) and for systems with heterogeneous services (i.e., services with different resource requirements), respectively. Simulation results indicate that, with the diffusive load balancing, a system with heterogeneous services is able to maintain a small variance of node performance when churn (i.e., node joining or leaving) is negligible. However, when churn is large, a system hosting homogeneous service is able to maintain the performance of the nodes within a reasonable variance and induces fewer service migrations than a system hosting heterogeneous service.

Our scheme is different from other load balancing schemes for peer-to-peer systems from two points of view. First, dynamic schemes like [5] and [8] reduce the variance of the utilizations of nodes. In case that the capacities of the nodes are different, this may lead to a large variation of the response times, even though the node utilizations are equalized. Our scheme reduces the variance of node performance by reducing the difference of the available capacities of nodes. The available capacity of a node is the processing power remains on a node after the node serves all the requests of its services. When a service migrates, the resource requirement of the service is transferred from the load sender to the load receiver, and both of the nodes have their available capacity changed by the same amount. The scheme in [7] decides node movement with different formulas for peer-to-peer systems, where the load of a cluster is shared among all the nodes of a cluster and the number of nodes in the sender and receiver cluster may be different. Second, our scheme does not rely on a specific overlay network structure to aggregate the load status of the system. Hence, our scheme can be adopted in any peer-to-peer system. Like the research in [8], we assume that the overlay network would update the destination of a shared object or a virtual server during a service migration.

We organize the rest of the paper as follows: Section 2 briefly reviews existing load balancing schemes for peer-to-peer systems and the diffusive scheme proposed for parallel computing systems. Section 3 presents our proposed diffusive scheme and its algorithms. Section 4 discusses the results of several simulation experiments, including the speed of load balancing and the number of service migrations involved. We conclude our paper in Section 5.

2   Peer-to-Peer Load Balancing and Diffusive Load Balancing

2.1   Peer-to-Peer Load Balancing

Peer-to-peer load balancing techniques can be distinguished by their different ways of performing load balancing operations. Some techniques perform load balancing operations when an object is inserted into a system or when a node joins a system. For example, a newly inserted object is placed on a node with the lowest load among the nodes randomly probed at that time [10], or a newly joined node hosts virtual servers that are taken from overloaded nodes [4]. Some techniques dynamically relocate objects between nodes that are consecutively connected in a ring or in a list. In order to further improve the load balancing speed, these techniques relocate an under-loaded node by making the node leave its original place and rejoin the network as a consecutive neighbor of an overload node [13] and [14]. Some load balancing techniques relocate virtual servers for load balancing [2], [5], and [8]. This kind of load balancing does not split or merge virtual servers, and adds less overhead to the overlay network than the other techniques. Our diffusive load balancing scheme relocates services like the methods in the last category. Load balancing techniques for peer-to-peer systems can be differentiated by the ways they collect status information and the ways that they select load senders and receivers. We will further compare our scheme with other methods in Section 4.

2.2 Diffusive Load Balancing

Synchronous and asynchronous diffusive load balancing can be distinguished. In the case of synchronous load balancing, all nodes run a load balancing operation at the same time. As shown in [11], this synchronized operation results in load exchanges that are similar to the diffusion of heat through a solid body. Asynchronous load balancing does not require synchronous operations on all nodes. The scheme in [3] specifies that any overloaded node (called a sender) should take the initiative to send part of its workload to under-loaded nodes (called receivers), and after such a load migration, the workload of the sender should still be larger than that of the receiver(s). Experiments in real systems have shown that diffusive load balancing with immediate neighbors deals well with dynamic changes of the workload [1].

Diffusive load balancing schemes can also be distinguished by how they deal with workloads of various sizes. Several papers assume fine-grain tasks, that is, the sizes of the workloads are very small compared with the resource capacity of a node. In this case, load balancing lets the workloads of all nodes converge to a global average [11]. Papers of [15], [6], and [9] considered that the resource requirement of each task is one (fixed sized) unit. The load balancing operations eventually lead to a global system state which is stable (that is, no further load exchanges occur), although this state is not completely balanced. In fact, the difference of workloads between any two nodes in a neighborhood could be as large as one unit (without leading to a load exchange). Therefore, the global load imbalance in the stable state, defined by the maximal difference of workloads between any two nodes in the network, is bounded by $\lceil \frac{D}{2} \rceil$ load units, where D is the diameter of the network.

3   Diffusive Load Balancing Scheme for Peer-to-Peer Systems

The proposed diffusive load balancing scheme allows load balancing operations periodically run on each node. An operation undergoes three phases. At first, the operation collects the load status of its neighbors in the information phase. Then, it makes decisions on service migrations in the decision phase. At the end, services are transferred from load senders to load receivers in the service migration phase. Operations executing on different nodes are not globally synchronized. These operations may run concurrently on different nodes, however, a node involved in one such operation will refuse the participation in another load balancing operation initiated by one of its neighbors. In this way, the load status information collected from a neighbor during an operation is always correct.

We describe in the following two algorithms that are used in the decision phase. One algorithm, named DIHomoService, is for a system hosting homogeneous services with the identical resource requirements. Another algorithm, named DIHeteroService, is used for systems hosting heterogeneous services with diverse resource requirements. These algorithms are derived from a directory-initiated (DI) algorithm where the running node works as a directory for locating senders and receivers. Our results in [7] show that the DI algorithm is superior to a sender-initiated or a receiver-initiated algorithm for load balancing.

We use here the following notations. The node that initiates a load balancing operation is called the running node of the operation and denoted as node i , the neighborhood of the operation is the overlay-network of the running node and is denoted as A_i . A node in the neighborhood is identified as node j. The number of nodes in A_i is denoted $|A_i|$. In case that a service, for example m , with resource requirement l_m migrates from node x to y, after the migration, we have the available capacity on nodes as $avc_y^{'} = avc_y - l_m$ and $avc_x^{'} = avc_x + l_m$ where avc_x and $avc_x^{'}$ are the available capacities of x before and after the service migration, respectively.

3.1 DIHomoService: DI Algorithm for Homogeneous Services

The DI algorithm decides service migrations between possibly several pairs of overloaded and under-loaded nodes within the neighborhood of the load balancing operation. The algorithm calculates the average available capacity of nodes in the neighborhood using the formula $\overline{avc_i} = \dfrac{\sum_{j \in A_i} avc_j}{|A_i|}$. Based on the average available node capacity $\overline{avc_i}$, it classifies the nodes j in the neighborhood as either overloaded (if its available capacity is smaller than $\overline{avc_i}$), under-loaded (if its available capacity is larger than $\overline{avc_i}$), or average loaded. The algorithm stores the overloaded nodes in vector SVect and the under-loaded nodes in vector RVect. Then the algorithm decides service migrations using the decision procedure shown in Fig. 1. A service has its resource requirement equal to l .

Decision procedure: Fig. 1.(a) shows the procedure. For a pair of nodes that have the largest difference of their available capacities among all of the nodes in the two vectors (line 3 and 4), the procedure resolves the load imbalance by calling the selection function shown in Fig. 1.(b) (line 5). The selection function returns the number of services to be transferred. In the case that no service can be transferred, the procedure stops since it will not be able to schedule any other service migration in this operation. In the other case the procedure decides the service migration. Then the procedure goes back to line 2 to find another node pair.

Selection function: The function is shown in Fig. 1.(b). It calculates the required available capacity for the sender and the provided available capacity for the receiver according to the differences between their available capacity and   (line 1 and 2). The minimum of the provided and the required available capacities is the load difference that the algorithm should resolve (line 3). In case that the minimum is larger than the resource requirement of a single service, the function returns the integer part of the ratio of the minimum to the resource requirement of a service (line 5). Otherwise, it returns 1 in case that the available capacity of the sender could be still less than that of the receiver right after the service migration. In this way, the algorithm keeps the available capacities of nodes closest to the average.

Decision procedure:
1 Do forever
2   if SVect and RVect are not empty
    // select a load receiver
3   select y such that
      $avc_y = \max_{j \in RVect} \{avc_j\}$
    // select a load sender
4   select x such that
      $avc_x = \min_{j \in SVect} \{avc_j\}$
5   w:= Selection(x, y);
6   if w > 0
7   decide the service migration
8   remove x from SVect
10   remove y from RVect
11   else break;
12 else break;

Selection(s,r)
1   $avc_{required} = avc_{A_i} - avc_s$
2   $avc_{provided} = avc_r - avc_{A_i}$
3   $avc_{moved} = \min\{avc_{required}, avc_{provided}\}$
4   if $avc_{moved} > l$
5   return $\left\lfloor \dfrac{avc_{moved}}{l} \right\rfloor$
6   else if $avc_s + l \le avc_r - l$
7   return 1
8   else
9   return 0

(a)   (b)

Fig. 1. The DIHomoService algorithm: (a) the Decision procedure, (b) the Selection function

We can see that, when following the above procedure, the diffusive load balancing eventually stops. We assume that the system has a static workload. This means that no new service joins or leaves the system, and the request rates of existing services do not change. We also assume now that the peer-to-peer system has no churn. Research in [15] presents assumptions for a general model of a partial asynchronous load balancing scheme. These assumptions assure that a scheme conforming to the general model is able to converge or stop in a system whose tasks have the same load size. We show that our scheme with the DIHomoService algorithm has stronger assumptions than the general model. First, the proposed scheme serializes the running of its operations in neighborhoods with common nodes. Compared with the assumption of partial asynchronous message passing of the general model, the local serialization guarantees that the load status of a neighborhood is fresh and correct during each operation. Second, the general model assumes a sender-initiated load movement. Since the scheme with DIHomoService decides service migrations for multiple pairs of senders and receivers, the scheme has a stronger assumption by invoking multiple sender-initiated service migration in its operations. Third, DIHomoService also guarantees that avc_s' is less than avc_r' for a pair of sender and receiver. Hence, like the general model, our scheme with DIHomoService will eventually stop service migrations (in a system with static workload) and the system enters a global stable state.

We further claim that after the system enters a global stable state, the local load imbalance of the system (i.e., the maximum difference of available capacities on nodes in a neighborhood) is $2l$. When the decision algorithm of an operation does not find any service migration to be done between two nodes, for example, between the sender $s1$ of S and the receiver $r1$ of R, either $\overline{avc_i} - avc_{s1} < l$ or $avc_{r1} - \overline{avc_i} < l$ holds as well as $avc_{r1} - avc_{s1} < 2l$. In the case that there are p nodes in R, and $avc(rp) \le \ldots \le avc(r2) \le avc(r1)$, then no receiver could be located as a receiver for $s1$. In the case that there are q nodes in S, and $avc(s1) \leq avc(s2) \leq ... \leq avc(sq)$, then no sender could be found for $r1$. Hence, in the global stable state, the local imbalance is the difference of the available node capacities between $s1$ and $r1$ which is at most $2l$.

Because of the local load imbalance, a maximal global load imbalance (i.e., the maximum difference of the available capacities of nodes in the system) can reach the value $2lD$ where D is the diameter (i.e., maximum of the minimum hop distance between any two nodes) of the overlay network. We use an example to derive the global load imbalance. We consider that a node $s1$ in neighborhood A_1 sends services to r_D in the neighborhood A_D in at most D hops. We construct a path connecting the nodes according to the service migrations in the form $s_1 \xrightarrow{A_1} r_1 / s_2 \xrightarrow{A_2} r_2 / s_3 \rightarrow \cdots \xrightarrow{A_D} r_D$ where r_i / s_{i+1} is a receiver in A_i and a sender in A_{i+1}. Since the local load imbalance is bound by $2l$, the global load imbalance between s_1 and r_D is bound by $2lD$.

3.2 DIHeteroService Algorithm: DI Algorithm for Heterogeneous Services

The DIHeteroService algorithm deals with heterogeneous services. Compared with the DIHomoService algorithm, the algorithm has a different selection function. The function returns a vector containing the services selected for service migration (Fig. 2.(a)). The function selects services with the minimal resource requirements (line 4) in order to assure that the total resource requirement of the selected services will not lead to a sender available capacity larger than the available capacity of the receiver after the load transfer. After one migration pair has been selected, the procedure removes the sender and receiver from the SVect and RVect and continues the decision phase until no further migration pair can be identified.

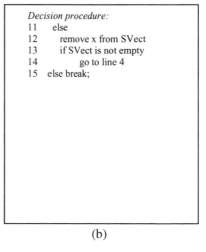

Selection (s,r):
1 W := { };
2 P := {service ∈ s};
3 Do
4       $l_{min} = \min\limits_{service \in P} \{l_{service}\}$
5   if $avc_s + l_{min} \leq avc_r - l_{min}$
6   then
7   add v to W if $l_v = l_{min}$
8           $avc_s := avc_s + l_{min}$
9           $avc_r := avc_r - l_{min}$
10   remove v from P
11   continue
12   else
13   return W

Decision procedure:
11   else
12   remove x from SVect
13   if SVect is not empty
14   go to line 4
15   else break;

(a)   (b)

Fig. 2. The DIHomoService algorithm: (a) the Selection function, (b) the segment replacing line 11 and 12 of the Decision procedure in Fig. 1.(a)

Following similar arguments as for the DIHomoService algorithm, we can show that the load balancing with the DIHeteroService algorithm will stop in the case of static workload. However, when the system reaches a global stable state, the local load imbalance might not be the smallest. For example, for the pair $s1$ and $r1$, even when there is no service of $s1$ that could be selected for a service migration, it is possible that there are still some services in other senders that could be migrated to $r1$ to reduce their available capacities. In order to improve the decision procedure, we replace the line 11 and 12 of the decision procedure in Fig. 1. (a) by the segment shown in Fig. 2. (b). The Decision procedure of the operation stops when there is no sender in S or no receiver in R.

Like the DIHomoService algorithm, the DIHeteroService algorithm reduces the variance of the available capacities of the nodes in each operation. Also, when the distribution of services in the system is unknown, at a global stable state, the local imbalance is bounded by $2l_{max}$ where l_{max} is the request rate of a service with the highest request rate, and the global load imbalance is bounded by $2l_{max}D$.

4 Experiments

The experimental measurements discussed in this section are obtained from a simulated peer-to-peer system. The system has a skip-list structured overlay network, as described for some classic peer-to-peer systems, like Chord and Pastry. In our simulated overlay network, nodes are connected into a ring, and each node is assigned a position numbered from 0 to $N - 1$. Node i at position i will take nodes at positions $(i + 2^0) \bmod N, (i + 2^1) \bmod N, \cdots (i + 2^{\lfloor \log_2(N-1) \rfloor}) \bmod N$ as its neighbors. In the overlay network, a node has $\lfloor \log_2(N-1) \rfloor$ out-degree connections and $\lfloor \log_2(N-1) \rfloor$ in-degree connections, and the diameter of the overlay graph is $O(\log N)$. We have built the overlay network with the simulator of the eQuus system [12] using one node per cluster.

In the simulation, load balancing operations are scheduled by a discrete event simulation library called "Ssim". During each operation, the running node collects the load status of its neighbors in the skip-list and uses the DIHomoService or DIHeteroService algorithm to decide service migrations. Service migrations are realized by updating the location of sevices to the nodes in the simulation. The time elapsed during an operation is not simulated since we assume that the neighborhood does not change in such a short time. We call a **round** a simulated time period in which each node runs one load balancing operation, and the standard deviation of the available node capacities and the number of service migrations are collected at the end of each round.

We investigate the effectivness of the diffusive load balancing agorithms in systems hosting homogeneous services or heterogeneous services; the impact of the resouce requirements of services is also examined by configuring small services (i.e., services with small resource requirements) or large services (i.e., services with large resource requirements) to these systems. The effectiveness of the load balancing is evaluated from three points of view. First, the speed that the system approaches the global stable state at is evaluated according to convergence ratios. The convergence ratio γ_τ of round τ is equal to the ratio of $\sigma(avc^\tau)$ to $\sigma(avc^{\tau-1})$, where $\sigma(avc^\tau)$ is the standard deviation of the available node capacities at the end of round τ. The ratio indicates the degree of reduction of the standard deviation of the available node capacities during one round. A smaller convergence ratio indicates a higher load balancing speed. Second, the number of service migrations that occurred for load balancing is concerned. We assume that each service migration spends the same amount of resources, such as CPU and bandwith, even though they may contain different numbers of services. A large number of service migrations indicates a high cost of load balancing. Third, the standard deviation of available node capacities when the system is in a stable state is concerned. This is the degree of load balancing that can be obtained; as we will see, it depends on the degree of churn (as can be expected).

The simulated peer-to-peer system is configured with 1000 nodes. In case of homogeneous nodes, the capacities of nodes (i.e., c) is 10 requests/second. In a simulated system, the sum of the resource requirements of services is equal to half of the total capacity of the system; therefore, the average available capacity of nodes is 5 requests/second (and the average utilization of the system is 50%). The simulated systems install either a workload of large services or of small services. These services are randomly distributed to the nodes at the beginning of the experiments. For example, for a system with large-sized homogeneous services, l is set as 2.5 requests/second for a service, which is in the same order as the node capacity. Therefore, a node can host at most 4 services in the system. For a system with small-sized homogeneous services, l is set to 0.25 requests/second, which is one tenth of that of a large service. A node can host at most 40 services in the system. For the systems hosting heterogeneous services, services have their resource requirements uniformly distributed between 0 and a preconfigured maximum, e.g., 2.5 requests/second for a system with large-sized services, and 0.25 requests/second for a system with small-sized services.

Table 1 shows the results collected from 20 runs of experiements. The mean value and the 90% confidence interval (CI) for the mean of each item are given. The convergence ratios of the first rounds γ_1 of all systems are smaller than the convergence ratios of the seconds rounds. This indicates that, when load balancing first starts, the balancing operations largely resolve the differences of available node capacities. Furthermore, γ_1 for systems hosting small services is smaller than that for systems hosting large services. This indicates that small services help the load balancing to reduce the differences of the available capacities between nodes. Since load balancing operations could select the small services in heterogeenous systems, the load balancing in these systems is able to further resolve the load unbalance and achieve a smaller standard deviation of available node capacities in subsequent rounds. However, moving services in the heterogeneous systems introduce more service migrations. The number of service migrations in a heterogeneous system is about three times of the number in a homogeneous system hosting the same services. From the Table 1, we also observe that the global load imbalance of the system in the stable state is much smaller than we expected in Section 3. The predicated global load imbalance is bound to $2lD$, but the experiment shows a value around l or $2l$.

Table 1. DIHomoService decision algorithm with skip-list overlay neighborhood and random neighborhood

		Homogeneous system		Heterogeneous system	
		Small services	Large services	Small services	Large services
number of service migrations	Mean	1825.9	617.65	5414.6	1608.05
	90% CI	25.44	5.86	64.46	17.17
γ_1	Mean	0.034	0.141	0.013	0.124
	90% CI	0.002	0.009	0.001	0.002
γ_2	Mean	0.88	0.99	0.324	0.99
	90% CI	0.039	0.005	0.016	0.001
Standard deviation	Mean	0.09	0.49	0.012	0.355
	90% CI	0.01	0.032	0.001	0.006
Global load imbalance	Mean	0.36	4.5	0.139	2.64
	90% CI	0.047	0.377	0.014	0.116

In the simulated system, churn is realized with the occurrences of nodes' joining and leaving. A newly joined node could be positioned at a random place in the ring, and an existing node could be randomly picked to leave the ring. At the beginning of an operation, the running node searches for its neighbors in the skip-list by their positions in the ring. We use a Poisson arrival model to simulate the churn occurrence in the system. We define a relative churn rate, i.e. the churn occurrence rate of the arrival model, as the number of node joining and leaving within a round. For example, when a system with 1000 nodes has a churn rate of 10%, the system would have a total of 100 occurrences of leaving or joining per round, and the mean time interval between two consecutive node joining or leaving is T over 50 where T is the duration of a round. In this way, the changes of available node capacities induced by churn and the deduction of the differences on available node capacities caused by the load balancing are evaluated in the same time duration. A joining node takes over half of the services of its successor after it locates its position in the ring, and a leaving node hands over its services to its successor. We assume that a node leaves and another node joins at the same time, so that, neither the total number of nodes nor the system's average available capacity changes. Without load balancing, the standard deviation of available node capacities always increases, and the degree of the increase depends on a churn rate. For example, in case the system has a churn rate of 10%, when the system has run for 50 rounds, the standard deviation of the available node capacities is increased by a factor of three. In case the churn rate is 90%, the standard deviation is increased by a factor of 7 after 50 rounds.

We compare the effect of the load balancing to the performance of the systems when they experience churn. When the systems have negligible churn, for example, one node joins or leaves in every 2 rounds, load balancing can quickly resolve the load unbalance, and its effectiveness is close to that shown in the previous experiments. Therefore, in this part, the systems with two different churn rates are investigated individually: a low rate as 10% and a high rate as 90%. Fig. 3 shows the standard deviation of available node capacities and the number of service migrations in the first 50 simulation rounds. The standard deviation slightly varies around a certain value as the system evolves, and we say that the system enters a steady state.

At a steady state, when the churn rate is 10%, the standard deviations for the four systems are around 0.75 with no significant difference (Fig. 3.(a)). However, the number of service migrations are largely diverse (Fig. 3.(b)). The homogeneous system hosting large services has the fewest number of service migration, and the heterogeneous system hosting small services has the largest number of service migrations. This observation indicates that the systems hosting large services are favored by the load balancing operations with fewer number of service migrations. Fig. 3.(c) shows the standard deviation of available node capacities when the churn rate is 90%. Compared with Fig. 3.(a), the standard deviation is increased. A heterogeneous system hosting small services has a distinct standard deviation of available node capacities around 2.2, and other systems have the standard deviation around 1.6. Fig. 3.(d) shows that a homogeneous system hosting large services has the fewest number of service migrations, and this further confirms our intuition based on Fig. 3.(b).

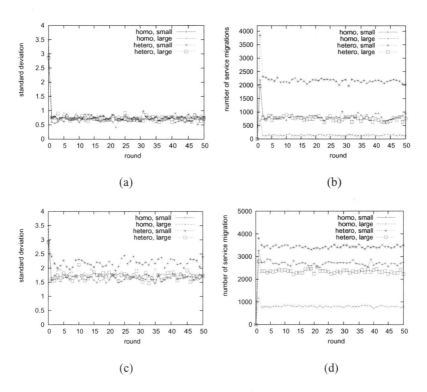

(a)   (b)

(c)   (d)

Fig. 3. Load balancing in a system with churn: (a) the standard deviation of available node capacities when churn rate is 10%; (b) the number of service migrations when churn rate is 10%; (c) the standard deviation of available node capacities when churn rate is 90%; (d) the number of service migrations when churn rate is 90%. (Note: "homo" is for homogeneous services, "hetero" is for heterogeneous services, "small" is for services with small resource usage, and "large" is for services with large resource usage)

We compare in the following our scheme with others proposed for peer-to-peer systems. We differentiate them in terms of load balancing policies. Similar to our scheme, these schemes have information, decision and load migration phases. However, some schemes have these phases run separately. For example, the schemes proposed in [13] and [14] require a global load distribution map for their decision phase. Their information and decision phases are separated. Research on dynamic load balancing has shown that this kind of separation could cause the load status information to become stale and thus reduce the effectiveness of load balancing. Also, aggregating a global map induces message overhead. Some schemes, such as [5], use random walks in their information phases, and they normally have a sender-intitiated policy in their decision phases. However, random walks cost extra messages, and a scheme with a sender-initiated policy converges slower than a scheme with a directory-initiated policy. Our work is similar to load balancing with a fixed number of directories [8].

We further compare our research with others in terms of the parameters collected from experiments. The research in the literature consider the maximum difference of loads among nodes [13] or the portion of failed requests [8] in the steady state of a dynamic system. We investigate the standard deviation of load distribution at systems' steady state, the convergence speed of the load balancing, and the number of service migrations during the load balancing. This approach allows us to analyze the effectiveness of load balancing from different perspectives.

5   Conclusions

We proposed a diffusive load balancing algorithm for peer-to-peer systems. The scheme reallocates shared objects on nodes and balances the available node capacities on nodes. Therefore, the performance of nodes is similar. The load balancing operations use the DIHomoService algorithm, i.e., directory-initiated algortihm for systems hosting homogeneous services, or the DIHeteroService algorithm, i.e., directory-initiated algorithm for systems hosting heterogeneous services. The results of the simulation experiments show that, when the churn is negligible, the small services hosted by a heterogeneous system facilitate load balancing. Hence, the node performance of a heterogeneous system has a smaller variance than that of a homogeneous system for the same services. The results also show that, when the systems have noticeable churn, the variances of the node performance of the systems are not significantly different. However, a churn with a higher rate brings a larger variance to a system. For example, when the churn rate is 90%, the variance of node performance is almost two times larger than that when the churn rate is 10%. The numbers of service migrations are also increased. A system hosting large services with homogeneous capacities always introduces the fewest service migrations.

Our load balancing scheme could be used to improve the performance of a large-scale distributed systems that have characteristics like those of a peer-to-peer system. In such systems, the variance of the delay of service requests is imperative. Also, our research indicates that, in order to have efficient load balancing, the system should have large-sized services in case that the system has heterogeneous services.

References

1. Corradi, A., Leonardi, L., Zambonelli, F.: Diffusive Load-Balancing Policies for Dynamic Applications. IEEE Concurrency 7(1), 22–31 (1999)
2. Zhu, Y., Hu, Y.: Efficient, Proximity-Aware Load Balancing for DHT-Based P2P Systems. IEEE Trans. Parallel Distrib. Syst. 16(4), 349–361 (2005)
3. Bertsekas, D.P., Tsitsiklis, J.N.: Parallel and distributed computation: Numerical Methods, Englewood Cliffs, NJ (1999)
4. Ledlie, J., Seltzer, M.: Distributed, secure load balancing with skew, heterogeneity and churn. In: Proceedings of 24th Annual Joint Conference of the IEEE Computer and Communications Societies, INFOCOM 2005, March 13-17, vol. 2, pp. 1419–1430 (2005)
5. Shen, H., Xu, C.: Locality-Aware and Churn-Resilient Load-Balancing Algorithms in Structured Peer-to-Peer Networks. IEEE Transactions on Parallel Distributed Systems 18(6), 849–862 (2007)
6. Song, J.: A partially asynchronous and iterative algorithm for distributed load balancing. Parallel Comput. 20(6), 853–868 (1994)
7. Qiao, Y., Bochmann, G.v.: A Diffusive Load Balancing Scheme for Clustered Peer-to-Peer Systems. In: Proceedings of 15th ICPADS, pp. 842–847. IEEE Computer Society, Los Alamitos (2009)
8. Surana, S., Godfrey, B., Lakshminarayanan, K., Karp, R., Stoica, I.: Load balancing in dynamic structured peer-to-peer systems. Perform. Eval. 63(3), 217–240 (2006)
9. Cortés, A., Ripoll, A., Cedó, F., Senar, M.A., Luque, E.: An asynchronous and iterative load balancing algorithm for discrete load model. J. Parallel Distrib. Comput. 62(12), 1729–1746 (2002)
10. Karger, D.R., Ruhl, M.: Simple efficient load balancing algorithms for peer-to-peer systems. In: Proceedings of the Sixteenth Annual ACM Symposium on Parallelism in Algorithms and Architectures (SPAA 2004), pp. 36–43. ACM, New York (2004)
11. Cybenko, G.: Dynamic load balancing for distributed memory multiprocessors. J. Parallel Distrib. Comput. 7(2), 279–301 (1989)
12. Locher, T., Schmid, S., Wattenhofer, R.: eQuus: A Provably Robust and Locality-Aware Peer-to-Peer System. In: Proceedings of P2P 2006, pp. 3–11 (September 2006)
13. Vu, Q.H., Ooi, B.C., Rinard, M., Tan, K.-L.: Histogram-Based Global Load Balancing in Structured Peer-to-Peer Systems. IEEE Transactions on Knowledge and Data Engineering 21(4), 595–608 (2009)
14. Li, M., Lee, W.-C.,, S.: DPTree: A Balanced Tree Based Indexing Framework for Peer-to-Peer Systems. In: Proceedings of the 2006 14th IEEE International Conference on Network Protocols, ICNP 2006, November 12-15, pp. 12–21 (2006)
15. Cedo, F., Cortes, A., Ripoll, A., Senar, M.A., Luque, E.: The Convergence of Realistic Distributed Load-Balancing Algorithms. Theory of Computing Systems 41(4), 609–618 (2007)

On the Dimensioning of an Aggregation Service for P2P Service Overlay Networks*

Adriano Fiorese[1,2], Paulo Simões[1], Fernando Boavida[1]

[1] Centre for Informatics and Systems of the University of Coimbra - CISUC
Department of Informatics Engineering - DEI
University of Coimbra - UC
{fiorese,psimoes,boavida}@dei.uc.pt
[2] Department of Computer Science - DCC
Santa Catarina State University - UDESC
890233-100 Joinville, SC, Brazil
fiorese@joinville.udesc.br

Abstract. An aggregation service (AgS) is a P2P overlay-tier whose purpose is to aggregate and optimize the searching of services and service components maintained by service providers in a P2P Service Overlay Network (SON). AgS dimensioning takes into account the AgS size, in order to allow it to adequately perform the searching when compared with P2P SON native searching mechanisms. Suitable AgS dimensioning helps service providers to plan their infrastructures and services, allowing them to keep costs under control. This paper presents an assessment of the dimensioning of an AgS overlay. The assessment takes into account the searching response time as metric in both the environments: 1) P2P SON and 2) AgS. The assessment also takes into account the AgS own maintenance overhead, in order to compare it with the searching response time in the P2P SON. The simulation results show that, on average, AgSs whose sizes are lesser than 90% of the P2P SON size present better searching efficiency than the same searching operations in P2P SON.

Keywords: Services Management, P2P, Service Aggregation.

1 Introduction

Service providers use the Internet connecting "fabric" to generate revenue, offering and operating a large variety of services. Particular services might be a composite of several intermediary services, which, in turn, are operated by third party service or service-component providers. Nevertheless, these services and service components need to be searched, grouped, composed and provisioned, in order to offer the final user a complete service.

In this scenario, service providers face problems in the reachability of the services they provide. A possible manner to cope with this problem is the

---

* This work was partially funded by Portuguese Foundation for Science and Technology (grant SFRH/BD/45683/2008).

I. Chrisment et al. (Eds.): AIMS 2011, LNCS 6734, pp. 136–147, 2011.

organization of the service providers into a Service Overlay Network (SON) [22]. This approach leads to added coverage, which allows service providers to target bigger markets and, at the same time, share infrastructural costs.

Even though the services are made available by the SON, the need for service search optimization remains. To cope with this, an Aggregation Service (AgS) was proposed by the authors in [11] [10]. AgS optimizes service and service components searching in a multi-domain environment composed of multiple service providers organized into a common P2P SON. In essence, AgS is a second P2P overlay-tier that executes on top of the P2P SON, aggregating the published services and, thus, making search processes faster and more efficient. Peers that belong to service providers and that are also part of the P2P SON constitute the AgS service. These peers play the role of aggregators and are responsible for the search optimization.

In this context, an open issue is to determine the AgS size, i.e., the number of peers making up the AgS service in order to improve the search efficiency and performance, when compared to the native searching mechanisms provided by the underlying P2P SON.

This paper addresses the problem of the AgS service dimensioning. Having in mind the stated goal and approach, this paper is organized as follows. Section 2 discusses related work. Section 3 briefly describes the AgS service. Subsequently, Section 4 describes in detail the simulated scenarios, presents the simulation results and discusses them. Finally, Section 5 summarizes the findings and discusses guidelines for further work.

2   Related Work

The AgS service and, consequently, its dimensioning, spans different areas in the field of network and distributed systems, briefly identified below.

2.1   Network and Services Management

Some indirect contributions from the network and services management area are relevant for the optimization of search services and their dimensioning issues.

Management by Policies is used to enhance services management [15]. Work in this area addresses managing performance service level agreements between internal service providers in a network through the enforcement of policy levels. However, these approaches depend on a series of agreements, adaptation and trust to be realized in cross-domain environments, which suggests the use of an appropriate Service Overlay Network (SON) to take care of this.

Currently, web services are the most developed approach to network and services management [24]. Also, they are the most popular solution for offering service interfaces and service composition [9], on which the Service Oriented Architecture (SOA) lays on [1]. Therefore, the searching of web services is a recurrent challenge. Works in this area comprises how to select and represent information about web services, as well as ways to overcome the limitations of the single centralized Universal Description, Discovery and Integration (UDDI) repository. Among others, proposes in this area includes searching web services by their operations based on the similarity of the desired operation [7].

2.2 Peer-to-Peer

P2P networks are generally classified into two categories: 1) unstructured and 2) structured. These terms relate to the topology of the P2P overlay network. When the topology is tightly controlled and content is placed at specific peers rather than at randomly chosen peers, the P2P network is said to be structured. Generally, this is accomplished using a Distributed Hash Table (DHT) as the core of the P2P network. Some examples of structured P2P overlay networks are: CHORD [21], Content Addressable Network (CAN) [18] and Chamaleon [5]. If the topology is not tightly coupled, which means the peers join the network according to some loose rules, then the network is classified as unstructured. In this kind of P2P networks there is not a coupling between topology and the location of data. Instead, peers form a random graph in a flat or hierarchical manner. Generally, in this kind of P2P network, peers use some kind of flooding to send queries (searches) to other peers, with a limited scope. Some examples of seminal unstructured P2P overlay networks are Gnutella [19] and FreeNet [6]. Reference [14] presents an extended discussion and comparison of structured and unstructured P2P overlay networks. Meshkova et al. [16] presents a survey of the discovery techniques used in some P2P overlay networks as well as in other types of networks.

P2P overlay networks are significantly used as supporting-tier application. In addition to the traditional file sharing applications, resource discovery is commonly executed by these overlays. Michel et al.   [17] proposed the exploitation of keywords and attribute-values co-occurrences for the improvement of keyword-based searching in P2P. An intelligent resource discovery mechanism based on weaving attributes into indexes, using locality sensitive hashing and performing searches based on the geographic location of the indexes in a structured P2P overlay is presented in [20].

Search enhancement by combining Grid and P2P was proposed in [4, 23]. Some ideas on this topic concern the use of routing indexes and mechanisms to easily spread them through the Grid; the utilization of bio-inspired algorithms in order to achieve overlay self-organization and selective search flooding, exploiting particular conditions on local caches, is proposed.

P2P used in the searching of web services has been addressed by several authors. For instance, approaches using semantics for web services searching are well studied [2, 3]. All these proposals claim that the P2P approach has some advantages for the service discovery process, when compared to centralized approaches, such as UDDI.

2.3 Service Overlay Networks

A Service Overlay Network (SON), is a virtualized network composed of interconnected nodes, whose generic purpose is to provide the required Quality of Service (QoS) to applications that execute on those nodes [22]. A difference between a SON and a P2P overlay network is that the latter regards providing efficient searching and retrieval. This difference is claimed in [22]. The formation of the SON does not require its own communication infrastructure. Hence, the problem of bandwidth provisioning in a SON composed of nodes that lease links from different link providers is studied in [8].

A P2P overlay network can also provide QoS services. We claim this can be accomplished when the participants are in a consortium of service providers that establish well-defined SLAs to regulate the contribution of each participant to the network. In this sense, these particular P2P overlay networks can be considered SON. This idea is based on the work of Zhou et al. [25]. They proposed a SON platform called ALASA. This platform uses a structured P2P overlay network on the Internet to describe, discover, compose, and repute services.

Taking this into account, this work will use a particular P2P overlay in order to assume a SON among several particular service providers belonging to different network domains.

Lavinal et al. [13] also uses P2P as support for the SON architecture. In that piece of work the authors also address the discovery of services, although they consider QoS aspects in their approach whilst we take into account performance aspects.

3   Services Searching Using Aggregation Service

The Aggregation Service (AgS) is an unstructured P2P overlay, meaning there is no tight coupling between overlay topology and information location/placement. It executes on top of a P2P SON created by service providers. AgS is composed of peers that belong to these service providers, interested in advertising their services.

The purpose of the AgS service is to aggregate service and service components. This is accomplished by concentrating the service offerings in the AgS peers (nodes), in order to facilitate and optimize the search process. The architectural design of AgS is depicted in Fig. 1.

AgS consists of a P2P overlay without coupling between its logical ring topology and the exact location of the aggregated services. Fig. 1 also shows the SON peers belonging to particular administrative domains announcing (publish) their services and service components to the aggregation peers.

The AgS service operates according to the model depicted in Fig. 2. The service or service component object is the central piece in the AgS model. It is part of the interactions with every subject in the model. It represents the Service or Service Component that actually executes on the SON peer and that is published in an aggregation peer. Aggregation peers (or AgS peers) are specialized SON peers, chosen among the peers that compose the P2P SON in order to form the AgS P2P overlay.

Each SON peer plays a double role. They execute the services and, in order to optimize the services searching, they also publish references to the available

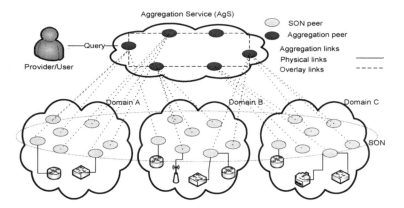

Fig. 1. Aggregation Service Architecture

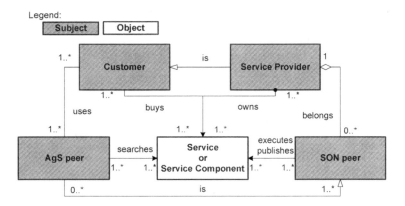

Fig. 2. Aggregation Service Model

services in several AgS peers. A single service offering can be spread over multiple
AgS peers in order to allow some redundancy and to overcome churn. The SON
peers make the services indirectly available (through interfaces encapsulated in
a service profile) to external entities (such as service composers and aggregators)
located in the same or other network domains.

As service providers are customers as well, they can act as third party
consumers of service components of other service providers. Nonetheless, to
accomplish this step, first of all, the service or service component needs to
be searched and found. According to the AgS model, the customer, which can
be a third party service provider, uses an AgS peer to accomplish this task.
The AgS service performs the search and makes the result available to the
customer. Searching for a service by means of the AgS framework results in
a set of references to SON peers that offer an interface to the services that
match the search criteria. This preserves the internal details of the service, since
the external entity is only granted with a mediated access (by means of the SON
peer), which may hide sensitive information and filter undesired operations.

The two-tiered AgS architecture enables the splitting of publish and search functionality from the services and service components management functions to be carried out in the P2P SON-tier. Thus, sensitive information and configuration of the services (e.g. the existing internal service provider management services, topologies, etc.) can be protected by only making available (publishing) a previously selected set of interfaces for services and service components.

The AgS working is based on a number of operations. Table 1 presents its key operations and the corresponding messages exchanged among peers.

Table 1. AgS Table of Operations and Messages

Operation	Goal	Executor	Message sent
Join	Form the Aggregation Service.	aggregation peer	JoinMessage sent by the requesting peer to its successor and predecessor in the overlay.
Leave	Leave the Aggregation Service (in a normal way).	aggregation peer	LeaveMessage sent by the requesting peer to its successor and predecessor in the overlay.
Query	Look for a peer that provides a particular service/service component.	aggregation peer	QueryMessage sent by the requesting peer to its successor in the overlay ring in a clockwise manner. The message is forwarded clockwise until it arrives at its goal or until the message reaches the requesting peer. When the desired information is found, a QueryReply message containing it, is then created. This latter message is directly transmitted to the requesting peer of the Query's operation.
Publish	Make the services to be searched available.	SON peer	PublishMessage sent by the SON peer to its aggregation peer(s), which makes the service(s) public.

4   Dimensioning the AgS

In order to dimension the AgS service, several simulations were performed in order to determine the search response time as a function of the number of nodes in the AgS layer. The response time is the time elapsed since a Query Message is sent from the requesting AgS peer until the reception of the corresponding Query Reply Message. By determining the response time for several sizes of the P2P SON and several sizes of the AgS overlay, it is possible to decide on the number of peers that should form the AgS overlay in order to obtain a certain search performance.

4.1   Definitions

Let's consider a set P of service providers that create a consortium to provide services to a large-scale community over a multi-domain environment. In order to do this, they create a P2P SON, in which the available SON peers are responsible for providing the services. In this case let $|P_n|$ be the number of peers a service provider p_n makes available as SON peers. Thus, $|SON| = \sum_{n=1}^{|P|} |P_n|$, and $SON = \{p \mid p \in P_n \in P\}$. On the other hand, the AgS overlay is constituted by the subset of the SON peers. Hence, in principle, $|AgS| \leq |SON|$. Let's define e as the search efficiency, which is given by the response time metric.

Thus, e_{SON} is the search efficiency in the P2P SON using internal, native searching mechanisms, which is inversely proportional to the response time, i.e., $e_{SON} = 1/rt$. On the other hand, e_{AgS} is the search efficiency in the aggregation service. However, in this case, rather than taking only into account the search performance, e_{AgS} must take also into account the AgS overlay set-up and maintenance performance, to which we collectively refer as overhead. Hence, $e_{AgS} = 1/(rt + ovhd)$, where rt is the response time and $ovhd$ is the overhead. This overhead results from the time spent by the AgS overlay in performing control operations. Each control operation, i.e. join (j), publish (h) and leave (l), takes a varying amount of time, which depends on the size of the exchanged messages and on the underlay bandwidth and latency. Thus, the objective of the AgS service is stated in equation (1).

$$(max|AgS|) \mid e_{AgS} \geq e_{SON} \tag{1}$$

4.2   Methodology

Fifteen hundred individual simulations were performed, involving a sample of thirty particular P2P SONs with different sizes, starting with 100 peers and going up to 3000 peers, at 100-peer steps.

Each particular SON executes, makes available and publishes its services, spreading them over 10 different domains. For the sake of simplicity, a particular SON peer can only publish, at most, seven services or service components, randomly chosen (using a uniform distribution) from the service set S={S1,S2,S3,S4,S5,S6,S7}. Each SON peer can only publish its service subset on, at most, 10 distinct, randomly chosen, aggregation peers (also following a uniform distribution). In the interests of simplification, the search concludes with the first match, though AgS has the ability to return all matches.

For each simulated P2P SON, four particular AgS overlays running on top of it were set up. Each one of these AgS overlays was composed of a percentage of the peers that form the P2P SON. These percentages were 10%, 50%, 80% and 90%.

Each execution simulated 50 hours of work. Each simulation performed 1,000 search operations, and they were repeated 10 times in order to get the averaged result. First, the P2P SON environment was simulated, executing the query operations. After that, each AgS overlay was simulated, over the previous simulated SON P2P, executing the same number of query operations. A configuration file with the query operations discrete-times was used to feed the simulations. Thus, the execution of the operations followed a pre-defined temporal sequence that was kept the same for all simulations.

In order to optimize the search process, caching of the search results was also taken into account. This means that when a Query Message found the desired information then a Query Reply Message containing that information was sent to the originating aggregation peer, which stored the information in its local cache. In a future query for the same service or service component started by aggregation peers located before the mentioned one in the ring, the search would then get fewer hops due to the cache hit, thus improving the search efficiency. The PeerFactSim.KOM [12] discrete events simulator was used in all simulations.

4.3   Results

The simulations primary result is the average response time (RT) of the search operations. When a search operation starts, the corresponding Query Message receives a time stamp (TS). Each peer along the search path forwards the Query Message in the case the service is absent from its local cache. When there is a cache hit, the time stamp of the Query Message is copied into the Query Reply Message. On reception of this message, the initiating peer can calculate the elapsed time. RT can then be calculated as the ratio between the accumulated time for all successfully accomplished search operations and the number of search messages, according to equation (3).

As already mentioned the AgS efficiency, which is expressed in (4), also depends on the overhead time. The overhead results from the time spent in setting up and maintaining the AgS overlay, by way of join (j), publish (p) and leave (l) control operations, according to equation (2).

$$ovhd = \sum_{m=1}^{n_j} time(j_m) + \sum_{m=1}^{n_p} time(p_m) + \sum_{m=1}^{n_l} time(l_m) \tag{2}$$

$$rt = \frac{\sum_{m=1}^{query\ msgs} (CurrentTime - TS_m)}{QueryReplyMessages} \tag{3}$$

$$e_{AgS} = \frac{1}{(rt + ovhd)} \tag{4}$$

Fig. 3 depicts the results concerning the response time and overhead for the simulated scenarios. It is worth mentioning the results rely on a confidence interval of 95%.

It is possible to notice that the AgS service is very efficient since, for the majority of results, AgSs whose size is up to 90% of the P2P SON size still lead to faster searches (even with overhead) than the plain P2P SON. Moreover, as one can see, the smaller the AgS overlay, the better. This can be explained by the high concentration of services in these relatively few peers, as is the case of AgSs with 10% of the P2P SON peers.

For some P2P SON and respective AgS sizes, a particular behavior can be observed. Especially in the cases of small P2P SONs (the ones whose size is smaller than 600 peers), one can observe that the search time (efficiency) of the AgS is worse than the search time for the P2P SON. All in all, the observation of this behavior in these conditions allows us to conclude that for small market niches, where service providers create small P2P SON, for the sake of searching, the AgS must not be greater than 80% of the P2P SON.

The influence of the overhead is stronger in the smaller P2P SON and respective AgSs. As services are equally heavily concentrated in the P2P SON

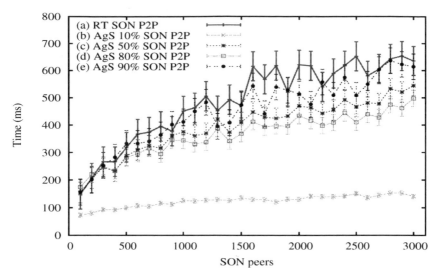

Fig. 3. AgS efficiency with overhead

and in the AgS overlay, the searches are fast. Thus, even a small AgS overhead has negative effects on the searching efficiency. The influence of the overhead can be seen in more detail in Fig. 4.

Fig. 4.(b) shows that even when 90% of the SON peers are part of the AgS overlay, AgS not only searches faster than P2P SON but also the entire e_{AgS} (i.e., search plus overhead) is greater than the e_{SON}. On the other hand, Fig. 4.(a) shows situations for which $e_{AgS} < e_{SON}$. These cases highlight that, for AgS sizes starting at 80% (as a matter of fact, with less than 80%) of the P2P SON size, the overhead is responsible for degrading the AgS efficiency. Nevertheless, it is worth mentioning that when the overhead is dismissed, e_{AgS} is always greater than e_{SON}.

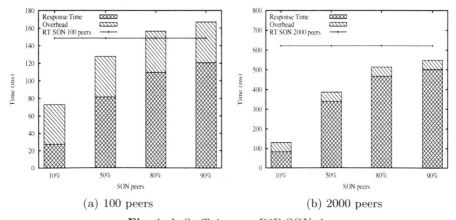

(a) 100 peers   (b) 2000 peers

Fig. 4. AgS efficiency x P2P SON size

Finally, Fig. 5 shows the histogram for the arithmetic mean values for all experiments. The average response time in the P2P SON is approximately 487 ms whereas for the AgS service it is approximately 77, 270, 403 and 448 ms for AgS sizes of 10%, 50%, 80% and 90% of the P2P SON size, respectively. The overhead is quite similar for all AgS sizes, with a value close to 47 ms.

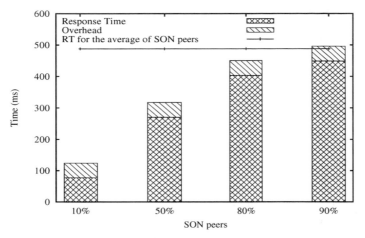

Fig. 5. Average AgS efficiency x P2P SON size

Looking at Fig. 5 it is possible to conclude that the AgS service can lead to very good performance gains relative to the plain P2P SON approach. In addition, the average overhead remains stable even with the increase in the number of aggregation peers. All in all, according the obtained results it is possible to claim that the AgS approach is highly beneficial and gives service providers ample freedom to decide on the number of 2nd-level peers without jeopardizing the performance gain.

5   Conclusions

The Aggregation Service under evaluation in this paper aims at improving the service search efficiency in large-scale, multi-provider peer-to-peer service overlay networks. When the number of peer increases, search operations can be performed more efficiently if a second-tier overlay is established, comprising special peers that maintain information of the various services available in and published by the peers belonging to the first tier.

Specifically, this paper addressed the issue of determining the relation between the number of peers in the Aggregation Service and the efficiency of service search operations. The results, obtained by simulation, clearly show that the proposed service has very good potential to improve the overall search performance when compared to the realization of search operations in a single-tier P2P overlay, at the cost of a very small overhead. The obtained results can easily be used by cooperating ISPs in order to dimension the Aggregation Service overlay.

Further work will address optimization of search operations, data consistency assurance, and robustness of the aggregation overlay.

References

1. Auer, L., Strauss, C., Kryvinska, N., Zinterhof, P.: SOA as an effective tool for the flexible management of increased service heterogeneity in converged enterprise networks. In: Proceedings of the 2008 International Conference on Complex, Intelligent and Software Intensive Systems, pp. 535–539 (2008)
2. Banaei-Kashani, F., Chien Chen, C., Shahabi, C.: WSPDS: web services peer-to-peer discovery service. In: Proceedings of the International Conference on Internet Computing, pp. 733–743 (2004)
3. Bianchini, D., Antonellis, V.D., Melchiori, M.: Service-based semantic search in P2P systems. In: European Conference on Web Services, pp. 7–16 (2009)
4. Brocco, A., Malatras, A., Hirsbrunner, B.: Proactive information caching for efficient resource discovery in a self-structured grid. In: Proceedings of the 2009 Workshop on Bio-Inspired Algorithms for Distributed Systems, pp. 11–18 (2009)
5. Brown, A., Kolberg, M., Buford, J.: Chameleon: an adaptable 2-tier variable hop overlay. In: Proceedings of the 6th IEEE Conference on Consumer Communications and Networking Conference, pp. 770–775 (2009)
6. Clarke, I., Sandberg, O., Wiley, B., Hong, T.: Freenet: A distributed anonymous information storage and retrieval system. In: Federrath, H. (ed.) Designing Privacy Enhancing Technologies. LNCS, vol. 2009, pp. 46–66. Springer, Heidelberg (2001)
7. Dong, X., Halevy, A., Madhavan, J., Nemes, E., Zhang, J.: Similarity search for web services. In: Proceedings of the Thirtieth International Conference on Very Large Data Bases, vol. 30, pp. 372–383 (2004)
8. Duan, Z., Zhang, Z., Hou, Y.T.: Service overlay networks: SLAs, QoS, and bandwidth provisioning. IEEE/ACM Trans. Netw. 11(6), 870–883 (2003)
9. Dustdar, S., Schreiner, W.: A survey on web services composition. International Journal of Web and Grid Services, 1–30 (2005)
10. Fiorese, A., Simões, P., Boavida, F.: An aggregation scheme for the optimisation of service search in Peer-to-Peer overlays. In: Proceedings of the 6th International Conference on Network and Services Management (CNSM 2010), pp. 481–486 (2010)
11. Fiorese, A., Simões, P., Boavida, F.: Service searching based on P2P aggregation. In: The 24th International Conference on Information Networking, ICOIN 2010 (2010)
12. Kovacevic, A., Kaune, S., Liebau, N., Steinmetz, R., Mukherjee, P.: Benchmarking platform for peer-to-peer systems. it - Information Technology 49(5), 312–319 (2007)
13. Lavinal, E., Simoni, N., Song, M., Mathieu, B.: A next-generation service overlay architecture. Annals of Telecommunications 64(3), 175–185 (2009)
14. Lua, K., Crowcroft, J., Pias, M., Sharma, R., Lim, S.: A survey and comparison of peer-to-peer overlay network schemes. IEEE Communications Surveys & Tutorials 7(2), 72–93 (2005)
15. Lymberopoulos, L., Lupu, E., Sloman, M.: An adaptive police-based framework for network services management. Journal of Network and Systems Management 11(3), 277–303 (2003)

16. Meshkova, E., Riihijärvi, J., Petrova, M., Mähönen, P.: A survey on resource discovery mechanisms, peer-to-peer and service discovery frameworks. Computer Networks 52(11), 2097–2128 (2008)
17. Michel, S., Bender, M., Ntarmos, N., Triantafillou, P., Weikum, G., Zimmer, C.: Discovering and exploiting keyword and attribute-value co-occurrences to improve P2P routing indices. In: Proceedings of the 15th ACM International Conference on Information and Knowledge Management, pp. 172–181 (2006)
18. Ratnasamy, S., Francis, P., Shenker, S., Karp, R., Handley, M.: A scalable Content-Addressable network. In: Proceedings Of ACM SIGCOMM, pp. 161–172 (2001)
19. Ripeanu, M., Iamnitchi, A., Foster, I.: Mapping the gnutella network. IEEE Internet Computing 6(1), 50–57 (2002)
20. Shen, H.: A P2P-based intelligent resource discovery mechanism in internet-based distributed systems. Journal of Parallel and Distributed Computing 69(2), 197–209 (2009)
21. Stoica, I., Morris, R., Liben-Nowell, D., Karger, D.R., Kaashoek, M.F., Dabek, F., Balakrishnan, H.: Chord: a scalable peer-to-peer lookup protocol for internet applications. IEEE/ACM Transactions on Networking 11(1), 17–32 (2003)
22. Tran, C., Dziong, Z.: Service overlay network capacity adaptation for profit maximization. IEEE Transactions on Network and Service Management 7(2), 72–82 (2010)
23. Trunfio, P., Talia, D., Papadakis, H., Fragopoulou, P., Mordacchini, M., Pennanen, M., Popov, K., Vlassov, V., Haridi, S.: Peer-to-Peer resource discovery in grids: Models and systems. Future Gener. Comput. Syst. 23(7), 864–878 (2007)
24. Vianna, R.L., Almeida, M.J.B., Tarouco, L.M.R., Granville, L.Z.: Investigating web services composition applied to network management. In: Proceedings of IEEE International Conference on Web Services, pp. 531–540 (2006)
25. Zhou, S., Hogan, M., Ardon, S., Portman, M., Hu, T., Wongrujira, K., Seneviratne, A.: ALASA: when service overlay networks meet Peer-to-Peer networks. In: Asia-Pacific Conference on Communications, 2005, pp. 1053–1057 (2005)

Impact of Dynamics on Situated and Global Aggregation Schemes

Rafik Makhloufi[1], Guillaume Doyen[1], Grégory Bonnet[2], and Dominique Gaïti[1]

[1] ICD/ERA, UMR 6279. Université de Technologie de Troyes
[2] GREYC/MAD, UMR 6072. Université de Caen Basse-Normandie

Abstract. Recently, numerous management approaches have emerged in order to manage networks and services in a decentralized and autonomous way. Some of them propose to minimize their cost by using a situated view when collecting aggregates for the decision making process, while others propose to improve their accuracy by using a more conventional approach which is global view. So far, little attention is given to the evaluation of situated view while many studies propose to evaluate global approaches. As a consequence, there is no work in the literature that compares the performance of situated and global aggregation schemes. Being able to choose the suitable approach for a given context is still a real challenge. Mastering it will ensure the efficiency of the autonomous management system. In this paper, we present a comparative study of situated and global schemes deployed over large scale and dynamic networks. We consider two factors: network and information dynamics. We implement typical aggregation schemes from each category and then we compare them according to the accuracy of the estimated aggregates and the efficiency of the decision making process.

Keywords: Autonomic Networking, Decentralized Aggregation, Situated View, Management Information.

1 Introduction

In the context of autonomous network management which is one of the most relevant class of management approches, the decentralized Autonomic Managers (AMs) are based on the control loop functions Monitor, Analyze, Plan, Execute (MAPE) [8]. Information used in the monitoring can come from both the local managed element itself or be the result of an aggregation of environmental informations provided by remote AMs. Two concurrent strategies are commonly deployed for this purpose. On one hand, it can be the result of a process involving all nodes in the network, thus providing a global view (GV), standard supporting algorithms that rely on tree and gossip schemes. These global schemes are expected to provide a good accuracy at the cost of a larger convergence time and overhead. On the other hand, the monitoring process can only consider a limited neighborhood, thus providing a situated view (SV). Approaches based on SV are expected to minimize their cost and to provide a high reactivity to AMs with a low accuracy.

I. Chrisment et al. (Eds.): AIMS 2011, LNCS 6734, pp. 148–159, 2011.

To date, there is no evaluation in the literature that compares the cost and the performance of situated and global aggregation schemes since the former have appeared recently. Thus, we do not know the exact behavior and the performance of these schemes while it is essential to precisely identify the appropriate context in which each of the aggregation categories performs better to design and deploy efficient autonomous management frameworks.

In this paper, we provide a comparative performance analysis of situated and global aggregation schemes. Since results coming from the use of such schemes in a static context are given by the protocols complexity, we focus our work on the resilience of such schemes to both the network and aggregated information dynamics. To this end, we implement three typical aggregation schemes, one situated view based and two global view based, i.e., gossip and tree. Then, we compare them according to two important performance criteria related to autonomous monitoring and control which are respectively the accuracy of the estimated aggregates and the efficiency of the decision making process.

The remainder of the paper is organized as follows. Section 2 presents the related work on the evaluation of aggregation schemes. Section 3 describes the aggregation schemes that we implement from each category. In section 4, we propose an evaluation of the developed schemes. Finally, in Section 5 we conclude and we present our working perspectives.

2   Related Work

Several research efforts propose to compare the performance of global aggregation schemes. The closest works to ours are given below.

In [1], the authors propose a set of aggregation schemes for estimating aggregates on a P2P network. They compare one gossip-based scheme Propagate2All to two other tree-based schemes: SingleTree and MultipleTree. This comparison shows that tree schemes outperform gossip ones in terms of convergence time, communication and computation costs, but they are less resilient to faults under a dynamic network. However, this study does not discuss the situated schemes.

A second work [17] proposes a comparison between GAP (Generic Aggregation Protocol), a basic tree-based aggregation protocol and G-GAP (Gossip-based GAP), a gossip-based protocol for continuous monitoring of aggregates. Surprisingly, in opposition to the first study, this evaluation shows that, for comparative overhead, the tree-based scheme GAP outperforms the gossip protocol G-GAP both in terms of accuracy and robustness even under a dynamic network.

Another study of the performance of aggregation schemes [2] discusses the strengths and limitations of gossiping. According to this characterization, gossip schemes present simplicity, bounded load on nodes, topology independence, ease of local information discovery and finally robustness to transient network disruptions. But, the small bounded message sizes and the relatively slow periodic exchanges limit the information carrying capacity of a gossip algorithm. Furthermore, gossip scales well in some dimensions but not for all. A node failure can also delay or even defeat the aggregation. This study provides only a qualitative analysis of the gossip's limitations and strengths without giving any quantitative result.

We recently proposed in [14] an evaluation study of typical global and situated aggregation schemes that we implemented in the context of a static environment. This work offers quantitative results on the costs and the performance of aggregation. However, this study does not compare these schemes in the context of a dynamic environment.

Globally, these studies address the global aggregation schemes but never compare them to the situated ones while the latter is massively used in autonomous management frameworks. Thus, we do not know the exact behavior and the performance of the situated schemes in comparison to the global ones. Situated schemes are expected to provide a high reactivity to AMs by minimizing the amount of maintained information by each AM. As for global schemes, they are expected to provide a good accuracy at the cost of a larger convergence time. Through this, we clearly observe that it is essential to precisely identify the appropriate context in which each category performs better in order to be able to design efficient management frameworks.

3   Developed Aggregation Schemes

In order to show under which conditions an aggregation approach outperforms the others, we implement and compare state of the art typical schemes that can be used for the computation of any aggregate function. In this section, we give a brief overview of them. The notations used in these algorithms are summarized in Figure 1.a.

3.1   Global View

In global aggregation schemes, each node collects information from the entire network. According to the global data structure, these schemes are either tree or gossip-based.

Tree. We implemented a simple push tree-based aggregation scheme that uses the typical aggregation process of GAP under the DHT-based deployment topology proposed in [13]. The latter is a structured P2P overlay where nodes communicate their local aggregates to a single root node that computes an overall aggregate and spreads it on all the interested nodes through a publish-subscribe mechanism. As shown in Algorithm 1, which describes the developed tree-based scheme, one active and one passive threads are executed on each node. The first one initiates the aggregation process by sending the value of each node to its parent. The second one waits for messages sent by an initiator to process them. Initially, each node i selects its parent p with the help of the getParent() method and sends it a couple $< X_i, 1 >$ on the form $< aggregate, weight >$ as given in lines a.1 and a.2. A node i that receives a message from a child node j computes a new partial aggregate according to a given aggregate function, updates its local state with the new values and then forwards them to its parent p as shown in lines b.2 to b.5. If node i is the root then it waits until it receives all its children's aggregates and it diffuses the computed global aggregate X_i over a publish-subscribe system on all the interested nodes as given in lines b.6 to b.9. Thus, each node that receives X_i from the root updates its partial aggregate with the global one as shown in lines a.3 and a.4.

Algorithm 1. Push tree-based algorithm executed on a node i

(a) Active thread	(b) Passive thread
1: $p \leftarrow$ getParent()	1: **loop**
2: send $(< X_i, 1 >, p)$	2: receive $(< X_j, w_j >, j)$
3: receive(X_j, j)	3: $state_i \leftarrow$ update(X_j, w_j)
4: $state_i \leftarrow$ update(X_j)	4: $p \leftarrow$ getParent()
	5: send $(< X_i, w_i >, p)$
	6: **if** (getParent()=null) **then**
	7: wait until receive all aggregates
	8: diffuse (X_i)
	9: **end if**
	10: **end loop**

Gossip. Unlike tree-based techniques where nodes are organized into a tree, gossip-based schemes do not require a particular structure to perform aggregation. In each round of a gossip, a node contacts one or more of its neighbors usually chosen randomly and exchanges information with them [2,5,7]. Initially, each node in the network has only its own raw management information. When messages are exchanged, nodes compute new partial aggregate and then decrease the variance over the set of all aggregates in the system. The gossip aggregation algorithm converges when the global aggregate is computed and available across all the network nodes.

In this category, we implemented a push-pull gossip scheme based on a typical gossip scheme [6]. As illustrated in Algorithm 2, with the help of the getNeighbors(1) method that selects uniformly at random one node j from a list of direct neighbors $\mathbb{D}_i$, each node i sends to j a message containing its partial aggregate X_i and waits for a response as shown in lines a.2 and a.3. When i receives a response (X_j, j) from j, it updates its local state through the update() method that computes a new partial aggregate according to the selected aggregate function as given in lines a.4 and a.5. The node i waits for a certain time and repeats the same process (line a.6). Similarly, when the passive thread of a node i receives an exchange request message, it replies with its local aggregate X_i and then it updates its local state as shown in lines b.2 to b.4.

Algorithm 2. Push-pull gossip-based algorithm executed on a node i

(a) Active thread	(b) Passive thread
1: **loop**	1: **loop**
2: $j \leftarrow$ getNeighbors(1)	2: receive(X_j, j)
3: send (X_i, j)	3: send (X_i, j)
4: receive(X_j, j)	4: $state_i \leftarrow$ update(X_j)
5: $state_i \leftarrow$ update(X_j)	5: **end loop**
6: wait(round duration)	
7: **end loop**	

3.2 Situated View

In opposition to the global schemes where global aggregates are computed over the entire network, situated view approaches like [9,12,3] propose to reduce the costs of aggregation by limiting the knowledge of a node to a bounded neighborhood. Thus, apart its own local information each node collects data from its direct neighbors or a subset of the network nodes to compute a partial aggregate representing its view.

In this category, we implemented a typical situated scheme inspired from the membership protocol HyParView (Hyper Partial View) [9] where each node maintains two views. In our implementation, each node executes Algorithm 3 to collect information from its view and then to compute a partial aggregate. As shown in Algorithm 3, each node i sends a query message containing the maximum number of hops h to all its direct neighbors obtained through the getNeighbors(all) method as given in lines a.1 and a.2. A node i that receives a request from j verifies if it does not previously answer to the same request (line b.2). If so, i answers by sending a response (X_{raw_i}, j) directly to the requesting node j (line b.3). The node i decrements the value h and tests if the maximum number of hops is not reached and then forwards the received request to all its direct neighbors as given is lines b.4 to b.8. When a requesting node i receives an answer (X_{raw_j}, j) from a neighbor j, it computes a new partial aggregate and updates its own state as shown in lines a.3 and a.4.

Algorithm 3. Pull situated view algorithm executed on a node i

(a) Active thread	(b) Passive thread
1: $\mathbb{D}_i \leftarrow$ getNeighbors(all)	1: **loop**
2: send ($h, \mathbb{D}_i$)	2: receive(h, j)
3: receive(X_{raw_j}, j)	3: send (X_{raw_i}, j)
4: $state_i \leftarrow$ update(X_{raw_j})	4: $h \leftarrow h - 1$
	5: **if** ($h > 0$) **then**
	6: $\mathbb{D}_i \leftarrow$ getNeighbors(all)-{j}
	7: send($h, \mathbb{D}_i$)
	8: **end if**
	9: **end loop**

4   Evaluation Study

In this section, we present the evaluation study that we carried out to compare the performance of the previously described aggregation schemes in terms of the accuracy of the estimated aggregated and the efficiency of the decision making process in a dynamic environment.

4.1   Dynamics Factors

We identify two important factors that can affect the performance of an aggregation process: network and information dynamics. For this, we propose to use the following models.

Network dynamics. The network dynamics, or churn, consists in the nodes arrivals in the system and their departures that can be planned or due to a sudden failure. Based on the analysis of the traces on different systems like mobile ad-hoc networks (MANETs) and P2P ones, many prior studies assumed a Poisson process of parameter λ for the node arrivals and an exponential distribution of parameter μ for the departures [10,11,15]. Thus, we adopt the same models in our experiments and we choose the values of arrival and departure rates so that they accurately represent existing networks. The values of λ and μ are chosen so that the average number of nodes, given by $N=\lambda/\mu$, will always be equal to 500. Thus, in our study λ varies in [0.0041;0.4166] and μ is ranging in [8.33×10^{-6};8.33×10^{-4}], corresponding respectively to average inter-arrivals $(1/\lambda)$ ranging in [2.4;240] seconds and to average lifetime durations $(1/\mu)$ in the range [20;2000] minutes.

Information dynamics. It determines the evolution degree of a management information over the time. It can be characterized through two criteria: (1) the changing frequency of the values on managed elements, for example a value X_{rawi} that changes every 1sec; (2) the changing degree of these values that is defined by the distance between two consecutive values. We generate realistic local values according to a triangular signal that could stand for a gauge associated, for example, to the quantity of traffic in a network. Thus, X_{rawi} is periodically incremented by α until reaching 100 and it is then decremented by the same α until 0. This allows us to control the information dynamics level. The local values are ranging in [0;100] for an α that we vary in [0.02;5].

4.2   Simulation Setup and Evaluation Scenarios

In order to evaluate the performance of the investigated aggregation schemes under realistic conditions, we carry out our experiments on the FreePastry simulator, an implementation of the Pastry DHT [16]. All simulations are done under the Euclidean network topology model, where nodes are randomly placed within a 2-dimensional plane in a uniform way. Concerning the tree-based scheme, we also rely on Scribe [4] to build and maintain a multicast tree that allows the diffusion of the root's global aggregates on all nodes that subscribed to the same diffusion group concerning the monitored variable.

Based on the realistic parameters summarized in Figure 1.b, we create a network where each node executes the previously described aggregation schemes to compute an average aggregate of the local values on nodes. We execute the situated scheme with a view limited to the direct neighbors (SV1) and also with a neighborhood limited to 2 hops (SV2). The gossip process is executed with rounds of duration 600ms that corresponds to the maximum time for to exchange and process an information between two nodes. The neighborhood degree in each scheme is limited to 8 neighbors per node. It is on the form 2×2^b of Pastry where b=2. The maintenance frequency of this neighborhood is fixed to 60 seconds like the one used by FreePastry to maintain the leaf sets. Concerning the local raw values, we assume that each 1sec a new value is generated on each node. In all our simulations, a 95% confidence interval is computed for each average value represented in the curves. These intervals are plotted as error bars.

Symbol	Signification
X_i	local aggregate of node i
X_{raw_i}	raw (non-aggregated) value of node i
w_i	weight of X_i
$state_i$	local state on i
h	number of hops
$\mathbb{D}_i$	set of direct neighbors of node i

(a)

	Parameter	Value
Constants	Aggregate function	Average
	Network topology model	Euclidean
	Topology maintenance	60sec
	Neighborhood degree	8
	Max. number of nodes	1000
	Value changing freq.	1sec
	Decision making freq.	30sec
	Gossip round duration	600ms
Variables	Node arrivals	$\lambda \in [0.0041; 0.41]$
	Lifetime durations	$\mu \in [8.33 \times 10^{-6}; 8.33 \times 10^{-4}]$
	α	$[0.02; 5]$
	Number of hops in SV	$h \in [1; 2]$

(b)

Fig. 1. Notations (a) and simulation parameters (b)

4.3   Evaluation Results

We propose here to compare the developed aggregation schemes according to their costs and according to two other important criteria, the accuracy of estimated aggregates and the efficiency of the decision making process.

Cost of situated and global schemes. Considering the cost of the aggregation schemes in a static context allows us to have a first idea on their expected performance in a realistic dynamic environnement. To this end, we compare the previously described schemes in the context of a static environment according to convergence time and communication cost. We notice in Figure 2.a that the convergence time is proportional to the number of nodes in the network. Under a network of 1000 nodes, gossip's convergence time is about 6 times higher than the one of the tree and about 23 times the one of SV2. This high delay is caused by the blind communication used to exchange messages at each round of gossip. As expected, the situated scheme, with a comparable delay between SV1 and SV2, is more scalable and converges more quickly than the global ones, because in a situated view only partial aggregates are computed by nodes. However, we see in Figure 2.b that SV2 involves more messages than the global schemes because it is based on a broadcast algorithm where each node floods its request message on all its h-hops neighbors. Numerically, under a network of 1000 nodes, the communication cost of SV2 is almost 3 times higher than the one obtained in the case of gossip and about 42 times the one of the tree. The tree causes the lowest communication cost, which corresponds to the messages sent in a bottom-up fashion to the root and those used by Scribe to spread the global aggregate.

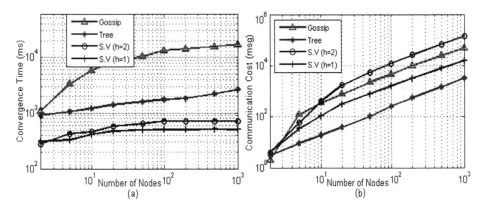

Fig. 2. Cost of SV and GV: (a) Convergence time; (b) Communication cost

Accuracy of estimated aggregates. We define it as the precision level of the aggregation scheme when computing global or situated aggregates. In order to evaluate the impact of network and information dynamics on this criterion, we look at the distribution of estimates over all the network nodes and we measure the distance between estimated aggregates and the actual global aggregate that should be computed. Thus, we show how far these estimates lie from the real average value by computing the average deviation $D_X = \frac{1}{N} \sum_{i=1}^{N} |X_i - X|$.

By varying the information dynamics level within a static network of 1000 nodes, we obtained the results shown in Figure 3.a. We see that, with a deviation that reaches 2 when $\alpha=5$, tree is about 5 times more accurate than SV1, about 3 times more than SV2 and almost twice more than gossip. Thus, it is the most accurate scheme under dynamic information. The situated scheme is less accurate than the global ones. This is caused by the computation of partial aggregates. Indeed, the deviation never reaches 0 like in the case of global schemes even under a static network and information. As predicted in [2], gossip is more sensitive to the information dynamics than the tree. But we do not clearly see here the evolution of the accuracy in function of the information dynamics level.

When we consider random fixed values on nodes (i.e. $\alpha=0$) and we vary the network churn level, we obtain the deviation measures illustrated in Figure 3.b.

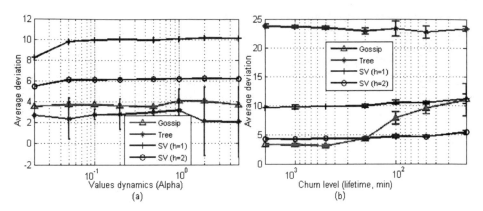

Fig. 3. Accuracy of estimated aggregates: (a) Information dynamics; (b) Churn level

We notice that in the case of the tree-based scheme, the network dynamics dramatically affects the accuracy of estimated aggregates with a deviation that reaches 24. This sensibility is caused by the departures and arrivals of nodes causing the continuously maintenance and reconstruction of the tree, whatever the churn level. The situated scheme is more resilient to churn than gossip and tree since we register the same deviation for it in the case of static and dynamics environments. Thus, SV2 is about 4 times more accurate than the tree and about twice more than SV1. This is explained by the fact that, in the situated scheme, a departure or an arrival of a node does not necessarily affect other nodes if it is not in their view. For the gossip, the deviation is proportional to the churn level because it is a community process where nodes are dependent upon the correct behavior of all other nodes. However, it is still the most accurate scheme under a low churn level where the average lifetime and inter-arrival are respectively higher than 200min and 24sec. In the other interval, SV2 is the most accurate.

Efficiency of the decision making process. In order to evaluate the efficiency of the decision making mechanism when using each of the implemented aggregation schemes, we implemented a simple threshold-based decision mechanism standing for a realistic case of control operations where each node makes decisions according to its last computed aggregate. The local values of managed elements are periodically retrieved by the AM to be used by the aggregation process (AP) and then by the decision process (DMP), as shown in Figure 4. According to Algorithm 4, each node i consults its local aggregate and makes a decision according to the defined threshold 50 (lines 2 to 7). Node i waits a certain time before renewing the same operation (line 8).

At the end of the aggregation process, we compare the resulting decisions on each node to the one that should be made in the case where we use the current actual global aggregate. Thus, we count the number of decentralized decisions that do not match with the actual one (i.e. the number of faulty decisions).

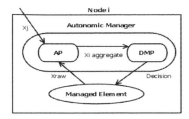

Algorithm 4. Decision making algorithm

```
1: loop
2:     if X_i >50 then
3:         decision←d1
4:     else
5:         decision←d2
6:     end if
7:     applyDecision(Decision)
8:     wait(round_duration)
9: end loop
```

Fig. 4. Decision making process

Under the same test conditions as in the evaluation of the aggregation accuracy, we obtain the results presented in Figure 5.

We observe in figure 5.a that the number of faulty decisions increases according to the information dynamics level. The information dynamics affects the aggregation process and then the decision making one. One can note that for all the aggregation schemes, the number of faulty decisions is ranging in [5;12]% when α=0.02, but when α=1 or 2 the number of faulty decisions reaches the interval [45;50]% where the decision making process is unable to take the right decisions. Globally, this error percentage is larger in the situated view while gossip offers the best quality of the decision making. Under churn, Figure 5.b shows that, in the case of gossip and SV2, the number of faulty decisions is comparable and lower than the one registered when using a tree or SV1. Moreover, it is proportional to the churn level. We also observe that churn hugely affects the quality of the decision making process on the tree where the average number of faulty decisions is about 45%. Thus, it is more relevant to use gossip or SV2 on a dynamic network.

To conclude, as expected, the situated view provides a higher reactivity to AMs than the global ones at the cost of a higher communication. SV1's convergence time is about 5 times lower than the one of tree and 33 times lower than

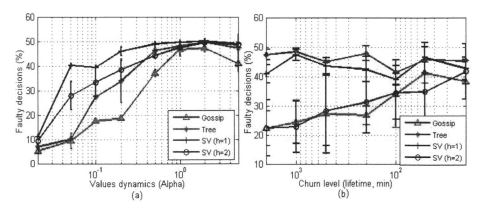

Fig. 5. Efficiency of the decision making: (a) Information dynamics; (b) Churn level

the one of gossip. Concerning the communication cost, the one of SV2 can be almost 3 times higher than the one obtained in the case of gossip and about 42 times the one of tree. As for the global schemes, under dynamic information, they offer more accuracy in the computation of aggregates and in the decision making. With a deviation that reaches 2 when $\alpha=5$, the tree-based scheme provides the best accuracy. It is about 5 times more accurate than SV1, about 3 times more than SV2 and almost twice more than gossip. Concerning the efficiency of the decision making, gossip provides the best performance. For all the aggregation schemes, the number of faulty decisions is ranging in $[5;12]\%$ when $\alpha=0.02$, but when $\alpha=1$ or 2 the number of faulty decisions reaches the interval $[45;50]\%$. In the presence of an acceptable churn, gossip performs better than the other schemes in terms of the aggregation accuracy and the efficiency of the decision making mechanism, followed by the situated view and then the tree. When the average lifetime and inter-arrival are respectively higher than 200min and 24sec, gossip is about 4 times more accurate than the tree and about twice more than SV1, with a comparable accuracy with SV2. However, when the average lifetime and inter-arrival are respectively lower than 200min and 24sec, gossip has a comparable accuracy with the one of SV1, and SV2 becomes the most accurate scheme. Thus, SV2 has a comparable performance of the decision making mechanism to the one of gossip. As for tree, it is dramatically affected by churn since the average number of faulty decisions is about 45%.

5   Conclusion and Future Work

In the context of autonomous network management, two concurrent approaches are commonly used to achieve the aggregation of management information which are situated and global views. However, we do not know the exact behavior and the performance of these different schemes. Moreover, it is crucial to precisely identify the appropriate context in which each of the aggregation categories performs better. To this end, we provide in this paper a comparative performance analysis of typical situated and global aggregation schemes. This work represents a first step in the evaluation of aggregation schemes. In an effort to enhance it, we are looking for ways to consolidate the obtained results by considering additional impacting parameters (e.g. the changing frequency of local values or various neighborhood degrees). On a long term, we will pursue this work by designing an adaptive system that combines the use of situated and global aggregation schemes. Such an autonomous management system would adapt itself to the supporting network operational behavior, bringing it self-optimization capabilities. A decentralized process will continuously analyze its environment to discover the current context of the management information and its environment and then selects the appropriate aggregation scheme that gives the best performance, in order to build efficient autonomous management frameworks.

References

1. Bawa, M., Garcia-Molina, H., Gionis, A., Motwani, R.: Estimating aggregates on a Peer-to-Peer network. Tech. rep. (2003)
2. Birman, K.: The promise, and limitations, of gossip protocols. SIGOPS Oper. Syst. Rev. 41(5), 8–13 (2007)
3. Bullot, T., Khatoun, R., Hugues, L., Gaïti, D., Merghem-Boulahia, L.: A situatedness-based knowledge plane for autonomic networking. Int. J. Netw. Manag. 18(2), 171–193 (2008)
4. Castro, M., Druschel, P., Kermarrec, A.-M., Rowstron, A.: Scribe: a large-scale and decentralized application-level multicast infrastructure. JSAC 20(8), 1489–1499 (2002)
5. Dietzfelbinger, M.: Gossiping and broadcasting versus computing functions in networks. IWACOIN 137(2), 127–153 (2004)
6. Jelasity, M., Montresor, A., Babaoglu, O.: Gossip-based aggregation in large dynamic networks. TOCS 23(3), 219–252 (2005)
7. Kempe, D., Dobra, A., and Gehrke, J. Gossip-based computation of aggregate information. In: FOCS (2003)
8. Kephart, J.O., Chess, D.M.: The Vision of Autonomic Computing. Computer 36(1), 41–50 (2003)
9. Leitao, J., Pereira, J., Rodrigues, L.: Large-Scale Peer-to-Peer Autonomic Monitoring. In: DANMS, pp. 1–5 (2008)
10. Leonard, D., Rai, V., Loguinov, D.: On lifetime-based node failure and stochastic resilience of decentralized peer-to-peer networks. SIGMETRICS 33, 26–37 (2005)
11. Li, J., Stribling, J., Morris, R., Kaashoek, M.F., Gil, T.M.: A performance vs. cost framework for evaluating DHT design tradeoffs under churn. In: INFOCOM, pp. 225–236 (2005)
12. Macedo, D.F., dos Santos, A.L., Pujolle, G., Nogueira, J.M.S.: MANKOP: A Knowledge Plane for wireless ad hoc networks. In: NOMS, pp. 706–709 (2008)
13. Makhloufi, R., Bonnet, G., Doyen, G., Gaïti, D.: Towards a P2P-based Deployment of Network Management Information. In: Stiller, B., De Turck, F. (eds.) AIMS 2010. LNCS, vol. 6155, pp. 26–37. Springer, Heidelberg (2010)
14. Makhloufi, R., Doyen, G., Bonnet, G., Gaïti, D.: Situated vs. global aggregation schemes for autonomous management systems. In: DANMS (2011)
15. Rhea, S., Geels, D., Roscoe, T., Kubiatowicz, J.: Handling churn in a dht. In: ATC, pp. 112–140 (2004)
16. Rowstron, A.I.T., Druschel, P.: Pastry: Scalable, Decentralized Object Location, and Routing for Large-Scale Peer-to-Peer Systems. In: Liu, H. (ed.) Middleware 2001. LNCS, vol. 2218, pp. 329–350. Springer, Heidelberg (2001)
17. Wuhib, F., Dam, M., Stadler, R., Clem, A.: Robust monitoring of network-wide aggregates through gossiping. TNSM 6(2), 95–109 (2009)

Towards Self-Adaptive Monitoring Framework for Integrated Management

Audrey Moui and Thierry Desprats

IRIT, Université Paul Sabatier
118 route de Narbonne, 31062 Toulouse cedex 9, France

Abstract. Integrated management copes with management of heterogeneous and complex systems in a multi-level dimension (network, systems, services). In this context, monitoring activity has to be concerned with efficiency and autonomy. This paper presents work in progress to define a framework for self-adaptive monitoring relying on the characterization of governability, adaptability and configurability.

1 Motivation

The multi-level dimension of integrated management (network, systems, services), the dependence between heterogeneous components and the affluence of management information make the management activity more and more difficult to perform. Currently, management is performed with the help of the classical MAPE loop [2]: the managed system is observed (M) and an analysis (A) is made to detect failures or every particular or relevant situations. If there are any, a technical decision is planned (P) and executed (E) on the system to improve its efficiency. The monitoring activity is a central point in integrated management. Indeed, monitoring aims at collecting from the various system components a set of relevant data: thus, its state and its behaviour can be known. Moreover, the monitoring activity makes it possible to detect all the perturbations occurring on the whole system or on one of its part. The monitoring can also have different purposes, like management optimization, protection, control, accounting or even maintenance.

But what are the requirements to be positioned on the collected data? Is it necessary to monitor everything, all the time, from all the components of the system? What is the importance of the **volume** of data to be stored and processed? How is it possible to select which data are useful, **relevant**, to be monitored? Have some quality criteria like accuracy, freshness, correctness to be taken into account or is it possible to collect data with a certain degree of **uncertainty**? May suitable or efficient decisions be taken with an important part of fuzzy or imprecise knowledge on the managed composite system state? Is the monitoring activity able to consider integrations and scalability of the managed domain? Mechanisms like event correlation, filtering and log can help dealing with the collected data: are they used by the current monitoring activity in the most efficient way?

I. Chrisment et al. (Eds.): AIMS 2011, LNCS 6734, pp. 160–163, 2011.

Finally, other contraints have also to be taken into account: system needs to be monitored at runtime, and the availability and the capacity of the technological ressources which support the execution of monitoring can constitute a restriction (storage, energy level, CPU load, bandwidth, etc).

So, we need to think about how improving the adaptiveness level of monitoring activities. Monitoring is required to become more flexible to autonomously tackle, in a relevant and efficient way, the variation of both "business" requirements and environmental constraints.

Numerous works already contributed to make the monitoring activity adaptable (e.g. [1] is not generic enough to be used in every management context – this one is based on SNMP –; RAP [4] is only concerned with polling adaptability; Ganglia [3] provides the ability to reconfigure the monitoring mechanisms according to the network context – but only for small networks). Note also that all these approaches only focused on network management, not on integrated management.

2   An Analysis to Deal with the Adaptability

Self-adaptive monitoring implies a self-governed and automatic behaviour adaptation of monitoring activity. The monitoring activity is a process which is based on the use, possibly combined, of polling and event reporting mechanisms.

The underlying mechanisms, and the way they are operated, must consider the high level business objectives. They have to provide relevant inputs for the analysis activity (why do we monitor?). Determining the nature of these mechanisms (how?), the managed elements they concern (what?) and the temporal mode by which they operate (when?) constitutes what we defined as a "monitoring strategy".

Our approach aims at creating a framework which would be able to support automatically the adaptation of the monitoring activity. An adaptation will result in a monitoring strategy change, and consequently will modify the monitoring activity behaviour. Automating monitoring adaptation requires to manage and control the monitoring activity. It becomes necessary to introduce a second management loop to control the monitoring. As shown in Figure 1, for

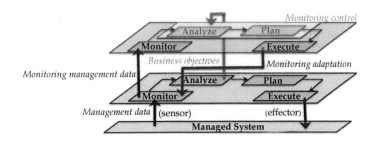

Fig. 1. The Adaptive Monitoring Framework

this loop, the managed system is the monitoring activity itself. We identified the three following levels of capabilities to be managed in order to perform on line monitoring adaptation:

1. The ability to detect a need of monitoring adaptation (*Governability*): this is the role of the "Monitoring control" plan (in purple) to decide if and how the monitoring activity has to be adjusted.
2. The ability to execute (in red) the monitoring adaptation (*Adaptability*) which has been decided by the "Monitoring control" plan, by performing operations on the set of mechanisms, with the objective to modify the current monitoring strategy.
3. The capacity of the monitoring mechanisms to be dynamically adapted (*Configurability*): parameters governing the behaviour of each monitoring mechanism can be modified dynamically at runtime and without disruption.

3   Global Approach and Work-In-Progress

Figure 2 depicts the global approach which governs the progression of our works:

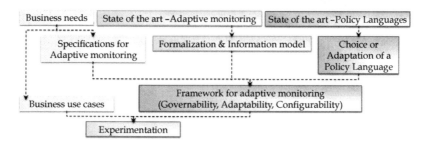

Fig. 2. Approach To Make Adaptable The Monitoring

The left axe (in yellow) is concerned with what we called "business requirements" and aims at bringing, in addition to several use case identification, the logics for determination and adaptation of a business-oriented monitoring strategy. The outputs stay at a high level of knowledge and has to be translated into more technical rules. They represent the content used by our "Monitoring control" plan.

The formalization of this logic (middle orange axe) is part of the current work. It is concerned with both the definition of generic management information models and the operators which will support the enforcement of a monitoring adaptation decision. They have to be generic enough to be used for business context adaptation requirements, or for monitoring self-optimization, or for adaptation in response to some constraints variations on technological ressources availability. The management information model scope is concerned at the same time with the configurability of the basic monitoring mechanisms (polling and event reporting) and with the monitoring strategy manageability. The enforcement operators allow the creation, deletion or reconfiguration of one or more mechanisms belonging to a monitoring strategy.

Moreover knowledge is necessary to take a monitoring strategy adaptation decision. Therefore, the framework must provide language facility to express, for one adaptation, both the triggering conditions and the resulting actions to be enforced. Thus, future works (right axe) will be concerned with the study, as a candidate approach, of event/conditions/actions-based management policies.

Finally, we will experiment concepts and derived tools of this framework on some business use cases.

4 Conclusion and Perspectives

Self-adaptive monitoring is an approach that aims at making the monitoring the less intrusive possible, by efficiently adjusting itself at runtime to every situations variation. This paper describes a work in progress which aims to obtain a generic model-based framework able to support the manageability of monitoring strategies. This approach relies on the characterisation of three complementary levels which respectively deal with configurability of basic monitoring mechanisms, adaptability and governability of monitoring strategy. Management information models and changing operators are defined to support adaptability automation. This automation will reduce the human operations over the system with an increase of effectiveness and fastness, and with an optimized adjustment of the monitoring activity. Some parts of this work have already been implemented on a CIM-WBEM environment [5]. Further works will focus on the governability level before experimenting the framework on a specific business environment where adaptive monitoring is required to improve real time diagnostic support in a case of integrated management.

References

1. Duarte Jr., E.P., Musicante, M.A., Fernandes, H.H.: ANEMONA: a Programming Language for Network Monitoring Applications. Internat. Journ. of Net. Managem. 18(4) (August 2008)
2. Kephart, J.O., Chess, D.M.: The Vision of Autonomic Computing. Computer 36(1), 41–50 (2003)
3. Massie, M.L., Chun, B.N., Culler, D.E.: The Ganglia Distributed Monitoring System: Design, Implementation, and Experience. Parallel Computing 30(7), 817–840 (2004)
4. Moghé, P., Evangelista, M.H.: RAP – Rate Adaptive Polling for Network Management Applications. In: Proceedings of IEEE Network Operation and Management Symposium NOMS 1998, pp. 395–399 (1998)
5. Moui, A., Desprats, T., Lavinal, E., Sibilla, M.: Managing Polling Adaptability in a CIM/WBEM Infrastructure. In: Int. DMTF Workshop on Systems & Virtualization Managt (SVM 2010), pp. 1–6 (2010)

A Novel Approach to Support the Visual Exploration and Management of Heterogeneous Home Area Network Devices and Services

Yuqian Song and Owen Conlan

Trinity College Dublin,
Dublin 2, Ireland
{yuqians,owen.conlan}@cs.tcd.ie

Abstract. With the advance of home networking technologies, people now enjoy increased communications convenience whilst occasionally suffering annoyance from trivial issues. The automated application of appropriate expertise can support ordinary users in managing and diagnosing their own network, despite being unfamiliar with the basic technologies. This presents a significant opportunity to increase user satisfaction and reduce support costs. As a part of my PhD research, this paper proposes an expert knowledge derived approach to manage, diagnose and resolve network problems in real time through a user-friendly visual interface derived from semantically annotated heterogeneous raw network monitoring data. This approach has been implemented in an early prototype – Home Area Network Monitoring System (HANMS). A detailed description of the current stage of this research and future work is addressed in this paper.

Keywords: Home Area Network; HAN; network monitoring; domain ontology; semantic visualization; semantic annotation; network management.

1 Introduction

As ICT (Information and communications technology) complexity increases, inexperienced users are continuously challenged and perplexed with even simple management and maintenance tasks. In a Home Area Network (HAN) scenario, normal HAN users are often puzzled by trivial wireless network issues. For example: a laptop suddenly suffers a quality degradation of the network connection, perhaps caused by a neighbor initiating some WiFi activity in the same channel – causing interference, or a signal weakens when the antenna of the wireless device is obstructed, or the laptop user may upload a large file which causes network congestion. Such events seem unremarkable but will impact on the end-user's perception of the quality of the service provided by the wireless network connection. Moreover, most users will not have the technical expertise to diagnose these problems in real time. Conversely, if the user could easily diagnose and solve these (often simple) problems, this would avoid unnecessary contact with support staff and reduce the operating costs for both the network provider and HAN users. To address this challenge, a novel approach is

I. Chrisment et al. (Eds.): AIMS 2011, LNCS 6734, pp. 164–168, 2011.

proposed to bridge the gap between the hard-learned knowledge of domain experts and the cognitive competencies of normal users in a HAN context. This approach aims to achieve the following objectives: to semantically enrich and correlate raw network log data from heterogeneous HAN devices and services with domain knowledge; to detect and analyze anomalies through a real-time diagnosis loop monitoring the constantly evolving HAN devices and services; to appropriately present the highly abstracted, correlated and annotated monitoring data for normal HAN users in a user-friendly visual interface; and finally, to leverage the high-level annotated monitoring data to perform high-level (but groundable) management actions. Related research already addressing some of these objectives will be briefly reviewed in the Related Work section. The Solution Overview & Evaluation section presents an early prototype of the Home Area Network Monitoring System (HANMS), followed by preliminary evaluation results. Future work and conclusions are described in the last section.

2 Related Work

One problem in the rapidly evolving smart home network management area is how to deal with the vast number of dynamic network log datasets. Driven by Semantic Web technologies, Semantic Annotation can be applied to transform and enrich the data and information with formal semantic meanings. In Handschuh and Staab's book [1], a broad range of technologies and methods is introduced for the explicit construction of semantic annotations, including approaches for data extraction, collaboration and translation into Semantic Web metadata. In particular, goal-oriented data extraction is valuable for network log data annotation, especially for monitoring and management purposes. By facing the challenges of evolution and heterogeneity of HAN technologies and varying user requirements in the complex HAN environment, Brennan et al. [2] presented a policy-based federated service management architecture that addresses these concerns for digital home devices participating in end-to-end communications services, while Jennings et al. [3] proposed an autonomic network management scheme, which allows a networked system to self-govern its behavior within the constraints of the human-specified goals. Another effective strategy is to perform network management by involving ontology-based modeling and reasoning. Hoag [4] presented an approach to apply semantic reasoning techniques for network management and resource allocation to avoid overbuilding and improve quality. Visualization is an effective strategy to align complex data by capitalizing on several human perception capabilities, and a novel interactive visualization system [6] was proposed as an approach to monitor the data collected from a home router and control bandwidth usage for family users. An interactive network management system, called Eden [7], delivered a simple conceptual model to help users understand key aspects of the network by eliminating the barrier and cost of the network technical minutia. Our research is also based on Conlan et al.'s work [9] to express a semantically enriched visualization approrch for non-expert users to monitor networks and services. Our work intends to combine the advantages of these research to propose a novel approach for HAN monitoing and management.

3 Solution Overview and Evaluation

This section describes a novel approach for HAN monitoring and management (Figure 1) established in our prototype, HANMS [5].

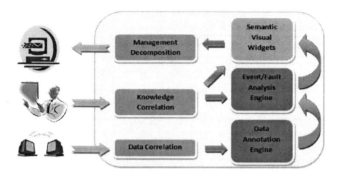

Fig. 1. HAN Monitoring and Management

In this figure, the data annotation process is implemented in a layered annotation engine to enhance large amounts of heterogeneous data with multi-level discrete semantic encodings according to the embedded network expertise to support the high-level processing. In the current HANMS prototype, the raw wireless log data are gathered from diverse wireless devices in a HAN test bed; expert domain knowledge is modeled into domain ontologies; and the annotation is applied in a two-level-annotation process. Through the Event/Fault Analysis Engine, real-time semantically enhanced data is observed in an analysis and diagnosis loop according to correlated expertise, in HANMS, modeled in network event ontologies. Using HANMS visual widgets (Figure 2), detected events/faults, and network information, is automatically and intelligently presented and highlighted. Management requests will be expressed through high-level management actions and these actions will be decomposed into lower level actions [8] to directly affect or control HAN services and devices according to expert defined ontologies and rules. The management decomposition is not supported by HANMS at this stage.

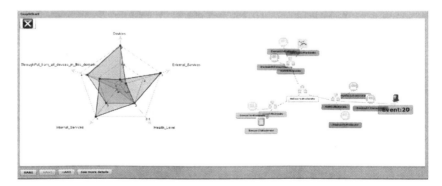

Fig. 2. HANMS prototype screenshot

The current HANMS prototype has been deployed and initial evaluation was carried out with two target groups: normal HAN users and domain experts. The majority of feedback (more than 70%) was positive, especially in the usability and UI design whilst identified limitations will be addressed in the future development.

4 Future Work and Conclusions

The current HANMS prototype is still under active development. For high-level network management, multi-resource HAN monitoring merits further development. As a part of the FAME project, HANMS has the potential to integrate with a number of prototype systems, e.g. smart home composite UPnP services. By consuming the knowledge models of UPnP events and faults [2], HANMS could present a more effective and efficient approach to diagnose the real time event/fault with high complexity. Based on this integration, high-level management goals can be decomposed into enforceable UPnP actions to control low-level devices and services. According to the up-to-date HANMS prototype deployment and evaluation results, this approach will assist ordinary end users to diagnose and resolve potential problems in a HAN, which presents a significant opportunity to reduce support costs and increase user satisfaction. This work will also show that it is possible to alleviate the difficulties of non-expert users in HAN scenarios by combining Semantic Web and Visualization technologies, while capturing and integrating domain experts' insights.

Acknowledgments. This work is partly funded by Science Foundation Ireland via grant 08/SRC/I1403 — Federated, Autonomic Management of End-to-End Communications Services (FAME).

References

1. Handschuh, S., Staab, S.: Annotation for the semantic web. IOS Press, Amsterdam (2003)
2. Brennan, R., Lewis, D., Keeney, J., Etzioni, Z., Feeney, K., O'sullivan, D., Lozano, J., Jennings, B.: Policy-based integration of multiprovider digital home services. IEEE Network 23, 50–56 (2009)
3. Jennings, B., et al.: Towards autonomic management of communications networks. IEEE Communications Magazine 45, 112–121 (2009)
4. Hoag, J.C., Hayes-Roth, F.A.: Semantic Reasoning for Adaptive Management of Telecommunications Networks. In: IEEE International Conference on Systems, Man and Cybernetics, Taipei, Taiwan (2006)
5. Song, Y., et al.: An Ontology-driven Approach to support Wireless Network Monitoring for Home Area Networks. In: 7th International Conference on Network and Service Management (CNSM 2011) (2011) (submitted)
6. Chetty, M., et al.: Who' s Hogging The Bandwidth: The Consequences Of Revealing The Invisibl In The Home. In: 28th International Conference on Human Factors in Computing Systems, New York (2010)
7. Yang, J., Edwards, W.K., Haslem, D.: Eden: supporting home network management through interactive visual tools. In: 23nd Annual ACM Symposium on User Interface Software and Technology (UIST 2010), pp. 109–118. ACM, New York (2010)

8. Keeney, J., et al.: Towards the use of Policy Decomposition for Composite Service Management by Non-expert Endusers. In: The 5th Network Operations and Management Symposium Workshops (NOMS Workshops). IEEE/IFIP, pp. 163–164. IEEE, Los Alamitos (2010)
9. Conlan, O., Keeney, J., Hampson, C., Williams, F.P.: Towards Non-expert Users Monitoring Networks and Services through Semantically Enhanced Visualizations. To appear in Proceedings of the 6th International Conference on Network and Service Management (CNSM 2010), Niagara Falls, Canada (2010)

Estimating Bandwidth Requirements Using Flow-Level Measurements

Ricardo de O. Schmidt and Aiko Pras

University of Twente
Design and Analysis of Communication Systems (DACS)
Enschede, The Netherlands
{r.schmidt,a.pras}@utwente.nl

Abstract. Bandwidth provisioning is used to dimension links so that a desired performance is met within a network (e.g. QoS metrics). Practical approaches for the estimation of bandwidth needs rely on rough traffic measurements overlooking traffic fluctuations that may have a negative impact on the network performance. On the other hand, effective theoretical solutions for estimating bandwidth needs require traffic measurements at very small timescales, which limit their applicability due to, for example, transmission rates. This paper describes our research goal of proposing a reliable and scalable solution for estimating bandwidth requirements by means of flow-level traffic measurements, as well as our proposed approach to achieve it. This research, currently in its initial phase, is planned to result in a Ph.D. thesis at the end of four years.

1 Introduction and Motivation

Link dimensioning plays an important role in network management, for example to support QoS provisioning. Usually, network operators make manual provisioning decisions based on empirical rules and on rough traffic measurements, like by using the Simple Network Management Protocol (SNMP) [1], and the Multi Router Traffic Grapher (MRTG) [2] for graphics, in timescales of 5 minutes. However, as proved in [3], traffic measurements in large timescales (e.g. interval of minutes) completely overlook traffic peaks that are detected in smaller timescales (e.g. intervals of milliseconds). This leads to imprecise estimations of bandwidth needs and, consequently, it results in non-optimal network performance. Both underdimensioning and overdimensioning of links can impact negatively in the network performance. The former can result in traffic bottlenecks caused by undetected traffic peaks, and the latter in waste of link resources when allocating more bandwidth than necessary.

Some of the solutions proposed so far for network dimensioning are application specific and, consequently, have reduced applicability scope. Solutions like [4] and [5] are focused on delay sensitive applications (e.g., VoIP) in backbone links, where the delay is resulted from queuing. By means of flow-level measurements,

I. Chrisment et al. (Eds.): AIMS 2011, LNCS 6734, pp. 169–172, 2011.

[6] and [7] focus on, respectively, dimensioning of TCP-connections throughput rates and congestion control.

A more general approach, i.e. applicable not only for backbone traffic, is proposed in [8] and [9]. One of the main contributions of this work is the dimensioning formula (1). It is used for calculating the minimal bandwidth requirements C for a given link, in a time scale of length T and with an acceptable error rate of ε, by adding to the average traffic rate μ a safety margin, which strongly depends on the traffic variance $\nu(T)$. The assumption of this formula is that the measured traffic at timescale T is Gaussian.

$$C(T,\varepsilon) = \mu + \frac{1}{T}\sqrt{(-2\log\varepsilon)\cdot\nu(T)} \qquad (1)$$

This formula was extensively validated and proved to be a good solution for the problem of link dimensioning. However, the drawback of this approach is that it requires packet-level traffic measurements, which may drastically reduce its applicability in high-speed networks (e.g., Gigabit Ethernet). Considering traffic loads currently observed in the Internet, packet-level measurements could often suffer from scalability issues. In addition, it may demand very specific, powerful and expensive hardware/software for traffic monitoring.

Given the increasing employment of flow-level measurements on network management and operations, e.g. Cisco IOS routers with embedded NetFlow [10], we believe it to be a promising approach for our research problem. Considering current transmission rates, the use of flow-level traffic measurement tools (e.g., Net-Flow and IPFIX [11]) would allow us to come up with a scalable solution when working with aggregated traffic information. Therefore, this paper describes our research idea towards the proposal of a solution for reliably estimating bandwidth requirements without recurring to packet-level traffic measurements.

The remaining of this paper is organized as follows. Section 2 presents our goal and research questions, as well as the proposed approach. The planned process to validate our findings is described in Section 3. Finally, Section 4 concludes the paper.

2   Goal, Research Questions and Approach

The goal of our research is **to determine how to estimate bandwidth requirements by means of flow-level traffic measurements**. In order to pursue this goal, we have defined the following research questions as the base of our research:

1. *What is the state of the art in flow-based bandwidth provisioning?*
2. *Which relevant data extracted from flow records can be used to estimate bandwidth needs?*
3. *Which statistical models describe the traffic measured at the flow-level?*

Research question 1 aims to raise information about main contributions and trends in the area of our research. To do so, we plan an exhaustive literature review. Interviews with network operators can also be considered as a possible way for obtaining information from real-world situations.

With research question 2, we want to identify what information (e.g., metrics) is relevant to our problem and how to extract it from the flow records. For instance, we aim to find out how to determine average traffic rate and variance from flow measurements in order to further apply these values in the dimensioning formula (1), as presented in section 1. It is important to remark that, as presented by [8], determining traffic variance from packet-level measurements (with smaller timescales) is not a complex task, due to the high level of information granularity, which allows for a high accuracy. However, the same task can be considered as a challenge in flow-level measurements, where traffic information is summarized into flow records and measurements occur at coarser timescales. In order to answer research question 2, we will use the knowledge acquired from research question 1 and further analysis on flow-level measurements of real-traffic.

In research question 3, we aim at identifying which traffic models fit better the traffic measured at the flow-level. More specifically, we want to investigate whether the measured traffic is Gaussian or not, in order to determine the suitability of the dimensioning formula from [8] for estimating bandwidth needs from flow-level traffic measurements. Once the traffic model(s) is identified, it will allow us to parameterize metrics such as average traffic rates and peaks (see [12]). We plan to use real-world network traces in order to identify such models.

3   Validation

In order to validate our final proposal, we intend to evaluate its correctness by analyzing real-world traffic, from different sources like GÉANT [13] and SURFnet [14]. We plan to compare the results from our solution with results obtained from the dimensioning formula in [8] with packet-level measurements. In addition, experimentations with real equipment and real-world traffic measurements will be done in the laboratory.

4   Final Considerations

This paper discusses the possibility of estimating network bandwidth requirements by means of flow-level traffic measurements. We have stated our motivation and planned means for achieving our goal. The long-term research goal, as described in this paper, is to be achieved in the period of 4 years, as a Ph.D. research. The research reported in this paper is supported by the SURFnet [14] and the FP7 ICT UniverSelf [15] (#257513).

References

1. Schonwalder, J.: Simple Network Management Protocol (SNMP) Context EngineID Discovery. RFC 5343 (2008)
2. MRTG: Multi Router Traffic Grapher, http://oss.oetiker.ch/mrtg/ (accessed in February 2011)

3. van de Meent, R., Pras, A., Mandjes, M., van den Berg, H., Nieuwenhuis, L.: Traffic Measurements for Link Dimensioning, A Case of Study. In: Proceedings of the 14th IFIP/IEEE Workshop on Distributed Systems: Operations and Management (DSOM), pp. 106–117 (2003)
4. Fraleigh, C.: Provisioning Internet Backbone Networks to Support Latency Sensitive Applications. PhD thesis, Stanford University (2002)
5. Papagiannaki, K.: Provisioning IP Backbone Networks Based on Measurements. PhD thesis, University of London (2003)
6. Bonald, T., Olivier, P., Roberts, J.: Dimensioning high speed IP access networks. In: Proceedings of the 8th International Teletraffic Congress (ITC), pp. 241–251 (2003)
7. Barakat, C., Thiran, P., Iannaccone, G., Diot, C., Owezarki, P.: Modeling Internet backbone traffic at the flow level. IEEE Transactions on Signal Processing 51(8) (2003)
8. van de Meent, R.: Network Link Dimensioning - a measurement & modeling based approach. PhD thesis, University of Twente (2006)
9. Pras, A., Nieuwenhuis, L., van de Meent, R., Mandjes, M.: Dimensioning Network Links: A New Look at Equivalent Bandwidth. IEEE Network 23(2), 5–10 (2009)
10. Cisco Systems Inc.: Cisco IOS Flexible NetFlow Configuration Guide. Release 12.4T (2008), http://www.cisco.com/ (accessed in February 2011)
11. Quittek, J., Zseby, T., Claise, B., Zander, S.: Requirements for IP Flow Information Export (IPFIX). RFC 3917 (2004)
12. van de Meent, R., Pras, A., Mandjes, M. R. H., van den Berg, J. L., Roijers, F., Nieuwenhuis, L.J.M., Venemans, P.H.A.: Burstiness predictions based on rough network traffic measurements. In proceedings of the 19th World Telecommunications Congress (WTC/ISS), 2004
13. GÉANT: Géant, http://www.geant.net/ (accessed in February 2011)
14. SURFnet: Surfnet, http://www.surfnet.nl/ (accessed in February 2011)
15. UniverSelf: UniverSelf FP7 project number 257513, http://www.univerself-project.eu/ (accessed in February 2011)

Using of Time Characteristics in Data Flow for Traffic Classification

Pavel Piskac and Jiri Novotny

Institute of Computer Science, Masaryk University,
Botanicka 68a, 62100 Brno, Czech Republic
piskac@mail.muni.cz, novotny@ics.muni.cz

Abstract. This paper describes a protocol detection using statistic information about a flow extended by packet sizes and time characteristics, which consist of packet inter-arrival times. The most common way of network traffic classification is a deep packet inspection (DPI). Our approach deals with the DPI disadvantage in power consumption using aggregated IPFIX data instead of looking into packet content. According to our previous experiments, we have found that applications have their own behavioral pattern, which can be used for the applications detection. With a respect to current state of development, we mainly present the idea, the results which we have achieved so far and of our future work.

Keywords: protocol detection, time characteristics, flow, IPFIX, pattern.

1 Introduction

Information about protocols on a network is very important in many areas. Planning of networks and their topology need to know how the networks will be used in order to their proper configuration. The security point of view needs to recognize protocols in order to find botnets, viruses, spam or intrusions. For example security teams get and analyze data in real-time, protocol detection represents interesting extension of their services and as such will be welcomed.

This work deals with an idea of protocol detection using extended information about a flow. In the first step, we used only inter-packet gaps which seem to be different for each protocol. Then we added information about packet sizes. The most difficult and unsolved problem yet is to find a method which will reduce variability caused by a network mainly jitter.

1.1 Related Work

The first attempts to detect protocols were done using well-known port numbers assigned by IANA [6]. Since the applications are able to change their default port numbers, this method is nowadays weak.

Looking for pattern inside packets is called deep packet inspection. Since each packet has to be read and its content compared with pattern database, this

I. Chrisment et al. (Eds.): AIMS 2011, LNCS 6734, pp. 173–176, 2011.

method is not suitable for high-speed networks. Another weak point is encrypted communication, because all the specific byte strings are hidden. In spite of these disadvantages, deep packet inspection so far brings the best detection accuracy.

Protocol detection on high-speed networks is based on aggregation which separates the important information and reduces computational power. Such methods use behavioral analysis or flow statistics. Data classification by host behavior looks for connection patterns of end points and deduces what the host is doing [7]. This method is not suitable for precise protocol detection, but it splits connections into groups (WWW, email, etc.) instead.

Extended flow statistics can carry various information about packets, e.g. inter-arrival packet times, packet direction, packet sizes, etc. [3]. Protocol detection based on these techniques is faster than deep packet inspection and it is able to classify the data even if it is encrypted [5]. Another approach detects protocols using only the first four packets of a TCP session [1].

2   Protocol Detection

Our first attempts were done in order to show the possibility of taking advantage of the extended flow statistics analysis. This approach was new at the time and we had to verify whether the time characteristics can be used for protocol detection or not. Since it was, as mentioned, a test, we did not try to achieve the best results, we wanted to verify the idea of time characteristics.

2.1   Early Phase of Research

FlowMon probes deployed at Masaryk University generate raw NetFlow data which is not capable to measure inter-packet gaps. Hence we decided to use Flow Time Statistic (FTS) tool which was developed as a testing tool for Liberouter project [8]. FTS generates IPFIX or text data where an additional information about time characteristics is included. Since FTS is a testing tool, it is not suitable for backbone networks monitoring due to insufficient speed of data processing. FTS was installed on our server where it listened to a network device and stored data in plain text format. This kind of data collecting was sufficient at this experimental phase of research. Data visualization was done as a plugin for NfSen [10].

The classification itself was done by vector matching algorithms. FTS computes statistics about flows and these values create a vector. There were obtained pattern vectors from captured data which were then compared with unknown connection vectors. Protocol detection is based on similarity of unknown and pattern vectors. Using this method, we are able to detect dictionary attacks on SSH protocol. There are better tools with higher accuracy but our goal was to show whether the time characteristics can be used for this purpose. As a first step, we used the following properties: number of packets and bytes, identification number of network and transport layer, minimal, maximal, average and standard deviation inter-arrival time of packets in a flow. These values were chosen according to results from previous experiments.

Vector comparison is done by methods which compute average distance between vectors, root-mean-square (RMS) distance, Euclidean distance and angle between vectors [2] in order to test which one is the most suitable for our purpose and which increases the detection accuracy. Experiments were made and we obtained results of around 90 % successful detection and around 7 % false positives. Average distance between vectors, RMS and Euclidean distance were the most accurate. We captured testing data on our network and it presented a real-life communication.

2.2   Current Phase of Research

Previous part showed that protocol detection based on time characteristics is possible. The results can be considered as acceptable because we did not use any specialized vector comparison method and the pattern vectors were also chosen manually which was sufficient at this stage. The current phase of development is devoted to making the method capable of detecting the whole protocols instead of one specific situation. The newest version of FTS was extended by computing statistics of packet sizes.

One of the most difficult parts of the detection is minimizing the influences in time characteristics caused by a network. Packet inter-arrival times always change as they go through the network and they are never the same. Thus we have to find techniques of how to compute and reduce the inadvisable variability. Another difficult part represents the number of situations which can occur during the communication, e.g. established connection, dictionary attacks, file transfer or tunneling other protocols, etc. These two points cause the biggest problems and we have to deal with them.

In order to detect more than one protocol, we make experiments with Quality Threshold (QT) clustering algorithm [4]. QT clustering provides automatic division into groups where the number of groups is not predefined and it gives always equal results for equal input data. The disadvantage is the speed of computation, which is slower than for example K-Means clustering algorithm [9]. No results from application of QT clustering algorithm are presented here, because they are currently being researched.

3   Conclusion

In this paper, we have shown that statistics about inter-packet gaps in flows can be used for detecting one specific situation of one protocol. Protocol detection is based on vector comparison where predefined pattern vectors are compared to unknown connections vectors. The disadvantage of this approach is that there has to be one pattern vector for each situation, e.g. successful or unsuccessful authentication.

This first part of our work was done in order to verify whether time characteristics are suitable for protocol detection. The result is that time characteristics have to be extended by some other statistics about flow which will increase accuracy and ability to detect various protocols. This work was the starting phase of the future work.

The biggest challenge is to reduce variability caused by network and find out which flow statistics are characteristic for each protocol. As soon as we will figure out how to do that, we can concern on practical implementation.

3.1   Future Work

Future work is an iterative process. At first, we have to reduce the variability in time characteristics and find the proper set of attributes which will the vectors consist of. Automatized division into groups and practical experiments will take place afterwards. We expect that these phases will repeat multiple times.

As soon as we will be satisfied with the detection algorithm, we can customize network probes in order to gain this information from the flows and export it in IPFIX format to our data store where the data will be processed and displayed to users. All the steps are leading towards more accurate and fast protocol detection and thus improved security on computer networks.

Acknowledgements. This material is based upon work supported by the Czech Ministry of Defence under Contract No. SMO02008PR980-OVMASUN200801.

References

1. Bernaille, L., Teixeira, R., Salamatian, K.: Early Application Identification. In: ADETTI/ISCTE CoNEXT Conference, Lisboa, Portugal (2006)
2. Deza, M.M., Deza, E.: Encyclopedia of Distances. Springer, Heidelberg (2009)
3. Erman, J., Arlitt, M., Mahanti, A.: Traffic classification using clustering algorithms. SIGCOMM (2006)
4. Heyer, L.J., Kruglyak, S., Yooseph, S.: Exploring expression data: Identification and analysis of coexpressed genes. Genome Research 9(11), 1106–1115 (1999)
5. Hjelmvik, E., John, W.: Breaking and Improving Protocol Obfuscation, Technical Report No: 2010-05, Department of Computer Science and Engineering, Chalmers University of Technology, Gothenburg, Sweden (2010)
6. Internet Assigned Numbers Authority (IANA),
   http://www.iana.org/assignments/port-numbers
7. Karagiannis, T., Papagiannaki, K., Faloutsos, M.: Blinc multilevel traffic classification in the dark. SIGCOMM (2005)
8. Liberouter, http://www.liberouter.org/
9. MacQueen, J.B.: Some methods for classification and analysis of multivariate observations. In: Proceedings of 5-th Berkeley Symposium on Mathematical Statistics and Probability, pp. 281–297. University of California Press, Berkeley (1967)
10. Netflow Sensor (NfSen), http://nfsen.sourceforge.net/

Intrusion Detection in Open Peer-to-Peer Multi-Agent Systems

Shahriar Bijani and David Robertson

Informatics School, University of Edinburgh. 10, Crichton St., Edinburgh, UK
s.bijani@ed.ac.uk, dr@inf.ed.uk

Abstract. One way to build large-scale autonomous systems is to develop open peer-to-peer architectures in which peers are not pre-engineered to work together and in which peers themselves determine the social norms that govern collective behaviour. A major practical limitation to such systems is security because the very openness of such systems negates most traditional security solutions. We propose a programme of research that addresses this problem by devising ways of attack detection and damage limitation that take advantage of social norms described by electronic institutions. We have analysed security issues of open peer-to-peer multi-agent systems and focused on probing attacks against confidentiality. We have proposed a framework and adapted an inference system, which shows the possibility of private information disclosure by an adversary. We shall suggest effective countermeasures in such systems and propose attack response techniques to limit possible damages.

Keywords: Security, Confidentiality, Multi-agent Systems, Electronic Institutions, P2P networks, Light Weight Coordination Calculus (LCC).

1 Introduction

We have focused on open peer-to-peer (p2p) multi-agent systems (MAS), in which *electronic institutions* [4] are used to form the interaction environment by defining social norms for group behaviour. An *open system* is a system that allows new components, which may have been created by different parties or for different objectives, not known at design time, to interact at runtime [5]. An open p2p *multi-agent system* is an *open system* in which autonomous peers can join and leave freely [4]. Open MAS have growing popularity (e.g. in social networks, e-commerce, social simulation and workflow systems) and are predicted to have many applications in the future [2]. In these open systems, peers may invent the protocols (*electronic institutions*) themselves and share them with others or use other (unknown) peers' protocols. We address confidentiality of open p2p MAS with dynamic protocols.

Although we focus on the open p2p MAS, we can extend the scope of our secrecy analysis without much difficulty to similar domains such as web services.

Even though openness in open systems makes them attractive for different new applications, new problems emerge, among which security is a key. Unfortunately there remain many potential gaps in the security of open MAS and little research has been done in this area. The focus of the related work is mostly on mobile agents and

I. Chrisment et al. (Eds.): AIMS 2011, LNCS 6734, pp. 177–180, 2011.

using conventional security mechanisms (e.g. cryptography and PKI) in agent communication layer.

Traditional security mechanisms resist use in MAS directly, because of the social nature of them and the consequent special security needs[7]. Open MAS using dynamic protocols are particularly difficult to protect, because we can make only minimum guarantees about identity and behaviour of agents and conventional security mechanisms, like authentication and encryption, are at best a small (though necessary) part of the solution. We have focused on confidentiality which is an important subset of security and is critical in many applications (such as healthcare systems). To best of our knowledge, so far there are no attack detection/response systems or methods for open p2p multi-agent system that use dynamic electronic institutions.

An electronic institution is an organisation model for MAS that provides a framework to describe, specify and deploy agents' interaction environments. It is a formalism which defines peers' interaction rules and their permitted and prohibited actions. There are a few choreography-oriented languages, from which we selected LCC [6] (as an example) to implement electronic institutions. LCC (Lightweight Coordination Calculus) is based on π-calculus and logic programming to execute electronic institutions (interaction models) in a p2p style.

2   Overview of the Suggested Framework

Our suggested framework for the secrecy analysis of interaction models in an open p2p multi-agent system is shown inFig. 1. The first three steps are optional and they only will be necessary if we want to extend our work to support other open systems that do not use LCC to create their interaction protocols. We briefly describe the framework in the following steps:

1. A multi-agent system (or a web service, a process management system ...) produces log files while running.
2. The process model of the system is extracted by a process mining tool (ProM[1]).

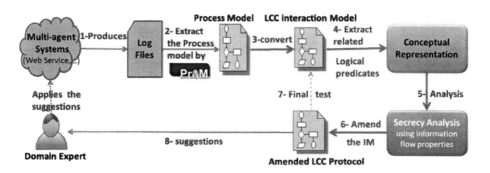

Fig. 1. A suggested framework for the secrecy analysis of open p2p multi-agent systems

---

[1] ProM is an open-source framework for implementing process mining tools in a standard environment (www.processmining.org). We selected it as a working example of process mining systems.

3. The extracted process model is converted to LCC interaction models.
4. LCC interaction models are converted to a conceptual representation. (Section 3)
5. The secrecy of the conceptual representation (that represents the interaction model) is analysed using an inference system that shows what an adversary could infer from the interaction model. (Section 3)
6. The interaction model will be fixed if there is any information leak exists.
7. Steps 4 to 6 will be repeated to double check the amended interaction model.
8. The source of the information leak problem and the amended interaction model with some annotations will be sent to the domain expert of the original system.

3 Probing Attacks and Countermeasures

We analysed possible attacks on open p2p MAS as a part of our work and selected probing attack to address it. We redefine the probing attack [1] in conventional network security to be applicable in MAS. A probing attack in network security is an attack based on injecting traffic into the victim's network and analysing the results.

In our case, an adversary could infer information not only from the interaction model itself, but also from the local knowledge of other peers. An adversary could control other peers' behaviour in an interaction, by publishing a malicious interaction model. Furthermore, it could access the private local knowledge (e.g. decision rules and policies) of the victim peer by injection of facts to the peer's knowledge-base, asking queries and analysing the queries result.

The first step in our secrecy analysis is converting interaction models to simpler logical representations in order to illustrate only the related parts of the LCC code to the security evaluation. What we need for our conceptual representation is a more minimal interpretation of LCC, which reflects information leaks or helps to find knowledge leakage. We should interpret interaction models for each scenario differently, to be able to discover information leaks and consequently to achieve more accurate secrecy analyses.

After the conceptual representation of interaction models we could analyse them to detect any possibility of a probing attack. We are going to use a security type system to analyse information flow properties in LCC interaction models. Meanwhile we used the Becker's inference system [3] for *detectability*[2] to analyse secrecy, because it was compatible with our conceptual representation. Although this inference system has been created for credential-based authorisation policies (such as Datalog), with some modifications, it could also be used to detect probing attack on open MAS. We want to know if an adversary injects expressions into the agent's private knowledge-base and asks a query, what else the adversary will infer from the knowledge-base. To answer this question we used the inference system in [3].

Two reasons that security problems might lead to probing attacks on choreographic systems are: (1) no distinguishing notion of private and public data in choreography languages (such as LCC) and (2) no mechanism for information leakage control in their interaction models. Hence, two countermeasures to these problems are adding

---

[2] Detectability (or non-opacity) is an information flow property that shows the ability to infer a specific predicate from a set of rules.

some access control features to the language and secrecy analysis of interaction models. The first solution for LCC is to label information in it and to add attack prevention rules in the LCC interpreter.

The second solution for probing attacks is secrecy analysis of interaction models using techniques such as using the introduced inference system to detect injection attacks before using the interaction models. This analysis could be implemented as a separate interaction model that receives other interaction models and after extracting the corresponding logical representation, check possibility of information leak using the inference system.

4 Conclusion and Future Work

We propose a programme of research that addresses secrecy of open peer-to-peer multi-agent systems by devising ways of probing attack detection and damage limitation. To analyse information leaks in these agent systems, we have suggested a conceptual representations of interaction models and adapted an inference system, which shows the possibility of private information disclosure by an adversary. Finally we have proposed two solutions to prevent and detect probing attacks in open p2p multi-agent systems. We intend to develop a security type system for LCC language to analyse information leakage in agents' interaction models. The evaluation of the suggested techniques has two stages. In the first stage, we will try to find detection and response methods for probing attacks and evaluation would be empirical by simulation of these techniques. In the case that no convincing detection method exists, we will analytically show it and disconfirm the hypotheses, as the second stage.

References

[1] Anderson, R., Kuhn, M.: Tamper resistance: a cautionary note. In: Proc. of USENIX Workshop on Electronic Commerce, vol. 2, pp. 1–11 (1996)
[2] Artikis, A., Sergot, M., Pitt, J.: Specifying norm-governed computational societies. ACM Tran. on Computational Logic (TOCL) 10, 1–42 (2009)
[3] Becker, M.Y.: Information Flow in Credential Systems. In: IEEE Computer Security Foundations Symposium (CSF), pp. 171–185 (2010)
[4] Esteva, M., et al.: Engineering open multi-agent systems as electronic institutions. In: Proc. of the National Conference on Artificial Intelligence (1999)
[5] Poslad, S., Calisti, M.: Towards improved trust and security in FIPA agent platforms. In: Workshop on Deception, Fraud and Trust in Agent Societies (2000)
[6] Robertson, D.: Multi-agent coordination as distributed logic programming. In: Demoen, B., Lifschitz, V. (eds.) ICLP 2004. LNCS, vol. 3132, pp. 416–430. Springer, Heidelberg (2004)
[7] S. Robles Trust and Security. Issues in Multi-Agent Systems: the AgentCities. ES Experience, Basel (2008)

Author Index